The Earthly Life of
Jesus, the Christ

The Earthly Life of Jesus, the Christ

A life in chronological, geographical and social context

Robert Duncan Culver

Mentor

© Robert Duncan Culver

ISBN 1 85792 798 2

This edition published in 2002
by
Christian Focus Publications,
Geanies House, Fearn, Tain,
Ross-shire, IV20 ITW, Scotland.

Previously published in 1976, 1984 and 1991 by
Baker Book House, Grand Rapids, USA

www.christianfocus.com

Cover design by Alister MacInnes

Printed and bound by
Bell and Bain, Glasgow

Scripture quotations are, unless otherwise noted,
from the Authorized (King James) Version.

Contents

Part 3 'I am leaving the world'

Part 4 'I am... going to the Father'

List of Illustrations

Maps

Diagrams

Tables

Introduction

The Lord Himself, during the last hours He spent with His disciples, delivered for the ages His own very succinct sketch of His earthly career: 'I came forth from the Father,' He said, 'and am come into the world: again, I leave the world, and go to the Father' (John *16:28)-from the Father,* the first stage; *to the Father,* the last; with *come into the world* and *leave the world* between. Albrecht Bengel called this verse the 'greatest recapitulation' of Jesus' career among men.[1] H. A. W. Meyer observed that this remarkable statement of Jesus is 'a simple and grand summary of His entire personal life.'[2]

In a distinctly observable manner, not only the entire Gospel of John (who alone reports this saying) but the whole corpus of the synoptic Gospels – Mark, Matthew, and Luke – is fully amenable to understanding under the rubrics of this fourfold structure. It is the outline of the present book.

Recent generations have produced a flood of literature – scholarly, pseudoscholarly, journalistic, fictional and otherwise – about almost every conceivable aspect of Jesus' person, career, message, and mission.

---

1 *Gnomon Novi* Testamenti, 2 vols. (Tubingae, 1850), 2:458.
2 *Critical and Exegetical Hand-book of the Gospel of John (New York:* Funk and Wagnalls, 1884), p. 455.

Some authors have presupposed that the genuine Jesus, the true prophet of Galilee, and His disciples must be sought in a reconstructed arrangement of the Gospel materials, employing archaeology, comparative religion, modern literary criticism, and other modern tools, insights, and techniques. Others have deliberately and openly sought to produce entertaining fiction, using the Jesus of the Gospel story as the main or a subordinate character. A smaller but significant number of sober men have treated the stories of Jesus, His disciples, and His detractors from the standpoint of devotion. Still others have sought to sketch out (some briefly, some fully) the actual historical data of the Gospels, producing a consecutive record of the career of Jesus of Nazareth that uses the Gospels as normative and modern discoveries and researches as supplementary. The goal is a systematically organized aggregate of all we know about His life here on this planet. This approach accepts the first three Gospels as both truthful and actually 'synoptic,' i.e., they go over essentially the same ground from slightly different points of view and with different emphases. The questions of mutual dependence or independence of the three, while not irrelevant, are not of prime importance here. This approach, adopted herein and followed by many older works and a sprinkling of recent ones, accepts the Fourth Gospel as a genuine late first-century document, probably Johannine, and consciously supplemental to the three Synoptics.

I have not treated every incident or journey in detail, nor interpreted every parable, nor sought to solve every problem or resolve all apparent discrepancies of the narratives. I have sought to include in the book plan every incident, every parable (or group of parables), and every sermon and miracle, while reserving for extended treatment a small number of typical examples. I have furnished sufficient of the journeys, incidents, teachings, parables, sayings, and climactic events of the Gospel records so that the reader can fit all into a tentative narrative scheme. For example, although not all of Jesus' conversations are discussed, His fascinating interview with that vital and intelligent 'woman at the well' of Sychar is presented in detail. Further, though many supposed discrepancies are left for the large commentaries to handle, the very typical and often noticed difficulties connected with our Lord's last passage through Jericho are discussed in a manner suggesting how all the others might be handled.

The discourses could not all be summarized in a relatively short work. The order and the geographical and chronological location of each, however, are noted, together with the tone, tenor, rising crescendo, and essential content of each.

My purpose is so to treat the accounts that the reader who consults his Bible as he reads, will obtain a substantial, interpreted summary of our Lord's career, seen in chronological and geographical context. We hope the student will be supported in the conviction that Jesus' career can only be explained as it was by those interesting villagers of Sychar whom He blessed with His presence and ministry as an honored guest for two days: 'We have heard him ourselves, and know that this is indeed the Christ, the Savior of the world.'

The value of the approach followed here was well put by an older author whose well-known 'life' of Christ I will cite often: '... if the elements of time and place are stricken from the Gospels, the Lord's life ceases to be a truly human and intelligible one; He becomes only a wandering Voice. The more fully we know the outward circumstances of His life, and His relations to those around Him, the more do His words gain in significance, and attest His discernment and wisdom. Thus it is of importance to know, so far as we are able, both the times and places of His utterances; and the labor spent in this study is not idle, but will yield rich reward.'[3]

---

3 ALOL, p. vii.

List of Abbreviations

ALOL   Andrews, Samuel J. *The Life of Our Lord upon the Earth.* Rev. ed. New York: Charles Scribner's Sons, 1891.

ANT   Alford, Henry. *The New Testament for English Readers.* 2 vols. London: Rivingtons, 1863-1866. Reprinted Chicago: Moody, n.d.

BA   *The Biblical Archaeologist.*

BASOR *Bulletin of the American Schools of Oriental Research.*

BGB   Baly, Denis. *The Geography of the Bible.* New York: Harper and Brothers, 1957.

BGHSG Burton, Ernest D., and Goodspeed, Edgar J. *A Harmony of the Synoptic Gospels in Greek.* Chicago: University of Chicago, 1947.

CLC   Cheney, Johnson M. *The Life of Christ in Stereo: The Four Gospels Combined as One.* Portland, Oreg.: Western Baptist Seminary, 1969.

EHL   Ellicott, C. J. *Historical Lectures on the Life of Our Lord.* London: Parker, Son, and Bourn, 1862.

ELTJM Edersheim, Alfred. *The Life and Times of Jesus the Messiah.* 2 vols. New York: Longmans, Green, 1907.

FANT   Finegan, Jack. *The Archaeology of the New Testament: The Life of Jesus and the Beginning of the Early Church.* Princeton: Princeton University, 1969.

FHBC   Finegan, Jack. *Handbook of Biblical Chronology.* Princeton: Princeton University, 1964.

FLAP   Finegan, Jack. *Light from the Ancient Past: The Archaeological Background of Judaism and Christianity.* 3rd ed. Princeton: Princeton University, 1974.

GCTNT Gregory, C. R. *The Canon and Text of the New Testament.* Edinburgh: T. and T. Clark, 1907.

GJM   Guthrie, Donald. *Jesus the Messiah.* Grand Rapids: Zondervan, 1972.

GSLC   Guthrie, Donald. *A Shorter Life of Christ.* Grand Rapids: Zondervan, 1970.

HDB   Hastings, James, ed. *Dictionary of the Bible. 5 vols.* New York: Charles Scribner's Sons, 1898-1904.

HWWJ   Hunter, Archibald M. *The Work and Words of Jesus.* Philadelphia: Westminster, 1950.

JFBC   Jamieson, Robert; Fausset, A. R.; and Brown, David. *A Commentary, Critical and Explanatory, on the Old and New Testaments.* 2 vols. Hartford: S. S. Scranton, n.d.

KBA   Kraeling, Emil G. *Rand McNally Bible Atlas.* Chicago: Rand McNally, 1962.

RELJ   Robertson, A. T. *Epochs in the Life of Jesus.* London: Hodder and Stoughton, n.d.

RHFG   Robinson, Edward. *A Harmony of the Four Gospels in English.* Rev. ed. Revised by Edward Robinson and M. B. Riddle. Boston: Houghton, Mifflin, 1890.

RHG   Robertson, A. T. *A Harmony of the Gospels for Students of the Life of Christ.* New York: Doran, 1922.

RHS   Reid, John Calvin, compiler. *His Story.* Waco, Tex.: Word, n.d.

SBCNT Strack, Hermann L., and Billerbeck, Paul. *Commentarzum Neuen Testament aus Talmud and Midrasch.* 6 vols. Muenchen: C. H. Beck, 1919.

SDB   Smith, William. *Dictionary of the Bible.* Rev. ed. Revised and edited by H. B. Hackett and Ezra Abbot. New York: Hurd and Houghton, 1875.

SDHF   Smith, David. *The Days of His Flesh: The Earthly Life of Our Lord and Saviour Jesus Christ.* 8th ed. London: Hodder and Stoughton, 1910.

SGG   Scroggie, W. Graham. *A Guide to the Gospels.* London: Pickering and Inglis, 1948.

SHJP   Schuerer, Emil. *A History of the Jewish People in the Time of Jesus Christ.* 5 vols. Translated by John Macpherson. New York: Charles Scribner's Sons, 1891.

SLC   Stalker, James. *The Life of Jesus Christ.* Chicago: Henry A. Sumner, 1881. Reprinted-Westwood, N.J.: Fleming H. Revell, 1949.

VIG   Vilnay, Zev. *Israel Guide.* 3rd ed. Jerusalem: Shiever, 1960.

WFHAB Wright, George Ernest, and Filson, Floyd Vivian. *The Westminster Historical Atlas to the Bible.* Philadelphia: Westminster, 1956.

Part I

'I came forth from the Father'

CHAPTER I

The Preparation for His Coming

People who begin their reading of the Bible with the New Testament find themselves in a strange world.

Although the men and women of this new world seem understandable enough, the things they say and do and the features of their society seem very remote. Their inner world of ideas – especially of faith - may be somewhat familiar, for the Bible is a part of Western culture; but it will have a strange feel. For example, the earliest pages of two of the Gospels cite many ancient prophecies concerning the career of Jesus and record two long genealogies. One of these genealogies (Matt. 1:1-17) traces Jesus' ancestry down from the first Hebrew, a man of the late third millennium BC named Abraham, while the other (Luke 3:23-38) traces His forebears back to the first human pair. The main actors are religious people whose ideas of devotion center in religious exercises of which most men today have never heard.[1]

The external world of men and things is almost as strange as the inner world of ideas. A certain Caesar Augustus rules 'the whole world'

---

1 The three mandatory religious pilgrimages (Exod. 23:14-17) and all the elaborate sacrificial rites involved in four major kinds of animal sacrifice (Lev. 1-7), plus all the innumerable regulations of the last four books of the Pentateuch, as interpreted by the religious leaders of the Jews, were observed as fully as possible in Jesus' time.

(Luke 2:1). Scholars from an unspecified 'East' visit the infant Messiah, and numerous rulers of overlapping or conflicting status rule the area. How, for example, is Herod (Luke 23:7) of Galilee related in jurisdiction to Quirinius (Luke 2:2) of Syria? or Pilate (Matt. 27:2), procurator at the trial of Jesus, to Philip (Luke 3:1), 'tetrarch of Ituraea,' and to a certain Lysanius (Luke 3:1), 'tetrarch of Abilene'? As the Gospels' story unfolds, a large variety of official and quasi-official persons appear: publicans, a procurator, ethnarchs, tetrarchs, priests and Levites, high priests, scribes, publicans, Herodians, Sadducees, Pharisees, Zealots, lawyers, and rabbis, to mention only the ones that come first to mind.

This external world of civil government, political geography, commerce, industry, and external religion is one that has long since passed away.

Though a thoughtful reading of the Old Testament will clear up most of the mystery and supply much of the missing information, there will be certain gaps. How can we fill in the gaps and otherwise understand the situation and outlook of the people whom we meet in the first four books of the New Testament? This opening chapter is devoted to these matters. We shall first look to the Old Testament preparation for and prophecies of His coming, then sketch the history of the Jewish people between the time the Old Testament closes and the New Testament begins, and after that describe certain Roman, Greek, and Jewish aspects of the world into which, in the fullness of time, the Son of God came.

THE OLD TESTAMENT

Matthew's Gospel alone directly cites or alludes to the Old Testament at least 129 times, 89 of these references being preceded by the phrase, 'in order that it might be fulfilled which was spoken of the Lord by the prophet,' or some similar expression. There are approximately 63 such clear references in Mark and about 100 in Luke. As for the Fourth Gospel, scholars agree that it is an insoluble mystery without the Old Testament because it is saturated with Old Testament thoughts, imagery, and language. More than 'literary dependence' is involved. An examination of these hundreds of references in the four Gospels will show that the authors regarded the events of the New Testament as the consummation of a redemptive history that began in the Old Testament. Jesus Christ of the New Testament is indeed the Messiah of Israel and the hope of the nations whom the Old Testament prophesies.

In addition to the numerous brief statements in the Gospels connecting this or that item of Jesus' career with the Old Testament, there are comprehensive, definitive texts which do the same, especially in Luke and Acts, the two books written by Paul's physician-companion, Luke. He reports that on the very day of His resurrection Jesus joined two of the disconsolate disciples on the way to their home at Emmaus and upbraided them for failing to see His career predicted 'in all the scriptures' (Luke 24:25-27). In the evening of the same day Jesus appeared to the same Cleopas and his friend, now at the meeting place of the Eleven at Jerusalem, and in different words connected His entire career, including even its issue in the church among all nations, with prophecies in the Law of Moses, the Psalms, and the Prophets. To correct their misunderstandings He specially 'opened... their understanding that they might understand the scriptures.' Thus the Old Testament, on the authority of Jesus Himself, is a Christian book, no more distinctly Jewish than the church itself, even though both began among Jews. It was decades after Jesus had enlightened their understanding that the Gospel writers, by His enablement, drew those hundreds of connections between Old Testament preparation and prophecy and their fulfillment in Jesus. In the same spirit the sermons of the Apostles in Acts almost invariably demonstrate that Jesus is the Christ of God by resort to the prophecy-fulfillment technique. Evangelists and apologists still do the same today.

At this point an important matter must be clarified. Jesus and the Apostles regarded all the Old Testament as preparatory and predictive, not just a few selected 'messianic' passages. This can be demonstrated beyond serious doubt. First observe the innumerable connections drawn by the Gospel writers. Then concentrate on Jesus' remarks cited above about 'Moses and all the prophets... in all the scriptures... all things must be fulfilled, which are written in the law of Moses, and in the prophets, and in the Psalms, concerning me... that they might understand the scriptures' (Luke 24: 24-27, 44-47). After that observe that all the Old Testament is regarded as written by prophets (Heb. 1:1, 2), and then turn to the four times that Peter, in sermons recorded in the Book of Acts, claimed that the prophecy of Christ and of the Apostles' gospel ministry is found in 'all the prophets' (Acts 3:18, 21, 24; 10:43). Paul charged that the Jerusalem Jews who condemned Jesus did so because 'they knew... not... the voices of the prophets which are read every Sabbath day' and that they 'fulfilled them in condemning him' (Acts 13:27). A few minutes with the Bible, letting these texts, in context, speak their message, will deliver the reader from the much-abused approach to Old Testament messianic prophecy of simple Old Testament 'proof texting.' Paul felt that any day in which a Jew attended synagogue services he would hear prophecy of Messiah read (see also Acts 24:14). Thus any list of so-called messianic texts out of the Old Testament, useful as it may be for certain purposes, may be misleading. The entire Old Testament is preparatory and predictive.[2]

It is not, however, all preparatory or predictive in exactly the same way. Discerning scholars have detected differing levels of precision in prediction. To these we now direct, attention.[3]

Every word of the Old Testament is certainly *messianic by way of preparation* for the coming of Christ. A basis for this observation is laid in Paul's words: 'But when the fullness of the time was come, God sent forth his son' (Gal. 4:4). The first eleven chapters of the Old Testament tell of the need for a savior of men, while all the rest - Genesis 12 through Malachi 4 - traces the history of the chosen people who produced the Savior-Messiah. When He was born into the degraded and corrupt heathen world of antiquity, Jesus' home was in an island of relative purity produced by Old Testament religion. His mother was a pure Jewish virgin when she came to her husband; his earthly 'father,' a true son of Abraham, understood righteous discretion; the cleanliness of the Jewish people, famous then as now, guaranteed that clean food be placed on the family table and that He sleep in a clean bed; the community of Nazareth understood the value of a latrine (something missing in many country villages of the Near East today). This came about because God had taught a pagan named Abram to worship God Most High. Later that man's descendants, grown numerous in Egypt, learned law and discipline in the wilderness. They then as a nation lived out hundreds of years of history in the 'land of promise' while a righteous remnant of them lived out both the letter and the spirit of their divinely imparted religion. That remnant, nourished by the Scriptures, was on hand – as the early chapters of Matthew

---

2 'The most important point here is to keep in mind the organic unity of the Old Testament. Its predictions are not isolated, but features of one grand prophetic picture; its rituals and institutions parts of one great system; its history, not loosely connected events, but an organic development tending toward a definite end. Viewed in its innermost substance, the history of the Old Testament is not different from its typical institutions, nor yet these two from its predictions. The idea, underlying all, is God's gracious manifestation in the world – the kingdom of God; the meaning of all – the establishment of this kingdom upon earth. The gracious purpose was, so to speak, individualized, and the Kingdom actually established in the Messiah.' ELTJM, 1:160, 161.

3 Extended discussion of these matters will be found in Robert D. Culver, 'The Old Testament as Messianic Prophecy,' *Bulletin of the Evangelical Theological Society 7* (1964): 91-97.

4 See especially in the reported character of Jesus' mother and earthly father (Matt. 1:18-25; Luke 1:26-56; 2:19-24), the parents of John the Baptist (Luke 1:3-80), and Simeon and Anna (Luke 2:25-38).

and Luke relate with great delicacy[4] – to produce and nestle the Messiah when He came. This readying of a society as home for Jesus during the 'days of His flesh' through Old Testament revelatory history constitutes that entire Book *messianic by preparation* and justifies in part, at least, the frequent Gospel formula, 'that the scripture might be fulfilled,' and Paul's 'according to the scriptures.' It is part of the function of the Law as *paidagôgos* (conductor of children) to lead the nation to Christ (Gal. 3:24 and 4:5).

Another category is Old Testament Scripture *messianic by extension.* Jesus claimed to fulfill the Law and the Prophets – i.e., the Old Testament. One important way in which He did this was simply for the first time in history to carry out every one of its moral requirements. The Psalmist, for example, could pronounce blessed the man who neither walks nor stands nor sits with evil in any way (Ps. 1:1, 2) and could describe the man who abides in God's holy hill, walks uprightly, and speaks righteousness in his heart (Ps. 15:1, 2), but these pronouncements were never truly and completely fulfilled until Jesus did it. By calling for human perfection the Old Testament calls for the Son of Man from heaven whose mission it was to produce just such human perfection. The practical wisdom of Proverbs, Job, Ecclesiastes, Song of Solomon, and other practical-morality sections are in a clear and definite sense deposits of messianic information and a call for Messiah's coming. In this way, Proverbs is quite as truly messianic as some often cited verses about Immanuel (e.g., Isa. 7-9) in the great prophecies of the Old Testament.

Another numerous class is sometimes called *divine parousia* (personal presence) *prophecies.* Numerous texts connect the coming salvation with the coming of God Himself (Mic. 1:2; cf. Mal. 3:1; Ps. 93; 94; 50:3) to deal in a direct and final way with the world's problems. 'For, behold the LORD cometh forth out of his place, and will come down.' These constitute predictions of the deity of the coming Christ, a fact which the Jews never fully understood and which renders a large part of the Old Testament distinctly messianic and, in a certain sense, exclusively Christian.

What certain contemporary writers call *royal messianic prophecy is* by an older generation called *indirect messianic prophecy.* This important class of material in the Old Testament is chiefly 'Psalms in which in keeping with the circumstances of the time at which they were composed, Messianic hopes were centered on a contemporary king, without, however, having been fulfilled in Him; so that in the mouth of the Church, which was still waiting for their fulfillment, they have become eschatological hymns, and we are perfectly justified in interpreting them *as such*, as well as in their bearing upon their own time.'[5] Psalm 72 – appearing in the hymnals of our day as 'Jesus Shall Reign' (Isaac Watts)is a notable example of this sort of messianic prophecy in the Old Testament.

Another variety, sometimes called *indirectly messianic*, might better be called *messianic by hyperbole*, i.e., by literary exaggeration. Commentators often point out this feature of passages wherein a psalmist, or other author, described his feelings and experiences in such a way that he was 'raised above his own individuality and time, and uses regarding himself hyperbolic [i.e., legitimately exaggerated] expressions, which were not to become full historical truth until they became so in Christ.'[6] Examples cited are usually related to persons who themselves are already typical of Christ (as David or Solomon). The 'Why hast thou forsaken me?' of Psalm 22 is an example. David felt forsaken, even though elsewhere he wrote, 'Yea, though I walk through the valley of the shadow of death, I will fear no evil: for thou art with me...' (Ps. 23:4). Yet, though David was never forsaken by his Creator and Redeemer, our Savior who made these His dying words was truly forsaken of God.

Typical messianic prophecy is a valid traditional category with which most Bible readers are fairly familiar. A steady feature of Christian use of the Old Testament from the beginning, and one that has sometimes been vastly overdone, has been the tracing of divinely intended typical connection (and, in that sense, *predictive* connection) between certain offices, institutions, persons, events, etc. in the Old Testament and important features of the Lord's earthly career.[7]

So, the very first chapter of the New Testament, after reporting the

---

5 Franz Delitzsch, *Biblical Commentary on the Psalms*, 3 vols. (Edinburgh: Clark, 1871), 1:93.

6 ibid.

7 This feature of the Old Testament, properly and specifically justified by reference to several New Testament statements, is called by at least five different names in the New Testament 'shadow,' skia (Heb. 10:1; Col. 2:16, 17); 'figure,' parabolé (Heb. 9:9); 'type' or 'figure,' typos (Rom. 9:14); 'pattern,' hypodeigma (Heb. 9:23); 'pattern' or 'example,' antitypon (Heb. 9:24). On this account the Book of Leviticus, large sections of Exodus and Numbers, events in Genesis and Joshua (in the view of many), as well as surely certain parts of the so-called books of poetry and prophecy, have a definite messianic (i.e., predictive-of-Christ) aspect.

On the very highest and most distinct level is direct messianic prophecy. The traditional Christmas texts employed in the great oratorios fall in this category (Gen. 3:15; 12:1-3; 49:10; Mic. 5:2; and many more). But so also does Isaiah 53, a chapter which so specifies the details of our Lord's passion and death that even enemies of Christianity can scarcely miss it. It has even been claimed that Jesus read the passage and deliberately-if morbidly-planned His last days on the basis of it.

first events connected with His birth, says: 'Now all this was done, that it might be fulfilled which was spoken of the Lord by the prophet, saying, Behold, a virgin shall be with child, and shall bring forth a son, and they shall call his name Emmanuel...' (Matt. 1:22, 23). Likewise, at the very opening of His ministry, Jesus could say, '... I am come [not] to destroy the law, or the prophets: I am not come to destroy, but to fulfill' (Matt. 5:17, 18); and at the very end of His earthly career He could say with reference to that program of fulfillment, 'It is finished' (John 19:30).

It is possible to treat these matters in a rigid, schematic, mechanical manner, as if Jesus, at every juncture from dawn of human consciousness until death, consulted the Bible to see what He should do next. A simple reading of the Gospels shows that, quite to the contrary, Jesus was the freest and most relaxed and natural of men. He was fully aware of the prophecies, but we are to understand that the same providence which rules our lives ruled His and thereby brought 'prediction and fulfillment' together.

Above all, this Old Testament preparation and prediction explains the expectation for the Messiah so prominent in the circle of devout persons at the time of His advent – the quiet expectation of Joseph and Mary; the believing response of Zacharias and Elizabeth, parents of the forerunner, to the angelic announcements; the worship of Magi, of shepherds, and of saints like Simeon and Anna. It also explains the frantic fears of the monstrous Herod.

The more we learn about the milieu of Palestine in the time of our Lord's first appearance at Bethlehem and Nazareth - as well as at His baptism and during His official ministry - the more important the prophecy and preparation become. The recent discoveries commonly associated together as 'the Dead Sea Scrolls,' considered against a deepening understanding of other extra-Biblical and secular literature from early times, show that Jewry and Judaism of all grades and varieties were near agog with excitement about the prophesied Messiah at the time he did, in veritable flesh, appear upon the scene.

JUDAISM 'BETWEEN THE TESTAMENTS'

Old Testament events and persons leave off at about the beginning of the last quarter of the fifth century BC. The last chapters of Nehemiah and the Book of Malachi report the situation in Palestine at the time. A few thousand Jews – surely scarcely more than 1,00,000 descendants of the approximately 43,000 Jews (Ezra 2:64, 65) who had returned from their captivities in the main contingent about a century before, plus a very few later returnees, all living mainly in and around Jerusalem – constituted the small Jewish population of Palestine. The bulk of Jewry were still in the Dispersion – then as now. They appear as a rather disconsolate island of only moderately prosperous Jewish farmers and traders, orthodox in religion but not especially vital in faith. Their chief concerns have turned from bare survival to advancement of material prosperity (Hag. 1:4-6). They have a modestly reconstructed temple, but the majority of the priests are faithless time-servers (Mal. 1:1-2:16), their chief assets in religion being a genuine aversion to idolatry, a large body of inspired Scripture (essentially the present Protestant Old Testament), and a core of vital believing servants of the God of Abraham and of Moses. Their final prophets appear to have been persuasive in turning the hearts of many to God (Ezra 5:1, 2; Mal. 3:16; 4:2).

But the land of promise was still sparsely populated and mainly in the hands of heathen foreigners and of apostates (Samaritans).

When our Lord began his ministry 400 years later, such vast changes had taken place that, had Malachi returned to visit, he might not have noticed much that was familiar. Many of the ideas, customs, institutions, and civil laws, and much of the political geography, were new and different. The people even spoke a different language – the Aramaic of the Exile had taken over from Hebrew, and Greek was now widely understood. Latin was heard in Roman administrative centers. Jews now constituted the majority of the population – numbering in millions – of the central portion of the land from Idumaea south of Hebron to the borders of Syria north of Galilee and in a large part of Trans-Jordan known as Peraea.

For the first hundred years after Malachi (who prophesied about 420 BC), the Jews enjoyed freedom and safety to develop their own community under the mild and friendly rule of the later kings of the Achaemenid Persians. The tone set at the beginning by Cyrus, the Persian, prevailed to the end of this century – closing 333/2 BC with the conquest of the Near East by Alexander of Macedon, apostle of Hellenism. We know very little about details. 'Though the general history of the ancient Orient is quite adequately known, during much of this time (particularly the fourth century) our knowledge of the Jews is very nearly a blank.'[8] We know the names of leaders at the very beginning – Ezra (Ezra 7:11, 12), the 'priest' and 'scribe' of fame in the books of Ezra and Nehemiah, was

---

8 John Bright, *The History of Israel* (Philadelphia: Westminster, 1959), p. 389.

there for a time beginning 428 BC[9] Nehemiah (Neh. 13:631) was there for a second time at the beginning of the period. A certain Jaddua – perhaps, though doubtfully, still in office in the time of Darius III, the last Achaemenid Persian king – at a very advanced age[10] was the high priest. There are bare names of citizens; but that is all.

Hellenism, that is, Greek culture, and a succession of Hellenistic overlords (the Ptolemy dynasty of Egypt, then the Seleucus dynasty of Syria) were brought by the conquests of Alexander. In the second quarter of the second century BC, the faithful of the Jews had to pay heavily to maintain their loyalty to Biblical religion when Antiochus IV, the current Seleucid king, sought to compel all Jews to worship idols and to conform to Greek ways of thinking and doing. At this time a priestly family of the Jewish village of Modin, known as the Maccabees, led the resistance, carrying on a guerilla warfare at first and later a succession of pitched battles which won renewed national independence for a few decades. During this time of violence and its aftermath, most of the religious and political parties whom we meet in the Gospels originated. The Maccabees, or Hasmoneans, as they are also called, ruled as priest-kings for several generations after 135 BC.

Just before the middle of the last century BC, the Romans assumed the real political suzerainty of the Near East. From 60 BC onward the Jewish civil and religious leaders (i.e., the high priests as well as kings, tetrarchs, ethnarchs, etc.) ruled as vassals of the Roman central power. The process of change is exceedingly complex, for at this time the revolutions that changed the Roman Empire from a form of republic to a genuine empire, i.e., imperial dictatorship, were taking place.

The first Hasmonean king, John Hyrcanus (135-104 BC), had expanded southward so as to include the Idumaeans (the Old Testament Edomites) then living in the land immediately south of Hebron and, in the process, had compelled the Idumaeans to accept circumcision, i.e., to become Jewish in religion. In one of the strangest reprisals of history, an Edomite governor, known to history as Antipas (or Antipater), by conniving with the Romans over a period of years, succeeded in having his son, Herod (the Great), named king of Judaea in 40 BC, though he was not able to assume the rule for three or four years on account of a Parthian invasion. This is the man who was king of the Jews when the wise men from the East came seeking another who was born 'king of the Jews' and desiring to 'worship him.'

---

9 ibid., p. 386.

10 John C. Whitcomb, Jr., "Nehemiah," in Charles F. Pfeiffer and Everett F. Harrison, eds, *Wycliffe Bible Commentary* (Chicago: Moody, 1962), p. 443; Bright, *The History of Israel,* pp. 386, 390, 393(n).

THE WORLD OF JESUS' TIME

Jesus would have modified all history afterward no matter at what time and place He entered it. To understand the particular impact and the response He generated, however, it is necessary to know something in particular about the Jewish nation of that epoch, for He lived out His life as a Palestinian Jew.

The entire New Testament falls within the period of the early strength of the imperial period of Rome. The Persian and Greek empires, which had preceded the Roman had enlarged and strengthened the geographical, commercial, cultural, and religious connections of all men to a degree. But it took the peculiar genius of the Romans to break all the ancient world in pieces, subdue it, and then put it all together again (Dan. 2:20; 7:7, 23) in one centrally administered complex, united by the finest network of roads the world was to see for thousands of years again and homogenized by common acceptance of the inherited Greek language and culture.

The Roman character of the world of Jesus' time is much less evident in the Gospels than a less focused narrative would reveal. There were, of course, some Roman soldiers with their accoutrements and symbols stationed at the procurator's headquarters in Caesarea down on the coast; there were Roman police and frequent official Roman visitors in Jerusalem – though most of the Roman military and civil officers had prudently maintained a very low profile in the Jewish capital. The scenes of the Savior's infancy, boyhood, and adult life were almost entirely, however, far from the Roman presence in Palestine. The persons we meet until the last week of His life are almost without exception Jewish provincials. They are Oriental - not European – in every respect. Though the Roman power and presence in Palestine is of some limited importance in understanding details of Jesus' life, it is of little importance to Jesus' life – appearing more in some oblique references in His parables than in personal incidents.

The Hellenization (i.e., prevalence of Greek culture) of the whole Roman world, especially among the Jews of the Dispersion, is of far greater significance in the life of Jesus than the Roman elements. It was this 'progressive' element in the national life that brought the life of the nation to a crisis point in the second century before His birth and that produced, by way of reception or reaction, many of the most significant currents of His time.

The thinkers of the Greek world three to six centuries earlier gave the world what today goes by the name of Western culture, especially on its literary, intellectual, and artistic sides. The names of the Greek philosophers (Plato, Aristotle, Socrates), the historians (Hesiod, Herodotos, Xenophon), scientists and mathematicians (Thales, Pythagoras, Archimedes), dramatists (Aeschylos, Sophocles, Euripides), etc. were names to conjure by in Jesus' time among all well-educated people – as they have been ever since. We are still amazed at their accomplishments, and the world will never outgrow them. They were the models of excellence at that time, and none were more interested in entering the circles of that culture and in excelling in them than those very Jews scattered throughout the Roman world and returning often to Jerusalem for the great annual feasts and temple rituals of their nation and religion. The roads of the Empire led *through* as well as by Galilee, and the Greek language was spoken by some throughout the region. It is pretty well accepted among scholars today that the Lord would have been conversant with the Greek language as well as with the Hebrew, the religious language of his people, and, of course, with the dialect of Aramaic prevalent in northern Palestine.

PALESTINIAN JEWS IN JESUS' TIME

Jesus lived out His brief life in a particular historical situation. His life began in a pious Jewish home in which Mosaic Biblical religion was fervently believed and carefully practiced. Modifications of that system of faith imparted by the Exile of five centuries earlier, by restoration, by submission to Persian and Greek overlords, by a briefly renewed national independence, and by resubmission, this time to the Roman conquerors, were familiar to Him. He showed Himself to be particularly aware of the special problems created by the Roman suzerainty and very adept at adjusting to it. The forms of Jewish life in that milieu now demand our attention. They shall be introduced briefly but as completely as our present knowledge and limitations of space allow.

Geography. The physical features of Palestine, modified somewhat by human use and misuse, have remained pretty much the same in all ages. The main changes are those characteristic of all the ancient Orient – loss of the forests, overgrazing and the resultant erosion of the soil. The distance from the south border of the land of the Jews at or near Beer-sheba in the Idumaea of Jesus' time to the north border of upper

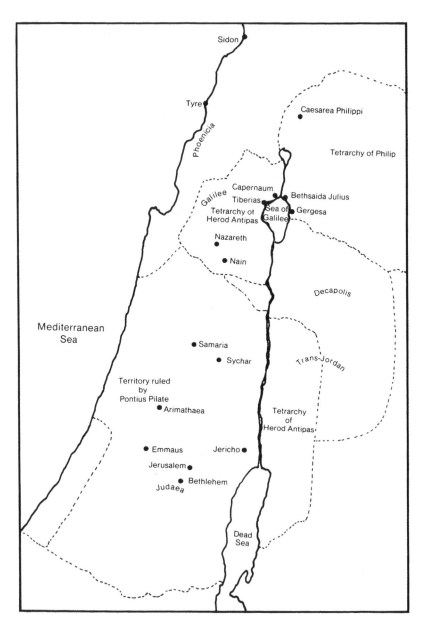

Map I. Palestine

Galilee is about 120 miles, somewhat less than 50 miles from Joppa on the sea to the Jordan near Jericho on the east and another 30 or 35 miles farther to the desert on the east, beyond Peraea and the Decapolis. The usual journey of a pedestrian pilgrim from Nazareth to Jerusalem would take him from an area of mountains up to 3,900 feet in height (though the town itself is situated at about 1,000 feet) to a depth of about 1,000 feet below sea level near Jericho and up again over the shoulder of the mount of Olives at over 2,500 feet. It is a land of rainfall varying from thirty to fifty inches annually in the hill country on both sides of the Jordan to less than fifteen inches in the areas about the Dead Sea and in southern and eastern deserts. The present-day traveler to the Holy Land is deceived about the prevalence of adequate rainfall in most of the inhabited areas simply because of three factors: (1) the exposure of rocks due to centuries of erosion; (2) the cutting of the trees throughout all ages, especially during the era of the Turks, who put a tax on trees, making their ownership a liability and resulting in the impoverishment of the natural beauty of the land and the above-mentioned erosion; and (3) the fact that most people visit Palestine in the summer months when the whole Mediterranean area tends toward aridity. It is an area of two seasons – wet from November to April and dry the rest of the time. Jerusalem gets about the same annual rainfall as Berlin or London, but it gets it all in a five- or six-month period. The ancients regarded it as a very fair land and peoples of southwest Asia today regard it the same way.

Political geography. The areas lived in or visited by Jesus during His ministry were divided into five political jurisdictions, though only four of them were parts of Palestine. Three of the political jurisdictions were based on a partition provided by the will of Herod the Great, who died in 4 BC, shortly after Jesus was born. Herod bequeathed to his son Archelaüs his title of king and his control of Samaria to the north, of Judaea adjoining on the south of Samaria, and of a portion of Idumaea controlled by Herod still south of Judaea. To another son, Herod Antipas (who executed John the Baptist and before whom Jesus appeared as prisoner on the day of crucifixion), he left Galilee, the northern territory above Samaria and west of both the Sea of Galilee and the upper River Jordan, together with Peraea, a band of territory on the east side of Jordan. Another son, Philip, received the territory east of the upper Jordan and south about the River Jarmuk. The fourth area, known as the Decapolis (Mark 5:20; 7:31; Matt. 4:25) – a Greek word meaning 'ten cities' – was a league of thoroughly Hellenistic and predominantly pagan towns mainly east and south of the Sea of Galilee but extending along the east side of Peraea as far south as old Rabbath-ammon (Philadelphia) and including the Plain of Jezreel around Beth-shan (Scythopolis). This part of Palestine was not very Jewish, and Jesus frequently visited there to get free of conflicts with Jews. It was not strictly a definite geographical jurisdiction but a recognized and legal league – its origin largely only surmised by modern scholars. The fifth area is Phoenicia, approximately identical with present-day Lebanon, in Jesus' time directly under the administration of the Roman governor of Syria. All five of these regions were parts of a basic geographic and political unity. Jesus could and did freely travel in all of these five areas without interference. All five areas were responsible to the governor of Syria. Ten years after the death of Herod the Great, complaints were lodged by residents of Judaea and Samaria against Archelaüs, with the result that Caesar Augustus deposed him, deported him to Gaul, and made the area a special kind of imperial province – that is, directly responsible to the emperor-governed by a procurator. Thus during Jesus' ministry the Roman ruler of Judaea and Samaria was the procurator Pontius Pilate, fifth Roman governor of Judaea.

Jewish religion. That which after the rejection of Messiah and the founding of the church could be disparagingly called merely 'the Jew's religion' (Gal. 1:14) was for Jesus a way of life that He voluntarily accepted and obeyed. The special features of that way of life were the wonder of the ancients, frequently noted, often resented by non-Jews, but sturdily defended by them.

The basic elements of Old Testament ritual religion were all observed in Jesus' time. There was the *temple* at Jerusalem. An ancient glorious king named Solomon had built the first permanent Jewish sanctuary there on a site divinely indicated to his famous father, David – whose descendant Jesus was. Solomon's structure had stood from the tenth to the first part of the sixth century BC, when it was destroyed by Nebuchadnezzar at the time of the Captivity of Judah. A very modest replacement was set up by the returned exiles at the end of the sixth century. This already ancient structure had now been magnificently and reverently replaced, stone by stone and piece by piece – services never being interrupted – by a superbly built edifice. The central house with inner and outer sanctuaries had about it an inner court of the officiating priests where the main altar of burnt sacrifice sat. Surrounding terraces contained a small court of Israel (i.e., for Jewish male laymen) on the north, east, and south sides; and a larger rectangular court which Jewish females as well as males could enter. Surrounding the whole site a very large enclosure (almost identical in area with the present Muslim Haram court-enclosure of the el Aqsa Mosque and the Dome of the Rock). This largest enclosure was known as the court of the Gentiles, for though non-Jews were forbidden on pain of death to go further toward the central sanctuary, any person could enter this area.

The ministers of this temple were the *priests,* all descendants of Moses' brother, Aaron, and their assistants the *Levites,* descendants of the third son of Jacob by his wife Leah. The procedures were regulated by the books of Exodus, Leviticus, and Numbers and involved mainly elaborate rituals for five main distinct *sacrifices* of animals, grains, and subsidiary elements. There were sacrifices regularly offered morning and evening as well as weekly, seasonally, and on special application by offerers. The temple was usually a busy place during all daylight hours. The outmost court provided space for stalls where money could be changed to proper ritual coin and where worshipers from afar could buy sacrificial animals and other materials, practices which degenerated into sharp dealing and corruption by the business agents there.

The *ritual calendar* prescribed by the Mosaic Law required every adult male in the land to appear before the central sanctuary three times a year: on the Passover and accompanying feast of Unleavened Bread in the first month (March/April); on Pentecost or Firstfruits fifty days after the beginning of Passover week; and in the fall the 15th to 22nd days of the seventh month (September/ October) called the feast of Tabernacles (literally, 'booths'). At this feast the families moved out of doors and lived in the open, as Mosaic Law prescribed, for in Palestine the crops – except perhaps a few olives – have by then all been gathered and the country has near perfect weather. It was certainly the highlight of the year for children, being, in a manner of speaking, a combination camping trip and Sunday school picnic, with overtones of a revival meeting.

These three annual family treks to the central sanctuary were the very heart of the national and family life of the Jewish people of Palestine in the time of Jesus. This made of Jerusalem necessarily a hospitality center. Enormous crowds are said to have assembled thereabouts at the time of main feasts. Note that Jesus and the Twelve walked in from as far as Bethany at the time of the last Passover.

The Jewish *Scriptures,* our Old Testament, known to them as the Law, the Prophets, and the Writings, are familiar to us and call for no comment. Though existing in Greek translation, they were read in the ancient Hebrew at the local synagogues according to a schedule. The readings were accompanied by formalized, orally preserved translations into vernacular Aramaic, called Targums.

The Jewish *synagogue* (from the Greek word *synagoge*, meaning 'assembly') was the central feature of Jewish life outside the home. Wherever Jews lived they associated with voluntary assemblies, much as free-church Protestants do today. The synagogue evidently arose and grew in popularity during the Exile when there was no ritual sacrifice or worship. The synagogue building was much like a Protestant church building of nonliturgical type, and its services were much like nonliturgical church worship. The leading teachers, who were not clergy but simply educated laymen (as in Protestant theory), were called *rabbis.* The rabbis studied in schools much like the seminaries of today. Some of the rabbis were denominated *lawyers,* rabbis who presumably were experts in interpreting the legal portions of the Scriptures and who had no official standing beyond that, though they would have been important persons in a land where civil and religious jurisdiction were not distinguished carefully. Apparently the highest order of teachers, or rabbis, were the *scribes.* Jewish tradition finds pairs of leading rabbis in succeeding periods of their history, both before and after Christ. Hillel (who died at about eighty-five when Jesus was about ten) and Shammai (Hillel's pupil and later rival) were the two teachers most honored in the period of Jesus' childhood. They were and still are cited by Jews with greatest respect.

In addition to the teachers (rabbis, lawyers, scribes), those who influenced opinion and official acts most were the leaders of two great politico-religious parties of the country. Those most thoroughly orthodox, most loyal to the national heritage in politics and religion but opposed to violent resistance to Rome, and most admired and followed by the common people were the party known as *Pharisees.* The party of accommodation, including the leading families of political influence (those close to the Hasmonean family), and of religious skepticism denying both immortality and the resurrection of the body – were known as *Sadducees.* They merit approval for their impatience with the growing body of *oral tradition* cherished by the Pharisees, but they were essentially worldly and irreligious, even though the nation's religious leaders (i.e., chief priests) were of the Sadducee party. But in spite of all this religiosity, religion had sadly declined. The externals had been multiplied, but the inner spirit had disappeared. However rude and sinful the old nation had sometimes been, it was capable in its worst periods of producing majestic religious figures, who kept high the ideal of life and preserved the connection of the nation with Heaven; and the inspired voices of the prophets kept the stream of truth running fresh and clean. But during four hundred years no prophet's voice had been heard. The records of the old prophetic utterances were still preserved with almost idolatrous reverence, but there were not men with even the necessary amount of the Spirit's inspiration to understand what He had formerly written.[11]

Another group unnamed in the New Testament but called *Essenes* (from an Aramaic word meaning 'holiness') by Josephus and Pliny, may be related to if not identical with the Jewish sect headquartered at Qumran, the people of the Dead Sea Scrolls. This sect, known mainly from the Dead Sea Scrolls and related literature, had abandoned both the ritual Judaism of the temple (presided over by the Sadducee high priesthood) and of the synagogue (dominated by the earnest but self-deceived Pharisees) in favor of a semi-ascetic life, partly in communal (cenobite) or solitary (eremite) monastic situations and partly in more normal married state within the village system of the land. Just how loyal to the faith of Abraham and the true spirit of Moses and the Prophets they were, is hard to say, though there are scholars who would make John the Baptist, and even the Savior Himself, one of their number.

Still another group were those celebrated only in 'the short and simple annals of the poor' – the ordinary working people of Palestine. Though attached via synagogue and natural sympathy with 'the party of warmth,' the Pharisees,[12] they really did not count greatly in national affairs. Into this class our Lord was born. There were good men in all the parties, but the New Testament shows that piety lingered longest then, as in all epochs, in the homes of the lowly. Just as in Martin Luther's time and as in ours there are those who believingly look beyond an elaborate, rigid liturgy to the living God, so 'among the common people there were those who, hearing the Scriptures read in the synagogues and reading them in their homes, instinctively neglected the cumbrous and endless comments of their teachers, and saw the glory of the past, of holiness and of God, which the scribes failed to see.'[13]

---

11 SLC, p. 28.
12 ibid., p. 31.
13 ibid.

Another element, pitiable in extreme, had no connection at all with religion and normal social life. These were the harlots and 'sinners' and the hated Jewish tax-gatherers, or publicans.

To this nation, 'lost sheep of the house of Israel,' the Messiah came. In sullen subjection to an oppressive foreign power, the people were ruled politically by the apostate dynasty of Herod and by oppressive foreign military officers. Their upper ruling class was selfish, skeptical, politicized, bureaucratized, and apostate. Their religious teachers and chief examples in religion rested in ceremonies, legalism, and formalism, 'their souls honeycombed with self-deception and vice; the body of the people misled by false ideals; and seething at the bottom of society, a neglected mass of unblushing and unrestrained sin'[14] – such was the condition of our Lord's people when He lived and died among them.

---

14 ibid.

CHAPTER 2

The Word Became Flesh and Dwelled Among Us

When the Desire of Nations and the Redeemer of Israel came forth from the ivory palaces, everything was ready for him - in the heathen world, in moribund Jewry, and in a godly home (Matt. 1:24) of Galilee. It takes a Christian eye to see it, but it is so. Providence had arranged so that He whom His countrymen knew to be a carpenter (Mark 6:3) of Nazareth (John 1:45) in Galilee; whom prophecy had declared would become flesh before the eyes of men at Bethlehem (Mic. 5:2); who would be a man of sorrows (Isa. 53:3) and yet a glorious king (Ps. 72); whom some would recognize simply as a Jew (John 4:9) but was truly the representative Man (John 5:27), the last Adam (I Cor. 15:45); who would veil His glory as God that men might judge Him for what He said and did as man – this One came forth from the Father when the time was ripe – in the very fullness of time (Gal. 4:4). Mark and John say almost nothing of this, but Matthew and Luke, each in his peculiar manner, makes it a matter of plain record in the first two chapters of their respective Gospel narratives.

As we read the short narratives of Matthew and Luke, our curiosity is aroused about what is left unreported. We remind ourselves that we are investigating the earthly career of the Messiah, not the biography of Israel's most famous son. No one will ever write a genuine biography of the Word made flesh; the materials are unavailable. We are granted vignettes of prenatal announcements to his 'parents' and some visions, crises, oracles connected with the appearance of John His forerunner. There are several tantalizing glimpses of the infant and His anxious parents, of kings, of imperial decrees, and of visitors from near and far. We learn of a sudden flight out of the country with a surreptitious return and settlement in Nazareth, and of necessary religious rites over a period of about thirty years, but that is all (Matt. 1; Luke 1, 2). We will follow the story through these materials, sifting some of the fruit of reverent investigation through the Christian centuries.

THE BIRTH OF HIS FORERUNNER

Luke
1:5-25
1:39-80
'The voice of one that crieth, Prepare ye in the wilderness the way of the Lord' (Isa. 40:3). This is the way Old Testament prophecy spoke of the announcement to Israel of Messiah's arrival. A few months before the formal opening of Jesus' ministry, a man named John appeared in the deserts of Israel proclaiming the presence of the long-predicted kingdom of God and calling on Israel to prepare to receive it by repenting. Jesus Himself acknowledged John to be the promised messenger, the fulfillment of Isaiah's prophecy, and submitted Himself to baptism at John's hands.

The miraculous wonder of John's conception and birth is, in the New Testament, exceeded only by Jesus' own.

In the hill country of Judaea – at a place generally acknowledged by pilgrims since at least the seventh century[1] and known as Ain Karim – there lived an aged priest named Zacharias and his aged wife, Elizabeth. After the Return in the sixth century BC, the Jewish authorities had organized the remnant of the sons of Aaron according to the family names of the original twenty-four clan orders of the times of Moses and David – though not all the clans were truly represented among the returnees.[2] They were settled about the country and given hereditary real estate rights. Zacharias's home (if indeed Ain Karim, 'Spring of the Vineyard') was a little less than five miles west of Jerusalem, in the midst of some rather steep hills (Luke 1:39, 65).

Luke relates how this couple, both 'well stricken in years,'[3] came to

---

1 FANT, pp. 3-5.

2 This information comes mainly from 1 Chronicles 1-8; Ezra 2:1-69; 8:1-36; Neh. 7:1-73; 10: 1-39; 11:1-12:47.

3 Later Zacharias said to the angel, 'I am an old man' (Luke 1:18). Just how old were Zacharias and Elizabeth? According to Numbers 4:3 and 8:24 a Levite began his work at the sanctuary at the age

have a child when for them, as for aged Sarai and Abram centuries before, such an event was simply not to be expected.

Each course of priests was on duty twice a year, so Zacharias had often served in the 'court of the priests,' but this was (if we may trust Alfred Edersheim's dictum)[4] to be the first and last time he would have the greatest privilege granted ordinary priests, that of offering incense upon the golden altar within the holy place of the temple! Two assistants would have accompanied him within, one to remove the ashes of yesterday (if this was the morning sacrifice), the other to spread fresh coals from the brazen altar upon the golden altar. But both had now gone outside to join other prostrate worshipers. The superintending priest had given the signal to spread the incense on the coals and sufficient time had passed to accomplish this, but Zacharias did not come out. He had been visited by an angel who promised him a child by his aged wife (Luke 1:11-17). The angel directed them to rear the son as a Nazirite and to name him John *(Jochanan,* 'the grace of the Lord'). John, the angel said, would prepare the people for the coming of the Lord (Luke 1:16). The astounded priest's response of doubting obedience, while not admirable, is understandable and gave occasion for the supernatural signs which confirmed the matter to the aged couple and all their neighbors (Luke 1:18-23, 57-84).

Rather strong inference (Luke 1:26, 39ff.) indicates that John was conceived about six months before Mary conceived her first-born, Jesus. So Mary and Joseph were not the first to know that the time of Messiah's appearance had come, for Zacharias had first learned that 'the Lord' (Luke 1:17) was about to appear.

ANGELIC ANNOUNCEMENTS OF HIS COMING

Six months later Gabriel ('Hero of God'), messenger of special revelation known to saints of old, broke the news to a maiden of Nazareth (Luke 1:26; cf. Dan. 8:16; 9:21). Christian devotion has emphasized the virgin's   Luke 1: 26-56 Matt. 1:18-25

---

of twenty-five (though evidently not admitted to certain service until thirty) and terminated it at sixty. The Bible, however, says nothing of the sort about any age beyond which a priest could not serve. Rabbinic sources furnish no proof otherwise in Jewish custom. *'Das Alter machte die priester nicht dienstunfnehig'* ('Age did not make the priests unfit for service'). SBCNT, 2:89. So Zacharias could have been more than fifty years of age, and his wife, also. Alfred Edersheim asserted, ' ... from *Aboth* [a Talmud tractate] v. 21 we learn, that sixty years was considered the commencement of agedness.' ELTJM, 1:135.

4 ELTJM, 1:135, 137; SBCNT is silent.

purity while critical scholarship has concentrated on the biological miracle of conception without impregnation. We can safely lay aside these somewhat overworked themes to concentrate on the concern of the divine messenger. Everything he said about the infant to be born the following winter, proclaimed: Mary shall conceive and bear the promised Messiah. The language of Hebrew prophecy underlies the angel's words, while specific messianic texts and ideas fill the announcement.[5] The correspondences between Gabriel's words and specific Old Testament prophecies inspired the famous lines:

> For lo, the days are hastening on,
> By prophet-bards foretold,
> When, with the ever-encircling years,
> Comes round the age of gold.

The angel solved just enough of the mystery of the Word becoming flesh to enable Mary to carry on, and she responded with obedient faith.

Shortly the careers (though prenatal in each case)[6] of the herald and the Messiah crossed (Luke 1:39-41) – never again to meet until that day when in mature young manhood the former baptized the latter in the Jordan and Jesus' active public career as Messiah began (Matt. 3:13; John 1:29, 35, 36). The ennobling thoughts of the two kinsman mothers-to-be, the one very young, the other very old for motherhood, do not require imagination alone to perceive, for each has given the church a song expressing in Holy Spirit-inspired language her exalted feelings on that day (Luke 1:46-55).

The announcement by the angel to Joseph supplements and finishes the one to Mary in every way.

---

5 Here are some of the correspondences: 'conceive in thy womb'='a virgin shall conceive' (Isa. 7:14); 'bring forth a son'='bear a son' (Isa. 7:14); 'call his name Jesus [Jehovah-Savior] '='call his name Immanuel' (Isa. 7:14), 'he will come and save you' (Isa. 35:4); 'he shall be great'='great is the Lord' (I Chron. 16:25); 'called the Son of the Highest'='the Lord, whom ye seek, shall suddenly come' (Mal. 3:1); 'the throne of his father David'='the throne of David' (Isa. 9:7), 'I will set up thy [David's] seed after thee' (II Sam. 7:12); 'reign over the house of Jacob'='and David my servant shall be king over them [the children of Israel; and they shall all have one shepherd' (Ezek. 37:24); 'he shall reign... for ever; and of his kingdom there shall be no end' – 'and they shall dwell in the land... they, and their children, and their children's children for ever; and my servant David shall be their prince for ever' (Ezek. 37:25; cf. Dan. 2:44; 7:14).

6 One is moved to ask: Did the young and delicate, pregnant virgin travel alone the seventy or eighty miles from Nazareth to Ain *Karim?* Did she reside in a place other than Nazareth where the holy family came to live later? Did her parents approve the journey? Did Joseph know of it and approve? There seem to be no answers.

It is not expressly stated by Luke that Mary, after a stay of three months (Luke 1:56), left Elizabeth before she was delivered of John, but it is the natural sense of the narrative.[7] The arithmetic makes sure that John's birth was imminent (Luke 1:24-26, 56). At any rate her absence from Nazareth had been long enough to make her pregnancy unconcealable (Matt. 1:18). Perhaps she discussed it with Joseph, though Matthew does not even hint at it. Formal engagement was marriage, before the Law, even if cohabitation had not begun. Joseph (being unwilling to accept an immoral woman as mother of his children) therefore had available two courses - either make charges at a public hearing before the officers of the local Sanhedrin, with possibility of severe punishment of the mother and a public scandal (Deut. 22: 13-21); or, without deciding on the (likely) guilt or (possible) innocence of the girl, give her a formal writing of divorcement before two discreetly chosen witnesses (Deut. 24:1, 2). Change of feeling was the only sufficient legal ground for this sort of divorce.[8] What Joseph's responsibility toward the yet unborn child would be is not clear. A 'just' man like Joseph, i.e., one whose life is directed by **all** the law of God, would remember mercy and take the gentler course (Matt. 1:19, 20).

The angel's message confirmed several features of his previous message to Mary: the babe was conceived by the divine power (with no suggestion of the frequent mythological pagan cohabitation of gods with women); the child shall be a son, and he is to be named *Jehoshua (Iésous* in Greek, Jesus in English) 'Jehovah-Savior.' This would likely have come out as *Yeshua* in the vernacular Aramaic of Nazareth. The angel also told Joseph that Jesus would 'save His people [in Joseph's understanding, Israel] from their sins.' This had been elaborated to Mary, except that sin as cause of their lostness had not been emphasized. That the Lord has 'people' among all 'peoples' was not yet widely understood by 'the lost sheep of the house of Israel.'

In the Greek text of Luke 1:35 the angel does not say 'The Holy Spirit shall come upon thee and the power of the Highest shall overshadow thee.' The definite articles are absent. A more literal and chaste (free from any dogmatic tendency) rendering would be 'holy Spirit shall come upon thee and power of Highest shall overshadow thee.' The second member ('power of the highest') explains the first ('holy Spirit shall come upon thee'). The specific point of the Angel is to answer Mary's

---

7 ALOL, p. 70.
8 SBCNT, 1:50-53.

question, 'How shall this be seeing I know not a man' (v34), Gabriel closes by emphasizing, 'For with God nothing shall be impossible.' Mary, therefore (and we as well) should understand not that the Third Person of the triune God is the father of our Lord's human nature but that His conception was by the power of the divine Spirit, God Himself, with whom all things are possible. The explanations by Calvin, Alford and more recently J. A. Fitzmeyer agree. (See *The Gospel According to Luke, I-IX, The Anchor Bible* (Garden City, NY: Doubleday & Co., 1981) pp350, 351.)

Thus the two announcements, though couched wholly in the mold of the Jewish world-view of Mary and Joseph, both obliquely suggest the larger mission of Messiah as the Savior of the world. This mission could be plainly made known to all only after Jesus was slain as the 'Lamb of God which taketh away the sin of *the* world' – not merely for Jewish sins.

HIS GENEALOGIES

_{Matt.} The purpose of each of these genealogies is to connect Jesus, by reason
_{1:1-17} of legal and natural descent, with three ideas of Old Testament promise
_{Luke}
_{3:23-38} and thereby secure His claim to be the promised Messiah. These intensely Hebraic notions are that the Messiah was to be (1) 'the seed of the woman,' (2) 'the seed of Abraham,' and (3) 'the seed of David.'

The seed of the woman (Gen. 3:15). The first promise of human redemption is that a seed (i.e., 'offspring') of womankind should crush the serpent's head. With profound insight and terrible earnestness, Paul traces the universal corruption, bondage, and guilt of man to the first man, Adam, in whom we all then were, who in one fateful act of disobedience brought this tragedy upon us all (Rom. 5:12-21; cf. I Cor. 15:45-48). The removal of sin's corruption, bondage, and guilt was to come by the last Adam – a descendant of Adam but free from Adam's guilt. When Eve, herself out of Adam's side, conceived seed by Adam and produced the offspring who were to carry on the race (Gen. 5:1-3), she did thereby procreate a vital, ongoing human unity: '... by man came death, by man came also the resurrection...' (I Cor. 15:21); '... there is one God and one mediator between God and men, the man Christ Jesus' (I Tim. 2:5). Luke's genealogy shows us that when God sent the Savior, He entered human history as a descendant of Adam and his wife. Starting with Jesus Himself, Luke traces the lineage back through Hebrew ancestry as far back as the first Hebrew, Abraham, and thence through Abraham's ancestors to Adam, the created Son of God. So, though His coming was announced by an angel, Jesus was not an angel incognito. 'Forasmuch then as the children are partakers of flesh and blood, he also himself likewise took part of the same... He took not on Him the nature of angels...' (Heb. 2:14, 16).

The seed of Abraham (Heb. 2:16). Paul calls attention to the special significance of the Hebrew nation. His memorable words describe the Israelites as those 'to whom pertaineth the adoption, and the glory, and the covenants, and the giving of the law, and the service of God, and the promises; whose are the fathers, and of whom as concerning the flesh Christ came...' (Rom. 9:4, 5). Their story begins with the original call of Abram. One of the central features of the call was that 'in thee [Abram] shall all the families of the earth be blessed' (Gen. 12:3). In Christ this promised blessing of all families of mankind came to pass. Hence Luke shows that Messiah's descent from Adam was through Abram. Matthew, whose focus of interest is less universal than Luke's, begins with Abraham, as is proper in his book, designed first to be read by the Jewish brethren of our Lord.

The seed of David (Luke 1:32, 33). It is emphasized in both genealogies that Jesus' descent was through David, the son of Jesse, the greatest of the ancient kings of Israel. At this point some acquaintance with the whole of II Samuel 7 is indispensable. The man who shall have an everlasting kingdom from which God's mercy shall never depart is 'thy [David's] seed after thee, which shall proceed out of thy bowels' (II Sam. 7:12). According to one of the prophets, the righteous king who shall renew the fallen creation and restore 'equity for the meek of the earth' will be 'a shoot *[netzer,* 'Nazarene'] out of the stock of Jesse' (Isa. 11:1-5; cf. 23:5, 6; 30:9). Another foresees that He shall be a 'branch of righteousness' who 'will grow up unto David,' in whose 'days shall Judah be saved and Jerusalem shall dwell safely,' for 'David shall never want a man to sit upon the throne of the house of Israel' (Ezek. 34:23, 24; Zech. 3:8; 6:12, 13; Isa. 4:2).

Two questions arise. First, How does the genealogy of Joseph in Matthew 1 connect Jesus with David, for Jesus was not Joseph's offspring? Joseph, by taking Mary as his legal wife, became unquestionably the father of Jesus in Jewish law and custom. The villagers of Nazareth accepted this. A close analogy is found in the law of Levirate[9] marriage

---

9 The word *levirate is* derived from the Latin word *levir,* 'brother-in-law.' Custom, enforced by Mosaic law (Deut. 25:5-10), strongly encouraged a man to marry the widow of his deceased brother, offspring of the union to perpetuate the name of the deceased.

(Deut. 25:5-10), whereby a brother married his deceased brother's wife and begat children by her in the brother's name. Jesus was Joseph's legal 'first-born' heir; hence if Joseph was a Davidic prince, so was Jesus. Strictly, Matthew's first chapter does not provide Jesus' natural genealogy, but Joseph's, though it does demonstrate Jesus' legal eligibility to accede to David's throne.

The second question relates to the genealogy in Luke: it appears also to be Joseph's. Without entering into the technicalities, it may be said that there are many reasons for holding this to be Mary's genealogy, not Joseph's. A simple shift of punctuation of Luke 3:23 ['Jesus himself being (as was supposed, the son of Joseph) the son of Heli'] allows the reader to understand that Jesus was the grandson of Heli, Mary's father, for Hebraic genealogical fashion normally omitted names of females in such registers.

Most reverent students who have registered opinions on this question – back to the earliest ages of the church – have held that Mary as well as Joseph was of the house of David, and many have contended that Luke gives her genealogical register. Scriptural evidence is of near-compelling force that Mary was of David's lineage. In Peter's first sermon he declared that in Christ was fulfilled God's oath to David 'that of the fruit of his loins, according to the flesh [not merely by Jewish laws about inheritance], he would raise up Christ to sit on his throne' (Acts 2:30). The original promise to David specified 'thy seed after thee, which shall proceed out of thy bowels' (II Sam. 7:12). 'Of this man's seed,' asserted Paul, 'hath God according to his promise raised unto Israel a Savior, Jesus' (Acts 13:23). Other equally impressive affirmations of a vital, lineal, biological connection between David and Jesus, infant son of Mary, may be read (see also II Tim. 2:8; Heb. 7:14; Rev. 22:16; Luke 1:32, 69; Isa. 11:1). Sitting on David's throne merely by legal right would not make Jesus 'the fruit of David's' loins in the clear sense which the Scriptures specify.

HIS PARENTS' JOURNEY TO BETHLEHEM

Augustus Caesar, the man who finished turning Rome from a republic into an imperial dictatorship, needed a better basis for taxing the far corners of his Empire. The basis might be provided by a universal census,[10] a device which even Israel's most noble king once unwisely

---

10 ALOL, pp 3-12; FLAP, pp 256-61; FHBC, pp. 215-55.

tried. So there went out a decree 'that all the world should be taxed [enrolled]' (Luke 2:1). The peculiar interest of modern Western people in dates has obscured the real meaning of that census. We want to know the history and politics of it; Luke is telling us how providence brought about fulfillment of an ancient prophecy (Mic. 5:2).[11]

Thus on an early winter day the newly formed household of Joseph, a carpenter of Nazareth, set out on an arduous, ninety-mile journey to the ancestral seat of the royal clan of David.

We can only imagine with what anxiety for his young wife Joseph set out and with what fatigue of body, coupled with exhilarating expectation of Messiah's birth from her own womb, the virgin wife accompanied him-afoot, or mounted on an ass, we cannot know for sure. But the Scriptures tell us the reasons of divine providence - why Octavius, self-praisingly called August, got to be emperor and why he used the position and power the way he did. The Messiah was to be called a *nazir* (or *netzer,* or Nazarene), said certain of the prophets, but another of their number affirmed that His birthplace would be Bethlehem. So 'the proud emperor drove southward the anxious couple. Yes; but another hand was leading them on – the hand of Him who overrules the purposes of emperors and kings, of statesmen and parliaments, for the accomplishment of His designs, though they know them not; who hardened the heart of Pharaoh, called Cyrus like a slave to His foot, and made the mighty Nebuchadnezzar His servant, and in the same way could overrule for His own far-reaching purpose the pride and ambition of Augustus.[12]

HIS NATIVITY

The strange modern preoccupation of 'clinical' and 'analytical' interest in every news event - giving the public such indiscreet morbidities as the length of Lyndon Johnson's abdominal incision and the precise location

Luke 2:6-38

---

11 Archaeology has recovered much about how such enrollments were conducted in the early imperial period. FLAP, p. 260. They were customarily taken every fourteen years. One of these census edicts is known to have been issued in AD 6. The next previous one would have been in 9 BC 'There is reason to think the actual taking of a census came in the year following that in which the order for it was given, in which case 8 BC would be indicated... and... it might have been delayed to 7 or 6 BC.' FLAP, p. 261. We also know about a prevalent practice of enrollment in the city of family residence by households. From the *Oxyrhynchus Papyri (VIII,* no. 1157) comes a clear example of a generally understood obligation *(subpoena)* to get to the ancestral home in person or by proxy for registration and payment of poll tax. FLAP, p. 251.
12 SLC, p. 11.

and direction of all of John Kennedy's fatal bullet wounds - is absent from Luke's reporting. Two verses – no more – are devoted to the mother's delivery and the infant's first care. In place of our statistics on length of time in labor, pounds and ounces, color of skin and eyes, we know only that there was no public lodging place for the parents to spend the night, presumably because many were in town to care for their own enrollment; that Jesus' first infant bed was some sort of manger; that He was born near the feeding place of animals; that apparently the mother herself bandaged the babe in a long linen cloth ('swaddling clothes') which she had prudently taken with her in expectation of delivery. All the news is in those two verses. The rest of Luke's report relates to: the worshipful respects paid to the newborn infant by some rustic shepherds who talked of angel choirs (fourteen verses); circumcision (one verse); presentation to the Lord (three verses); the blessing of aged Simeon (eleven verses); the thanksgiving of Anna (three verses).

This emphasis is certainly intended to teach believing readers something about the true sense of the Biblical narrative and thereby also of reality in spiritual things. The parents *obeyed* the Word of God in every detail of ritual instruction, presenting their first-born with the appropriate sacrifice at the temple; the shepherds *worshiped* Jesus; the aged Simeon found in Jesus the true *Star of lifelong saintly hope;* while the devoted, aged Anna, speaking *for* and *to* 'all that looked for redemption,' *gave thanks* to God for His unspeakable gift.

Learned negative criticism has attacked every historical detail of Luke's nativity story, and devout scholarship has defended it successfully. The miracle of virginal conception can neither be attacked nor defended on strictly empirical-logical grounds. Wise believers will respond as did the parents of Jesus, the shepherds, the wise men, Simeon, and Anna with worship, obedience, dedication, strengthened hope, and thanks to God.

HIS FAMILY'S FLIGHT TO EGYPT

Matt. 2:1-23 Luke 2:30 Luke says nothing of the family's flight to Egypt and the circumstances attending it, though he does refer to their return to Nazareth. We are indebted wholly to Matthew for this part of the story.

The order and time relation of three events connected with this period of Jesus' life have always puzzled students, lay and learned. Did the dedication of Jesus at the temple, when Simeon and Anna appear in the story, come on the normal fortieth day after birth or, as some say, on the way back to Nazareth from Egypt? Did the wise men visit Him shortly after His birth at Bethlehem (The feast of Epiphany, long celebrated in East and West on January 6, rests on the assumption that they did)? Or did Joseph and Mary go to Nazareth with the babe before the departure for Egypt, and did the wise men find them at Bethlehem on a later occasion? Eusebius (fourth century) and Epiphanius (d. AD 403) reasoned from the fact that Herod slew the children of Bethlehem up to two years of age that a year or two had passed.

A commonly received and defensible arrangement places the purification at the normal fortieth day, the visit of the wise men shortly after that.[13] We know from Matthew 2:21, 22 that Joseph probably planned to rear David's greater son in David's town – Bethlehem – and so secured a 'house' (Matt. 2:11). Very shortly after the purification the wise men came, and almost immediately after that the holy family, on the night of the angelic visitation, departed for Egypt (Matt. 2:16). Three assumptions seem both justifiable and helpful: (1) all these things may have transpired in a few weeks; (2) that Herod killed infants of Bethlehem up to two years of age signifies only that Herod was unconcerned about the dimensions of the atrocity; and (3) nothing definite is indicated about the age of Jesus at the time.

Thus Scripture telescopes the Christmas narrative. If we will rest content to view the story in that literary context, ignoring our modern curiosity about time and sequence, we will come up with the composite impression the authors of Scripture intended. It will represent to us the arrival of the prophesied Messiah in the fullness of time, at the right place, under the right circumstances, creating the responses which will be normal for His entire subsequent career and to the present moment.

Let us look at the circle of interested parties gathered, so to speak, about the cradle of the infant Messiah.

There were *representatives* of *heaven* – *the angel* Gabriel who broke the news first to Mary, then to Joseph, and finally, accompanied by a 'multitude of the heavenly host,' to the shepherds. Heaven's messengers were obviously interested. The Old Testament was mediated by angels (Heb. 2:2), so they no less than God's ancient holy people were passionately interested in the outcome as Peter so strikingly avers when he says that these things 'angels desire to look into' (I Peter 1:12). Angels

---

13 ALOL, pp. 89-93.

appear at several critical junctures of our Lord's earthly career. An angel (the word means 'messenger') also notified the virgin and her espoused husband of the impending arrival of Israel's Hope. We find angels later standing beside ardent missionaries (Acts 5:19) who tell the good news, and an angel shall publish the everlasting gospel before that last great day of the Lord comes. Who knows what assistance (Heb. 1:13, 14) they even now provide the messengers of the good news of Christ's person and work? There was a heavenly 'multitude' (Christian imagination calls it a choir) who praised God for sending His peace to earth in the hearing of the startled shepherds (Luke 2:13-15). How lavish God is with His gifts in the strangest places! As the famous elegy puts it:

> Full many a gem of purest ray serene
> The dark, unfathomed caves of ocean bear;
> Full many a flower is born to blush unseen,
> And waste its sweetness on the desert air.[14]

There was a small group of expectant godly *Jewish believers.* Mary and Joseph are only the most prominent among the pious people who viewed the Savior, or knew of Him, in His infancy. The mother was intelligently – if innocently – troubled, curious, submissive, joyous, patient. '... she was troubled... and cast in her mind what manner of salutation this should be' (Luke 1:29) 'How shall this be, seeing I know not a man'? (Luke 1:34). 'Behold the handmaid of the Lord; be it unto me according to thy word' (Luke 1:38). 'My soul doth magnify the Lord, and my spirit hath rejoiced in God my Savior' (Luke 1:46, 47). 'But Mary kept all these things, and pondered them in her heart' (Luke 2:19). Joseph was simply believing, obedient, and discreet. All that a loving godly husband should be, he was. As a tradesman, rather than as a farmer fixed to his fields, this simple man was able and willing to break up his residence several times in two or three years in order to protect the infant and His mother from the designs of wicked men. Both Mary and Joseph are models of Christian parenthood. The shepherds were men who cared for sheep intended for sacrifice at the temple not far away – evidently spending the entire year in the fields.[15] It is significant that these humble and, perhaps, despised rustics were privileged to hear and see what no pontiff or Jerusalem ecclesiastic was allowed. Their hearts

---

14 Thomas Gray, 'Elegy Written in a Country Churchyard.'
15 ELTJM, 1:186.

were pure and therefore received this supreme blessing of the Lord (Ps. 24:4, 5). Simeon and Anna, together with the wondering shepherds, stand for the genuinely righteous element, those who 'in an honest and good heart, having heard the word, keep it, and bring forth fruit with patience' (Luke 8:15). The centuries of suffering had plowed these Jewish hearts rather than hardening them. Their hearts had mutely prayed for the consolation of Israel (Luke 2:25); therefore they had the spiritual insight to recognize Him when He came.

The *Gentiles are* represented also, for the Magi, or wise men of the East, were likely Gentiles of a learned class who, following astrological principles and knowledge gained from Jews in dispersion, and divinely guided by the mysterious star, came seeking the Savior of the world. They represent another line of Old Testament prophecy and the special working of the Spirit out in heathendom (Isa. 42:1, 6; 49:6, 22; 60:3; Matt. 12:18-21; Acts 14:7) preparing a few to find the strait gate leading to eternal life.

In the indifferent citizens of Bethlehem, the callous-hearted innkeeper, and the proud ecclesiastics of Jerusalem (neither discerning the presence of the Lord at presentation and circumcision nor heeding the inspired voices of Simeon and Anna), there is *the perennially indifferent crowd of ordinary humanity, eager* to accept the solace and social pleasures of customary religion but unwilling to understand, much less to obey, its demands or deeper lessons.

Finally, Herod represents the greatest of all our Savior's enemies – the princes of this *world (I* Cor. 2:8). They never know the true Prince of life. Since He challenges their view of reality, they hate Him. They therefore killed Him and still persecute all His seed (John 7:7).

HIS CHILDHOOD IN NAZARETH

After that hasty flight from Herod to Egypt, the holy family settled at Nazareth of Galilee and stayed there. A number of writers have referred to this period as the silent years at Nazareth, and so they are except for the trip to Jerusalem at the end. This does not mean, however, that we are without dependable information about – if we dare so to call them – 'formative influences' on Him in the most impressionable years of His life. Certain it is that there were influences emanating from the community on His social, intellectual, and spiritual development, quite as much as there were influences from the terrain He walked, the air He breathed,

Matt. 2:23 Luke 2:40

and the food He ate upon His physical development. 'It would be easy to exaggerate the influence which they may be supposed to have exerted on His development. The greater and more original a character is, the less dependent it is on the peculiarities of its environment. It is fed from deep well-springs within itself, and in its germ there is a type enclosed which expands in obedience to its own laws and bids defiance to circumstances. In any other circumstances, Jesus would have grown to be in every important respect the very same person as He became in Nazareth.'[16]

There was first *the countryside.* The town was located in a region which, though surrounded by hills (some very high), was reputed for fertile fields, healthful climate, and pleasant scenery, and which had sufficient economic base for a relatively dense, stable population and a prosperous citizenry. No one should have gone hungry in Galilee. In spite of its seeming remoteness (to the Jerusalem elite), Galilee was crossed by several international trade roads and was in close touch with the Greek, Roman, and Arab world at its borders. The Judaea of Jesus' time, at the other end of Palestine, was already showing the ecological wear and tear of the violent centuries. It is exceedingly barren today in large part. But it was far different in Galilee, as it also is today. Though his Jewish enthusiasm for the land may have somewhat carried him away, Edersheim is essentially correct in saying, 'A more beautiful country – hill, dale, and lake – could scarcely be imagined... According to the Rabbis, it is easier to rear a forest of olive trees in Galilee than one child in Judaea. Corn grew in abundance, the wine... was rich and generous. Proverbially, all fruit grew in perfection, and altogether the cost of living was about one-fifth that in Judaea.'[17] Josephus may have exaggerated some, but again he may not, in saying there were about 240 towns and villages of Galilee, each with at least 15,000 inhabitants.[18] That would be at least 3,600,000. Americans especially, unacquainted generally with how *utterly* the ancient Mediterranean world perished in antiquity and how the Near East has suffered repeated and continual drain on all its natural resources (especially its forests and soils) up to the end of Turkish domination as recently as 1918, find it hard, when they see the region, to imagine the vast populations it once supported.

16 SLC, p. 23.
17 ELTJM, 1:224.
18 ibid.
19 A reading of a good historical geography of Palestine will set these matters in perspective. Though somewhat brief on history, BGB is excellent and of manageable size.

Jesus would have grown up with a sense of the Father's bountiful provisions for all His creatures, as His sayings amply indicate.[19]

There was above all the *orthodox Jewish home* of Joseph and Mary, shared by Jesus and several brothers and sisters. From His saintly and wise father, as was the Jewish custom, He learned the trade of carpentry (Matt. 13:55; Mark 6:3) and actually worked at it, making 'ploughs and yokes, thus setting before them symbols of righteousness and teaching an active life.'[20] From Jesus' words on the cross to John (John 19:26, 27) and the omission of any mention of Joseph's name or reference to him after Luke 2:51, it is generally assumed that Joseph died in Jesus' youth.

The most decisive influence on His growth was His mother's. What kind of woman she was is manifest by the angel's message, her response to it, the various notices throughout the Gospels, and especially her song, the Magnificat (Luke 1:46-55) – 'a woman religious, fervently poetical, and patriotic; a student of Scripture, and especially of its great women, for it [the Magnificat] is saturated with Old Testament ideas and molded on Hannah's song; a spirit exquisitely humble, yet capable of thoroughly appreciating the honor conferred upon her... pure, saintly, loving, and high-souled.'[21] Jesus grew up in the tender love and care of this marvelous mother, both of which He cordially returned.

The brothers and sisters of Jesus (at least the brothers) did not accept His messiahship until after His passion. His sisters – several of them were apparently married before He began His ministry, lived in Nazareth. The four brothers – James, Joseph (or Joses), Simon, and Judas – and the sisters[22] do not seem to have mixed much socially or familiarly with Him. His saying that a prophet is without honor in his own house (Mark 6:4; cf. Isa. 53:3) is one of greater pathos if we think of it as indicating experiences of rejection during the silent years. This large household is presented as being under Mary's immediate supervision and her husband Joseph's support and protection. There is no hint of a previous marriage of Joseph by which these children came to be, nor any Scripture cause for making them cousins. The

---

20 Justin Martyr, quoted in ALOL, p. 110.

21 SLC, p. 17.

22 Information on Jesus' brothers and sisters is at Matt. 13:56; Matt. 12:46-50; 13:33; Mark 6:3; Luke 7:19; John 2:12; 7:3; Acts 1:14; 1 Cor. 9:5; Gal. 1:19. There is a very adequate treatment of them in ALOL, pp. 111-23. Also helpful are: J. A. Alexander, *Commentary on the Gospel* of Mark (New York: Scribner, 1864; reprinted-Grand Rapids: Zondervan, n.d.), pp. 141-45; and John J. Gunther, 'The Family of Jesus,' *The Evangelical Quarterly* 46 (1974): 25-41. See also the various Bible encyclopedias under titles 'Brethren of the Lord' and 'Holy Family.'

Greek words used are normal for the primary relationship of children of the same parents. The so-called perpetual virginity of Mary is not a Biblical teaching but 'is either an article of faith, as with the Greeks and Romans... or a matter of feeling.'[23] 'After all it is not so much a matter of reason or of faith as of taste and sensibility.'[24] The social discipline, however, of living in a large family throughout life no doubt affected Jesus toward that orderly manner of life He ever manifested.

Synagogue joined with home in the teaching of the national religion and the Scriptures on which it rested. The synagogue promoted all the peculiar features of Jewish social life – feast, fast, ritual, marriage, human relation – and it enjoined the observance of Mosaic morality. We know that at this time the synagogue supplied basic education for children in reading and writing.[25] From Jesus' manner of quoting Scripture, it is quite certain that He could read Hebrew as well as the vernacular Aramaic of the populace. Though there is no reason to believe He ever read the Greek classics, He must have known how to read Greek. Hebrew was then a 'dead' language, but it was the original language of the Old Testament and was the only language in which Scripture was read in the synagogue. Hebrew is similar to Aramaic but sufficiently strange that those whose tongue was Aramaic could not thereby understand Hebrew. So an oral paraphrase – the Aramaic word is targum – by then probably a fixed traditional rendering, was given by the rabbi after reading the Hebrew text. It is probably correct to think of the lad Jesus as poring over the rolls of the Torah (Law), *Nebhi'im* (Prophets), and *Khetubhim* (Holy Writings) at the synagogue.

We must not overlook the educative influence of immemorial village life. The bulk of Western people today, recently removed from it and inchoately longing for it, have missed this form of social experience. In the large cities, though we see multitudes every week, we know none of them, for we see only the facade of life. In the village almost nothing of life – good or evil, significant or trivial – can be hid. Elsewhere Nazareth was considered a wicked place (John 1:46; 7:41, 52). The scandalous treatment accorded Jesus on His visit to the synagogue there early in His ministry demonstrates how

23 ALOL, p. 121.
24 Alexander, *The Gospel of Mark*, p. 143.
25 ELTJM, 1:230-33 cites extended references from the Talmud and Josephus.

spiritually stupid and morally perverse the inhabitants were. Jesus clearly reacted away from His fellow villagers. They really never did accept Him. Yet it did not render Him an aloof person, for women and children and strangers were attracted to Him throughout His ministry. Jesus loved social intercourse – a truly convivial person.

The *geography of* the district had a clearly discernible influence on Jesus' preaching and on His devotional habits. Nazareth lies in a small valley just north of the great Plain of Esdraelon but separated from it by low hills. Less than twenty miles north are the highest mountains of Palestine west of Jordan. On one of these is Safad - a famous rabbinic city in Medieval times, perhaps the 'city set on a hill' visible from the neighborhood of Nazareth. A few miles east, looking like a flat-lander's idea of a wooded mountain, isometric Mt Tabor rises from the plain. Round-topped hill peaks, four to five hundred feet high, border the town on north and west. On those slopes, wandering as a boy, our Savior gathered in the orderly features and processes of nature and country life that pour forth in profusion in all His discourses. What boy who has ever climbed a mountain on a day of good weather in May can doubt that He gained the habit, evinced regularly in the Gospels, of going out into a mountain alone to pray.

During His remarkable brief ministry Jesus attracted people of every social class. Children flocked to Him; young men were captivated; many women sought His company – in groups and in private (Jesus was no prude). Roman army officers, Jewish tax farmers (for the emperor), lay leaders of local synagogues, learned scribes and Pharisees – both believing and unbelieving – cynical Sadducees, aloof Herodians, even a Jewish king and a Roman procurator found in Him much to attract and interest, if not always to admire. 'The common people,' especially, 'heard him gladly' (Mark 12: 37). Yet Jesus Himself was a simple member of the working class, turned rabbi while still short of middle age. He was also, an exception from Jewish custom, which recommended marriage at age eighteen, a bachelor. Literate but not learned, He had no official or social standing to capture the attention He attracted. And when on that last occasion He entered Jerusalem in what the church has come to call the triumphal entry, the people of Israel with their chief priests and elders and scribes, together with Herod and Pontius Pilate, knew they had a most formidable man and movement with which to deal.

THE END OF HIS CHILDHOOD

Luke
2:41-52

Only once does the Bible narrative break the veil of silence between the return of Mary and Joseph with the child[26] Jesus and His appearance as a man before John the Baptist at Jordan. This was the occasion of His first visit to the temple with His father and mother on one of their annual treks to the Passover feast at Jerusalem. He was twelve years old at the time. Females were not required to go, but Joseph took his wife. This was the last year Jesus would be treated as a dependent minor child. At thirteen years of age the Jewish boy became a son of the Law (bar *mitzveh).*

No matter what route one takes to Jerusalem from Nazareth and back again, it is a walk through history. Every turn provided an inspiring reminder of national and spiritual history, something for devout parents to talk to children about. The round trip was at least 160 miles – a week of walking for a pilgrim caravan. The destination was a city enshrined in the hearts of Jews, then as now, as no other capital or sanctuary town in earth's history, a place to fire the eyes and thrill the heart. This we see even at the end of passion week in the exclamations of Peter and Andrew with James and John (Mark 13:1ff.). The occasion of this trip was Passover, celebration of the national birthday nearly fifteen hundred years before in events of supernatural wonder in the house of bondage down in Egypt (Exod. 12, 13). It is not surprising that after the Passover day itself and a day or two of the week of Unleavened Bread immediately following, the party left the crowded ways of Jerusalem's environs, nor is it surprising that such a lad should want to linger.

What do we learn from the incident? We learn that by His twelfth year, for sure, our Lord was aware of the nature of His mission: He knew

---

26 'Considering what loving care watched over Jewish child-life, tenderly marking by not fewer than eight designations the various stages of its development, and the deep natural interest naturally attaching to the early life of Messiah, that silence, in contrast to the almost blasphemous absurdities of the Apocryphal Gospels, teaches us once more, and most impressively, that the Gospels furnish a history of the Savior, not a biography of Jesus of Nazareth.' The eight terms referred to are *'Yeled,* the newborn babe, as in Isa. 9:6; *Yoneq,* the suckling, Isa. 11:8; *Odel,* the suckling beginning to ask for food, Lam. 4:4; *Gamul,* the weaned child, Isa. 28:9; *Taph,* the child clinging to its mother, Jer. 40:7; *Elem,* stripling, a child becoming firm, 1 Sam. 17:56; *Naar,* Gen. 21:12, the lad, one who shakes himself free, or youth; and *Bachur,* the ripened one, young man, Judg. 14:10.' ELTJM, 1:221.

that the temple was His Father's house and that the ritual there and the Law with its interpretation were His Father's business. We would like to know if and *when* Mary and Joseph told Him of the remarkable circumstances surrounding His birth, and if not, how and when He learned of His divine mission. When did the eternal Logos, eternal Son of the Father, become self-conscious in Jesus, the carpenter of Nazareth? People have always wondered. Learned books have been written about it. Really no one knows or can know for sure, but most readers will agree with James Stalker: 'With His reply to His mother before me, I cannot trust myself even to think of a time when He did not know what His work in this world was to be.'[27]

We learn also that even in His own home our Lord was a comparative stranger. Even His mother did not quite understand Him. Over and over again, though her love and loyalty never failed Him, she was amazed at the things He said and did. The better one comes to know Jesus, then and now, the more fully aware he becomes, both of His likeness to us 'in all points,' sin excepted, and at the same time aware of the immense difference and distance from all *things merely* human. The danger of crashing either on the Scylla of docetism (denial of His genuine humanity) or the Charybdis of Ebionism (denial of His genuine deity) is not limited to the second and third centuries. It derives from the very nature of the incarnation, and thus was present from His first day on earth and is no less so today.

Our Lord's next eighteen years were days of growing and waiting, until one day in ripe young manhood He suddenly appeared on the banks of Jordan, offering Himself in symbolic surrender to the will of God for a short but pivotal ministry for all generations of mankind.

---

27 SLC, p. 22.

Part 2

'I have come into the world'

CHAPTER 3

His Emergence Into Public Life

The New Testament passes by the next eighteen years of Jesus' life in silence. Then abruptly He appeared in public at Jerusalem with five or six Galilean disciples. Yet it was not as sudden as it seemed at Jerusalem, for He had left Nazareth about four months before. Deliberate, official inauguration of that ministry and mission could not take place in a day, and there is a definite preliminary stage – the ministry of John.

Jesus' opening stroke came at the temple in Jerusalem just before the annual Passover festival. It took the form of an assertion of messianic authority over His 'Father's house' (probably spring AD 27). The series of critical incidents leading up to that event is the subject of this chapter.

HIS FORERUNNER'S MINISTRY

The chronological significance of the rather full information supplied by Luke (Luke 3:1, 2) must be assessed. It would be normal for John – priest, son of a priest – to enter upon his life work when thirty years old.[1] Tiberius – second emperor of Rome, successor and stepson to that Augustus under whom both Jesus and John were born, an unsocial man

Mark
1:1-8
Matt.
3:1-12
Luke
3:1-18

---

1 Levites entered service at age thirty (Num. 4:3, 47).

See also
Acts
1:5, 22
10:37,
13:24
18:25,
19:1-7 without affection, melancholy, affecting decency in public but 'prince of hypocrites,' in his latter days indulging every lustful and perverted propensity – was the reigning Caesar throughout Jesus' ministry. Pontius Pilate was governor of Judaea (including Samaria) wherein lay Jerusalem. The misdeeds of Archelaüs (Matt. 2:22), son of Herod the Great, had cost him the throne of Judaea. Pilate, a man careless of human life, was fifth in the succession of procurators which replaced the Herods in Judaea. Herod (Antipas) was tetrarch of Galilee and Trans-Jordan [or Peraea] – a man who, lacking his father's great abilities, had preserved his vices. Philip, another son of Herod, ruled the area east of the Sea of Galilee and of the upper Jordan. Annas, a man of very evil reputation, greedy, avaricious, was head of the Jerusalem Sanhedrin and manager of the priestly 'take' in connection with sales of sacrificial animals and money-changing at the temple, and, though unable to keep the high-priesthood proper for himself, he had managed to keep it for his family, including a son-in-law, the present incumbent, Caiaphas – a man worthy of his unscrupulous patron in every way. These men are the leading civil and religious dramatis personae throughout the public career of Jesus and on into the early part of the Book of Acts.

John, the son of Zacharias and Elizabeth, had grown up not only under the regime of a son of Aaron destined for priesthood but also, as the angel directed Zacharias, as a Nazirite,[2] i.e., a religious ascetic (Num. 6:3; Judg. 13:4-6; I Sam. 1:11). His manner of dress and of taking food marked him out in this special way and gave him standing in the Jewish community as one who should be listened to in religious matters. Furthermore, John broke the 400 years of suspension of the office and function of prophet – a silence mourned predictively in the Psalms ('We see not our signs: there is no more any prophet: neither is there among us any that knoweth how long' [74:9; cf. I Sam. 3:1]) and, being a judgment of God, a blow to the well-being of the nation. Unlike the scribes, who only preserved the letter of Scripture, or the rabbis, who sought to make a legal bondage of it, John had a fresh message from heaven (John 1:19-25). And, in a brief time, he came to be widely accepted as a prophet, perhaps even the Messiah or his forerunner, Elijah.[3] John knew himself to be one officially sent of God on a preliminary mission.

---

2 A Nazirite in Old Testament usage is someone or something withheld from customary use. For religious reasons parents might declare offspring to be Nazirite (as the case with John) or the person himself might do so. Nazirites abstained from all fruits of the vine-fresh, dried, or fermented-and they did not shave or cut their hair. Such vows were normally for a specified period of time. Jesus was a Nazarene but not a Nazirite, as was John, with whom He is contrasted (John 11:18, 19). See the excellent article: J. Barton Payne, "Nazirite, Nazarite," in Merrill C. Tenney, ed., Zondervan Pictorial Bible Encyclopedia, 5 vols. (Grand Rapids: Zondervan, 1975), 4:392, 393.

3 The Old Testament closes with a prophecy that God will send Elijah the prophet to do a work of

If the people had not perverted their way, if their leaders had been willing to allow the Old Testament prophecies of the spiritual side of Messiah's kingdom to season and shape their political expectations, such preparatory work would have been unnecessary. But now that the kingdom had arrived in the person of the King Messiah, men expected Messiah to sound a call to arms, then to lead a successful war ridding Israel of foreign rulers, and after that to extend Jewish hegemony over the world (for all of which, Old Testament prophecy could be cited). They did not, however, ponder or apply the weight of prophecy regarding spiritual and moral (Jer. 31:31-34; Ezek. 36:23-31) aspects of Messiah's reign to affect their expectations. The 'righteous and devout, looking for the consolation of Israel' (Luke 2:25), of whom the pious circle around the holy Infant were typical, were exceptional. Finding in the prophecies of Isaiah (Isa. 40:3; cf. Matt. 3:3) his authority, his message, and his mission, John appeared one day in the desert near Jericho preaching a revivalist's message: sin and judgment; repentance and forgiveness. He attacked the prevalent Jewish trust in descent from Abraham as sufficient ground for divine favor (Matt. 3:9). He denounced prevalent sins, proclaimed God's axe already 'laid unto the root' of every evil tree, called for repentance accompanied by change of life, and promised divine forgiveness if these conditions should be met. He offered no social panaceas, but he laid the basis of social reform calling for honesty, covenant keeping, and peaceful order in all relationships, and recommending generosity toward all in need.

All this was distinctly Old Testament ground, the very righteousness described in the Law, recovered by the Prophets, praised by the Psalms, and distilled in the Wisdom literature. 'He was the lamp that burneth and shineth,' and they 'were willing to rejoice for a season in his light' (John 5:35).

A sacred rite of immersion in water by the baptizer was the outward confession of the repentance demanded. All Israel knew that national repentance was a prerequisite for the manifestation of Messiah – one often-cited rabbinic saying having it that if Israel would repent for a day, the Son of David (Messiah) would come.[4] There were also various

---

spiritual renewal in Israel "before the coming of the great and dreadful day of the Lord" (Mal. 4:5, 6). Whether John was the fulfillment of it and if so, how? and if not, why? are matters of rather fierce controversy in discussions of Biblical prediction and the nature of the kingdom of God in the Gospels.

4 SBCNT, 1:164, lines 29, 30. Psalm 95:7 is cited by the rabbis to this effect. SBCNT cites several pages of rabbinic statements that 'repentance' is the 'condition of messianic redemption.' 1:162-65.

lustrations and washings, possibly even immersion in water, among the orthodox (Pharisees) and the Essenes. (There is no clear precedent of water baptism for such purposes in Israel's previous history.) In these, however, the candidate washed himself. John was the first to lead the candidate into the water, and, as administrator of the rite, immerse the repentant one. Thus he was called 'the baptizer,' or as it has come to be said, 'the Baptist.' It was a preparatory rite, though it seems likely that disciples drawn from John's circles were not ordinarily again ritually immersed upon becoming Jesus' disciples.[5]

John preached and baptized down at the Jordan, not only opposite Jericho, but also in the area near the ancient crossing to Bethabara (also called Bethany beyond Jordan, or Bethany of the Ford or House of the Ford) not far from where Jordan leaves the Sea of Galilee.[6] He attracted attention from everywhere. John's announcements of the presence among them of the long-promised Coming One drew both the curious and the repentant from all walks and levels of Jewish society – including five stalwart young men from Capernaum and Bethsaida of lower Galilee: Andrew and Simon, John, Philip and Nathanael, and probably also John's brother James.

HIS BAPTISM BY JOHN

It is reasonable to suppose that John ranged the length of Jordan in his baptizing and that either Bethabara or Aenon (John 3:23), about six miles south of Scythopolis (Beth-shan) and not over twenty miles from Nazareth[7] is where Jesus came. Traditions and pious conjectures have

---

5 This has been a matter of intense doctrinal controversy, but it is not sufficiently relevant to the discussion here to merit extended treatment.

6 The exact location and name of this place are both in question, but what we do know about it tends to support the view advocated here regarding the place of Jesus' baptism and the location of the mount of temptation. It was apparently here that the messengers from the Jerusalem leaders found John the Baptist shortly after he baptized our Lord (John 1:28). The similarity in spelling with Beth-bara of Judges 7:24, situated near the Jordan apparently in the tribal territory of Ephraim, suggests the northern location. The Received Text of John 1:28 furnishes the spelling Béthabara. The Hebrew of Judges 7:24 is the same except for the omission of the first a. At some time before the fixation of the vowels by the Masoretes (Medieval Jewish scribes), the a may very well have been customarily pronounced. The brief note in *Wycliffe Bible Encyclopedia* (Chicago: Moody, 1975) is helpful: 'The name survives at the ford called Abarah, twelve miles S of the Sea of Galilee and NE of Bethshean. This is the only place where this name occurs in Palestine. This site is as near to Cana as any point on the Jordan, and within a day's journey.' 1:221. Manuscript evidence for Bethany is not especially stronger than for *Bethabara*, though most recent versions read *Bethany*.

7 ELTJM, 1:278.

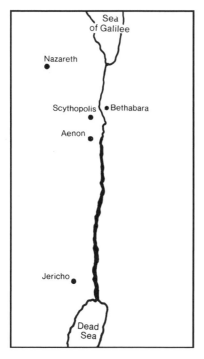

Map 2. The Site of Jesus' baptism

put the baptism and mount of temptation fifty miles south,[8] but we may safely assume that the Lord and His new disciples came to John when he was near their own homes in Galilee.

Though reared apart and perhaps never having met, even though kinsmen, it seems likely the two men knew of one another. Jesus, at the end of His long vigil, heard in Nazareth the report of His kinsman's ministry. Thus, as John approached Galilee, and after - we may be sure - much reflection and prayer, Jesus broke the ground which would never be laid back in place. Apparently alone, He left Nazareth one morning and the next day, probably in very early (January) AD 27, showed up among the crowd of John's auditors, requesting baptism. The face of Jesus – the same that convinced Nathanael a few weeks later, that silenced enemies and drew friends with irresistible power enlightened John as to the identity of the applicant for baptism. Perhaps John had been expecting Him, though hardly in the crowd of penitents; hence John's consternation.

---

8 So-called holy places have a way. of being moved by promoters of pilgrimages to places easy for the traveler to get to. The traditional mount of temptation and supposed site of Jesus' baptism, both near Jericho, are a short trip from Jerusalem. The site advocated here involved several days of foot travel going and returning for pilgrims already at Jerusalem. Maps that mark a spot near Jericho are traditional and conjectural, not necessarily historical.

Why did Jesus seek baptism? Why did the sinless One participate in an ordinance associated with confession of sins, repentance, and forgiveness? The history of interpretation furnishes no less than a dozen answers. Of the event itself, it has been said to be (1) contrary to fact and unhistorical; (2) 'staged' by John and Jesus to attract public attention; (3) a confession by Jesus that He was a sinner in need of repentance like us all. Other more reverent views have been that (4) He thereby publicly became representative of the sinful race of men or (5) their sin-bearer. It is held that He accepted the baptism required of all (6) to show solidarity with His people or (7) to separate Himself publicly from Israel's sins. It is said to be (8) a surrendering to death (by ritual burial), (9) an act of public approval of the Baptist and his work, (10) a token (sign) of messiahship, (11) a vow to observe the Law, (12) a commencement and consecration of Himself to, or a way to receive spiritual qualification for, His messianic work. It has even been suggested that it was (13) to gain the favor of John's disciples. Many of these suggestions (especially numbers 6[9] and 8) have merit and seem to come under Jesus' dictum, 'thus it becometh us to fulfill all righteousness.' Yet none is quite 'on target.' The Son of God was circumcised simply because His parents were carefully obedient to Mosaic law — even though that rite, in part, signified the putting away of the corruption of the carnal nature. The offerings of His parents on the fortieth day and all family sacrifices thereafter, including Passover, had a 'sin-atoning' reference for all others, though not for Him. So what the ordinary Israelite did when he obediently submitted to John's baptism was to signify confession, repentance, forgiveness; but not so with Him. He did it because, as required of godly Jews, He ought to do it. Jesus' submission to baptism was only one of many examples (though an exceptionally striking one) of the perfect, non-ulterior, 'active' obedience of God's Son. To those ever since who have shown some reluctance about submitting to water baptism after adult conversion, Jesus' example has been the most persuasive argument.

The descent of the Spirit as a dove and the voice of the Father in approval are without precedent in Jewish history, as the best authorities agree.[10] John and Jesus were the only witnesses. The crowds neither

---

9 GSLC, p. 80.

10 *Bath qol*, an Aramaic expression meaning 'daughter of the voice,' is explained by certain scholars as a rabbinic idea appearing here as a literary device of the Gospel writers. SBCNT (1:125-34) does not support this: 'Man hörte nicht die Stimme, die vom Himmel ausging, sondern aus dieser

heard nor saw anything. God's design was to confirm the Baptist's assurance that his work had been done well and was now essentially at an end, while at the same time it set the Lord up with marvelous support for the temptation in the forty days immediately to follow, assuring Him anew that indeed in Him the work of the Servant Son of Jehovah prophesied by Isaiah would be carried to successful completion.

HIS FORTY-DAY TEMPTATION

Immediately after His baptism, the Gospels say, 'the spirit driveth him into the wilderness. And he was there in the wilderness forty days, tempted of Satan; and was with the wild beasts...' (Mark 1:12, 13). 'Then was Jesus led up of the spirit into the wilderness...' (Matt. 4:1). 'And Jesus being full of the Holy Ghost, returned from Jordan, and was led by the Spirit into the wilderness' (Luke 4:1). There is no hint as to what wilderness. Further, though a mountain is the scene of one of the temptations, it is by no means certain that He spent the forty days there. Popular opinion places the scene of the forty days in the southern Jordan, near the supposed scene of baptism at Jericho and the mount of temptation nearby. The view taken here is that the baptism and temptation were near the Sea of Galilee (as many reliable authorities agree).[11] It might even have been an uninhabited spot in Galilee. The statement of Luke that after His baptism Jesus 'returned from Jordan' (Luke 4:1) before the temptation strongly suggests an area in lower Galilee. If so, then Tabor might be the mount of temptation. Mt. Quruntan at Jericho seems to the pilgrim to be what the wilderness and mount of temptation 'ought' to look like, but the tradition for it is late,[12] and like so many so-called holy places, just may have been located there by ancient tour directors for ancient pilgrims' sightseeing convenience!

As Paul spent a period of three years in Arabia before embarking on his life's work and Moses a much longer period, so Jesus added to His preparation forty days alone with God, wild beasts, angels, and the

---

Stimme ging eine andre Stimme hervor; wie wenn ein Mensch mit Gewalt einen Schlag ausführt und man hört einen zweiten Ton, dur in der Ferne aus ihm (dem Schlag) herforging. Eine solche Stimme hörte man; deshalb nannte man sie "Tochter der Stimme."' - This German sentence means that when the teachers of Jewish piety spoke, after the cessation of prophecy, they spoke not as God's voice but only as the echo (SBCNT uses this word) of the true voice of God in prophetic Scripture (1:125). Hence the rabbis were not voices of God but echoes of God's oracles spoken by prophets of old. Alfred Edersheim's discussion (ELTJM, 1:385, 386) is informed and excellent.

11 ELTJM, 1:300; ALOL, p. 155; EHL, p. 106.
12 ALOL, p. 155

tempter, away from human habitation. Speculation as to the nature of His trials – whether subjectively or obectively real, whether it were possible for Him to yield to the temptation or not, etc. – are not irrelevant, but they are not a part of the record and are incapable of answer satisfactory to every reverent inquirer.

The heart of the matter lies in considerations on the grander scale of what the whole Bible teaches. His whole earthly life was one of temptation by Satan, beginning with the efforts of Herod to kill Him as an infant and on to the horror of drinking the cup of the Father's will in Gethsemane. The forty days capsulize all of it.

Jesus is set forth as the believers' strength and example in their own temptations. He 'was in all points tempted as we are, yet without sin' (Heb. 4:15). How many 'points' are there in which men can be tempted? Three. Only three.

John declares that 'all that is in the world' – he aims to be comprehensive – which comes to man's heart to entice to sin comes by one of three channels: the appetites of the body, called 'the desires of the flesh'; the social impulses, to see and be seen by others with approval, called 'the lust of the eyes'; and the acquisitive impulse to own and control, called 'the pride of life [bios, 'possessions contributing to life']' (I John 2:15-17). So Eve in the first satanic temptation on record, 'saw that the tree was good for food' (appetite of the body), 'that it was pleasant to the eyes' (the social impulse), and that it was 'to be desired to make one wise' (i.e., wisdom as possession) (Gen. 3:6) – thus illustrating the complete range of sin's enticement. The temptations in Jesus' case are the same and, in Matthew and Mark, in the same order as in Genesis 3.[13]

It is of utmost importance to observe that each channel represents a proper interest of normal people. We are always amazed to find that the largest prospective temptation comes from the direction of our legitimate interests – bodily health and normal function; social interests and legitimate expression; the impulse to secure a minimum of goods and properties to make life secure, useful, and interesting.

In our Lord's case He recognized that each of these interests (impulses, desires) must, in the will of God, come, first, by righteous, lawful means and, second, at the divinely appointed time. It is well to recognize the

---

13 These three triads can hardly, especially in view of John's evident intention to give a comprehensive summary, be merely accidental. They are of great practical and homiletical value precisely because they by revelation conduct the Bible reader to bedrock reality in analysis of the possibilities of sin's enticement.

same for ourselves – physical desires are divinely given, to be expressed in God's time by proper means. Fornication is a striking example of violation of these twin principles. Jesus' willingness to fast until the divinely designated moment illustrates holy expression of the physical impulse, that is, bodily appetite. Five days after the forty days He partook of a wedding feast quite within the Father's will. Social impulses also must be met only in God's time and by right means, as must our desires for a kingdom of possessions – however large or small.

Satan ('tempter... devil... old serpent') has mastered the best 'devices' for results, and he confronted Jesus with them all. Two words of Matthew's account key in two of them. 'Then' – after the flush of glorious spiritual victory, always the weakest moment for every man – Satan came with his assailing doubts and feelings of post-ecstatic letdown. Also 'when he had fasted forty days and forty nights' and, being 'hungered,' every cell of His body cried out for food, Satan attacked Him at what at that moment must have been His weakest spot. So he always does, usually with success; but not with Jesus.

Our Lord's resource, the means which enabled the human nature to be a proper and holy vehicle of the divine, was decisively the fullness of the Holy Spirit. In God's providence this great trial could not come until after the special descent of the Spirit at His baptism. It was this special conferral which enabled the divine-human Christ to perform miracles. It was later extended to the Apostles and the 'Seventy' and certain others on whom the Apostles laid hands. This indument enabled them to perform the mighty works associated with the first steps of Christianity. There was also – and very prominently – our Lord's mastery of and complete reliance on the inspired Holy Scriptures, meeting each assault of the enemy broadside or head-on by clear statements of Scripture. This was accompanied by a will to resist – 'Resist the devil and he will flee from you.'

The results for Him were the consoling ministrations of angels and respite from trial for a while; for us they are that we have a high priest who is 'touched with the feeling of our infirmities,' having been 'in all points tempted as we are,' and to whom we may 'come boldly' for grace, mercy, and help 'in time of need' (Heb. 4:14-16).

HIS FORERUNNER'S TESTIMONY TO A SANHEDRIN COMMITTEE

John 1:19-34 This section of John immediately before us (1:19-2:11) is almost a day-by-day report. It was the first week[14] of our Lord's ministry – opening steps, not quite yet public and not yet with a large following. Nevertheless, during these days He drew to Himself the nucleus of the apostolate of the Twelve, five men of the Capernaum-Bethsaida area at the northern end of the Sea of Galilee and one of Cana, a town north of Nazareth.

On the very day Jesus' forty days of temptation in the wilderness came to an end, a committee from 'Jerusalem, priests and Levites,' – i.e., the Sanhedrin – arrived at Bethabara (Bethany) to demand a clarification of John's mission. All that John had been saying, though strictly within the bounds set by Pharisaism and the Saducean administration of the temple services, disturbed the leaders of both parties. Though declaring Messiah's kingdom to be already present, John had not as yet identified Messiah, making no claim for himself beyond that of Messiah's herald. Furthermore, they knew the Old Testament required Israel's repentance. They also knew something of the ambiguity of Messiah's manifestation, humiliation to be followed by victory. Yet they really had no place in their thinking for spiritual preparation by confession of sin, turning from it, and humility toward God. John repeated his regular message for the committee's benefit, stating that he was not Messiah, nor Elijah, the one to prepare for Messiah, nor the popularly expected one known as 'that Prophet.' But, said he, the One who is to follow me – i.e., the Messiah – is standing 'in the midst of you.' He is now here; though recognized by me, He is still unrecognized by you.

A few weeks later Jesus was to appear in Jerusalem, make bold exercise of Messiah's authority, and begin His campaign to win the nation. This committee's report to their sponsors of what the herald had said did certainly set the stage at Jerusalem. Jesus did not talk among the Galileans about His being Messiah; He only asked for their hearts to acknowledge Him as the Savior sent from God. At Jerusalem, however, over and again by His actions He set forth His claims to the messianic office. Strangely, even at Jerusalem He did not say in so many words, 'I am Messiah.'

It may be that before that committee left the vicinity of Bethabara, John had opportunity to point out to them the face of the very man of whom he spoke and about whom they and their cohorts at Jerusalem

---

14 See John 1:19, 29, 35, 43; 2:1. The last day, the wedding at Cana, would have been, by Jewish custom, a Wednesday.

would have to make a fateful decision. For Jesus – no doubt gaunt and lean from forty days without food – the next day turned up among the crowds gathered about the Baptist. John thereupon publicly declared that though he had long known that someone would soon be manifested to Israel as the long-expected One, he had not long known Him by face. We must assume that the details regarding Mary's visit to Elizabeth thirty years before and the prophecies of Mary and Elizabeth on that occasion had been told to John by his parents and always cherished by him, but that owing to the distance (a week of travel, to and from), the two kinsmen had never met face-to-face until Jesus' baptism. John says that the God who sent him to herald Messiah's arrival had informed him how to recognize Him: the Holy Spirit would descend on Him. John concludes his witness – and if the committee had gone already, it was reported to them quickly – '... I have seen, and have borne witness that this is the Son of God' (John 1:34 ASV). By this announcement John in effect ended his ministry. The herald was no longer needed. The coming One had arrived and John had pointed Him out, though this greatest-of-those-born-of-women[15] did continue to preach and to baptize for a few months more.

HIS GATHERING OF THE FIRST APOSTLES-TO-BE

Jesus chose and won the first six of the men who were to compose His apostolate on the third and fourth days after the end of His forty days of temptation. These six only were to company frequently with Him for some months, though they would go home part of the time and ply their trades also. John 1:35-51

We have no direct knowledge of the kind of men our Lord sought for the apostolate. We only know whom He chose and by inference what sort of men they already were and were to become. We are best acquainted with these first six, chiefly through the reports passed on to us by one of the first two, for it may hardly be doubted that John, who tends to cover his identity throughout his Gospel, was the man with Andrew that day and that they were the first.

Early on that Sabbath morning (the working day starts early in the

---

15 The greatness of the man and the heart of what he had to say, plus the verdict of others, will be seen by examining the following passages: Matt. 3:1-17; Mark 1:1-11; Luke 3:1-23; John 1:6-15, 19-37; John 3:22-30; Matt. 11:2-19; Luke 7:18-35. See also Matt. 21:25; Mark 11:30; Luke 20:4; Acts 1:22; 10:37; 13:24; 18:25; 19:3 - each in its context.

Near East) the Baptist stood with two of his disciples – and whom else we cannot say – two who had learned well from him and truly in their hearts had prepared a highway for God. They had heard their rabbi's declarations (to the committee) about Jesus the day before, and now, hoping to hear more about Him, in the early quiet of the Sabbath they saw the Messiah standing before them. 'Behold the Lamb of God,' exclaimed the Baptist. It was John's way of dismissing them forever to another's care. Without any leave-taking and drawn by an overwhelming impulse, they followed Jesus. Perhaps they knew not why; it is enough that He knew them and drew them on, forerunners of the millions through the centuries who have been drawn irresistibly to the uplifted (that is, crucified) Lamb of God (John 12:31, 32). Jesus, turning backward, asked, 'What seek ye?' and they answered, 'Master, where are you lodging?' And He invited them, 'Come and see.' Wherever the conversation may have occurred – perhaps only a bare spot between the boulders of Bethabara's countryside – they spent that Sabbath day with Him.

Incidentally, in this first time-of-day reference in John, it appears clear that the author, now in the latter part of the first century, a long-time resident of the Roman province of Asia and far removed from Jewish modes of life, employed the Roman mode of reckoning the hours from midnight to noon and from noon again to midnight. Otherwise John would not say they spent 'that day' with Jesus, for the tenth hour according to Jewish reckoning would already be at day's end (see diagram I).

Andrew 'first' – probably indicating that John also looked for his brother[16] James – found and brought Peter to Jesus. This may have been the most important thing Andrew ever did. The next day (Sunday) Jesus, taking the initiative, sought and found Philip, who like Andrew and Simon was a resident of Bethsaida. But it was Philip who fetched Nathanael. The remarks of each, plus the rapid progress of events, give the impression of 'intense excitement' among the new disciples. They never recovered from that excitement, though it led all save one to martyrs' deaths.

These verses in John tell us more of the evident veracity and convincing power of the Savior Himself, and of the conviction of certainty in His simplest words, for those whose hearts had been prepared. His cryptic

---

16 Skilled exegetes have insisted that the language requires (cf. Mark 1:19) that the unnamed John sought and found James, then brought him to Jesus, as Andrew had already ('first') brought Peter. See John Peter Lange, Commentary on John, 2 vols, trans. Philip Schaff (Edinburgh: Clark, 1872; reprinted-Grand Rapids: Zondervan, n.d.) on John 1:41

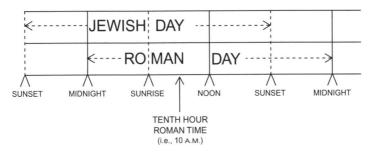

Diagram I. The Jewish and Roman days

'Come and see' is yet today at once the unavoidable final stage in Christian persuasion. 'O taste and see that the Lord is good: blessed is the man that trusteth in him' (Ps. 34:8). Over a century ago Philip Schaff wrote *The Person of Christ: The Miracle of History,* a truly great book on this theme.

In this amazing section we observe the finest men their country could produce, upon their first meeting with 'Jesus of Nazareth, the son of Joseph,' spontaneously proclaiming Him Master, Messiah, Him of whom Moses (in the Law) and the Prophets had written, the Son of God and King of Israel. On His part, Jesus calmly accepted each title and encomium, connecting Himself with their father Israel and with Daniel's prophecy of the Ancient of Days and the Son of man. His deity is not denied by the expression 'the Son of man,' but it is obscured. All these titles and encomiums were in the finest tradition of rabbinic Judaism, yet some of them – especially 'Son of God' – were soon to be invested with greater meaning. They would not just yet be led deeper into the mystery of the incarnation than their immature state would permit.

Our Lord now has five disciples – Andrew, John, Peter, Philip, Nathanael – and, if John did indeed find and bring his brother James, a sixth. We shall assume that he did.

HIS EMERGENCE INTO PUBLIC NOTICE: THE MIRACLE AT CANA

Cana was the home of Nathanael, one of the original six disciples, though we do not learn about that until near the end[17] of John's Gospel. The location of this village preferred by recent archaeologist-geographers is

John 2:1-11

---

17 John 21:2; cf. Matt. 10:4 where Cananean may mean 'of Cana.'

not the long favored Kafr Kenna, four or five miles northeast of Nazareth, but a place known locally to Arabs as Khirbet [ruin of] Qana some ten or twelve miles due north of Nazareth. It is called Cana of Galilee (John 2:1) to distinguish it from a town near Tyre (Josh. 19:28). During the three or four days while Jesus gathered those first six disciples, a messenger delivered to Him an invitation to a marriage in this place. Perhaps mother Mary had some arrangement with her Son as to where He would be at this time and sent the message to Him there. At any rate, Jesus, now recognized as a rabbi, 'and his disciples' were invited. It would have been a leisurely hike for the small party, leaving Bethabara to the east of Jordan, across from Scythopolis (Beth-shan), on Monday to have arrived for the wedding on Wednesday, perhaps visiting home at Nazareth on the direct route.

The Jewish home itself being a sacred instrument, marriages were truly 'solemnized' – with enormous incubus of tradition, solemnity, 'protocol.' But it had its merry aspects too. Jesus was present at it all, His mother, likely as a kinswoman, taking some responsibility. The celebration reported by John would likely have been in the evening at the home of the bride's father, the groom furnishing the feast. Arguments that the home was a poor one are unconvincing except that the groom had failed to provide sufficient wine. Whatever the cause, the wine failed.

Many have conjectured the meaning of Mary's words to her Son and His strange answer. That, as some have suggested, she meant to indicate that now would be a discreet time to leave is to make too little both of her words and of His response. To claim that she was now asking Him to vindicate her purity in His motherhood by some miracle or to 'launch a march' to the kingdom by a manifestation of great power seems to make too much of them. More likely, she meant, as His mother, simply to call the host's dilemma to His attention.[18] His response was to let her know that the old relationship was at an end. Mother she would ever be, but her interests and directions must now forever be subordinate to those of the kingdom of God, as He understood it.[19] His words, then, enforce another rejoinder eighteen or so years earlier: 'Wist ye not that I must be about my Father's business?' David Smith captured some of the significance of the whole incident: 'The great crises are wont to come in simple guise. Had Jesus found Himself confronted by some mighty task like cleaving the sea... He would never have hesitated; but the supplying

---

18 ELTJM, 1:352-58.
19 ibid., 1:361.

of wine to a company of peasants seemed so trivial, so unworthy of the Messiah, so insufficient for the inauguration of the Kingdom of Heaven. 'Can this be the call of God?' was the question which he was debating with Himself, still unresolved, when Mary's appeal broke in disturbingly upon Him. It was a momentous crisis; and in the hour of perplexity, searching of soul, and inquiring after the Father's will, it was revealed to Him what 'the works of the Messiah' [at that season, at least (Matt. II:2ff.)] must be — not dazzling marvels, as the Jews expected, but lowly deeds of service and compassion.'[20]

John summarizes the meaning in a threefold way (John 2:II): (I) It was a 'beginning of miracles.'[21] News of it travelled, with Galileans soon to attend Passover, to the national center at Jerusalem, where it augmented His budding fame. It is of the first of the 'signs' selected by John to draw his readers to faith and salvation. (2) Further, in this miracle Jesus first 'manifested forth his glory.' There is more than immediately meets the reader's eye. It did, of course, put His unique power on display. It was, however, a very chaste and disciplined display. More to the point, it showed what the glory of the Messiah was really to be — gracious work of rescuing men from their failures and mistakes as well as sympathetic rescue from their lost condition. The Messiah was not above joining common people in homely pleasures, sharing the joy of bride and groom. He would even rescue the bridegroom from embarrassment, 'saving' the social occasion. This showed what a true Savior of men He was, sent not to destroy men's lives but to save them. The world for Jesus is no unholy territory, even though its unholy prince rages boldly in it. He did not frown on mirth and joy but hallowed them by His own presence and participation. 'It was intended... to strike the key-note of His ministry as different from the Baptist's. John was an ascetic hermit who fled from the dwellings of men and called his hearers out into the wilderness. But Jesus had glad tidings to bring to men's hearts; He was to mingle in common life, and produce a happy revolution in their circumstances, which would be like turning the water of their life into wine.[22] (3) Because of the miracles 'his disciples believed on him.' We are to understand that their previously existing faith-commitment to God, manifest in their submission to John's baptism and exercised in immediate acceptance of the Messiah when they beheld Him, was now deepened

20 SDHF, p. 55.
21 See excursus I, p. 87.
22 SLC, p. 50.

and confirmed. As the latter part of John's second chapter displays, any faith grounded in miracles alone is vulgar and unseemly, bearing no true likeness to saving Christian faith.

HIS PRELIMINARY TRANSFER TO CAPERNAUM

John 2:12 At this stage in His career, Jesus changed His residence from Nazareth to Capernaum. For a while His brothers and mother resided there. (The sisters presumably married and settled at Nazareth.) We are not given any reason. It was an exceedingly well-favored area, a crossroads of the world if such was to be found in northern Palestine. Words spoken there would ultimately travel the length of the land and into the heathenism beyond. Besides, all six disciples except Nathanael resided nearby. They would desire to attend to family duties. Peter, at least, had a wife. We may suppose Jesus' brothers had not yet rejected Him and that they were interested in hearing more of what their strangely endowed older brother was saying. We may imagine the family as guests all the while in homes of relatives and of the disciples in nearby Bethsaida.

This brief residency at Capernaum was the end of any peaceful existence on earth for Jesus. Though already a remarkable teacher, He was still only 'Son of man' – i.e., a common person – in quiescent Galilee. He would enter Jerusalem in a few days with obvious messianic claims, to perform obvious messianic deeds at the temple and to be for evermore a famous public person. The Jewish authorities never ceased to seek His destruction after that. At Capernaum. of Galilee, He was still moving discreetly and slowly. Soon He would set the whole nation on its ear, and He would do so deliberately.

Excursus I – The Recorded Miracles of Jesus

Allowing the possibility of slight variation on account of questions of whether certain accounts really duplicate others or not (Are Luke 11:14, Matthew 9:32 and 33, and Matthew 12:22 the same?), the four Gospels report thirty-five distinct miracles, in addition to many others not described particularly (Matt. 4:23 24; 9:35; 11:21; Mark 6:53-56; Luke 4:40, 41; 5:15; 6:17-19; 7:21; John 2:23; 3:2; 4:45; 20:30; 21:25).

Four Greek words are employed by the Gospels to designate what we call miracles: (1) *teras*,' 'wonder or marvel' (Mark 13:22); (2) *dynamis*, 'power,' that is, 'innate strength' (Mark 6:2, 5, 14); (3) *simeion*, 'sign'

(Mark 8:11, 12); (4) *ergon*, 'work or deed.' The first emphasizes the effect on the minds of the observers; the second, the divine power by which they were wrought; the third, the truths, the meaning or import of the event; and the fourth, the event *per se*, happening in objective history.

The loose usage of the word miracle in popular speech today imperils our understanding of the idea of miracle in Scripture. The Biblical miracle is an objective event in the external world, observable to the senses, attributed by the performer to the Godhead, explicable only on the basis of power which comes from God, and always directed toward some distinct moral end.[23] Thus a remarkable answer to prayer for conversion or a striking healing or a notable concomitance of events (such as one car rolling ahead in time to be missed – or hit – by a runaway truck) are not, strictly speaking, to be called miracles.

The miracles of the Gospels, while valuable as certifying Jesus' claim to be God (Acts 2:22), were means by which Jesus taught the crowds and teaches us. '... His miracles were parables in deeds. Bishop Westcott has said that the miracles and the parables "are exactly correlative to each other; in the one we see the personality and power of the Worker, and in the other the generality and constancy of the Work; ... in the one we are led to regard the manifoldness of Providence, and in the other to recognize the instructiveness of the Universe."'[24]

See W. Graham Scroggie's useful listing and classification of all the recorded miracles of Jesus in table 1.[25]

---

23 This is the definitive, variously phrased in books of Christian apologetics, philosophy of religion and systematic theology. In popular speech miraculous and miracle mean scarcely more than marvellous and amazing.
24 SGG, p. 553.
25 Taken from ibid., p. 554.

Table I. The recorded miracles

In One Gospel

	Matt.	Mark	Luke	John
1. *Water becomes wine				2:1-11
2. Nobleman's son healed				4:46-56
3. Impotent man healed				5:1-9
4. First draught of fish			5:1-11	
11. Widow's son raised			7:11-15	
12. Blind, dumb man cured	12:22			
17. Two blind men healed	9:27-31			
18. Dumb demon exorcised	9:32,33			
22. Deaf, dumb man healed		7:31-37		
24. Blind man healed		8:22-26		
26. Tribute money provided	17:24-27			
27. Congenital Blindness cured				9:1-7
28. Dumb demoniac healed**			11:14	
29. Woman's infirmity healed			13:10-17	
30. Man cured of dropsy			14:1-6	
31. Lazarus raised				11:17-44
32. Ten lepers healed			17:11-19	
35. Malchus's ear healed			22:49-51	
36. Second draught of fish				21:1-14

*Numbers indicate chronological order.
**Could be identical to no. 18 or no. 12.

In Two Gospels

	Matt.	Mark	Luke	John
5. Demoniac		1:23-28	4:33-37	
10. Centurion's servant healed	8:5-13		7:1-10	
21. Gentile girl healed	15:21-28	7:24-30		
23. Four thousand fed	15:32-38	8:1-9		
34. Fig tree cursed	21:18-22	11:12-14		

In Three Gospels

	Matt.	Mark	Luke	John
6. Peter's mother-in-law cured	8:14, 15	1:29-31	4:38. 39	
7. Leper cured	8:2-4	1:40-45	5:12-16	
8. Paralytic healed	9:2-8	2:3-12	5:18-26	
9. Withered hand healed	12:10-13	3:1-5	6:6-10	
13. Storm stilled	8:23-27	4:35-41	8:22-25	
14. Two demoniacs liberated	8:28-34	5:11-20	8:26-39	
15. Issue of blood staunched	9:20-22	5:25-34	8:43-48	
16. Jairus's daughter raised	9:18, 19	5:22-24	8:41, 42	
	9:23-26	5:35-43	8:49-56	
20. Walking on sea	14:25-33	6:45-52		6:16-21
25. Epileptic boy cured	17:14-18	9:14-29	9:38-43	
33. Two blind men healed	20:29-34	10:46-52	18:35-43	

In Four Gospels

	Matt.	Mark	Luke	John
19. Five thousand fed	14:15-21	6:35-44	9:12-17	6:1-14

Table 2. Jesus' first year of public ministry and the four Gospels

Treated only by Synoptics	Treated only by John	Treated by all Gospels
Mark (through 1:13), Matthew (through 4:11), and Luke (through 4:13) take the story through the temptation.	John (2:13–4:45) reocrds the trip from Bathabara, or Bethany (baptism and temptation), the wedding at Cana, the visit to Capernaum, the pilgrimage to Jerusalem for the first Passover of Jesus' ministry, and the extended ministries in Judaea and Samaria. This period covers nearly one year, and in it Jesus calls only six of the Apostles.	Mark, Matthew, and Luke follow with the Galilee ministry as if there were no passing of several months. John also follows, in 4:46, with the ministry in Galilee,

CHAPTER 4

The Initial Crisis and His Judaean and Samarian Ministries

Matthew and Mark only hint at the passing of time between Jesus' temptation and His return to Galilee for the long ministry He gave that province. Luke, in his peculiar manner, does not even drop a hint of it. One would scarcely guess that the large part of a year falls between Mark 1:13 and 1:14, and between Matthew 4:11 and 4:12 as well as between Luke 4:13 and 4:14. Except for John's account we would not be aware that there was a brief trip from Bethabara to attend a wedding in Cana of Galilee, then a brief visit to Capernaum, followed by a pilgrimage to the Passover – a pilgrimage extended to ministry in Jerusalem, Judaea, and Samaria, and lasting nearly a year before Jesus returned to Galilee. (See table 2.)

John 2:13 -4:45
Mark 1:14
Matt. 4:12
Luke 4:14

If John had not seen fit to report this period of our Lord's ministry, we would know nothing of the first miracle – turning water into wine at the wedding feast of Cana – and the first cleansing of the temple, nor would we know about the interview of Nicodemus and His fascinating conversation with the woman at the well of Sychar.

Because John wrote these matters down, there is a basis for constructing a feasible chronology of our Lord's ministry. That chronology is made possible by John's reports of certain festival seasons, of which the first is in this part of Jesus' ministry. What scholars have made of this information and some related questions are not essential to understanding this portion, however interesting. So they are discussed at the end of this chapter (in excurses 2 and 3) rather than at this point. The reader may pass them by without loss to understanding of the essential story.

HE ASSERTS MESSIANIC AUTHORITY BY CLEANSING THE TEMPLE PRECINCTS

John
2:13-22
This incident occurred in that part of the temple area which was outermost and reserved for 'Gentiles' – i.e., for proselytes of a certain degree and other non-Jews. The ostensible purpose for the traffic in coin and animals for slaughter was twofold: (I) To change coins from all the countries of the Dispersion, whence many of the pilgrims came, into the proper money for payment of a temple tax due on or before that time of year. Though the authorities cited the single precedent of 'atonement money' from Exodus 33:13, there was no Biblical command that a fixed annual tax be paid by every adult Jewish male in the world.[1] Though ostensibly to pay for the daily morning and evening sacrifices commanded by Moses, and hence of religious value for every Jew, the Law provided that voluntary offerings should provide them – hence Jesus' comment about this tax that 'the children are free' (Matt. 17:26). He approved payment only by way of concession. (2) To make it possible to buy sacrificial animals and other materials for Passover and for the temple sacrifices. The priests in charge, however, had moved the whole business from the streets outside, where there might be economic competition, to the precincts of the temple, where they could monopolize the traffic. Several wrongs were involved. (I) Sharp dealing cheated the people and thereby provided graft money for the priesthood (Luke 19:45, 46). (2) The animals – doves and pigeons in large cages, as well as the common slaughter animals – physically polluted the precincts. (3) The house of God reeked with odors from the urine and dung of animals. The area rang with the inevitably noisy oriental haggling. These were a distraction from quiet worship. Furthermore the people who had a right to the area – the Gentile worshipers – were callously disregarded, being deprived of any decent place of worship at all.

As Jesus Himself later acknowledged, the nation's leaders had a duty

---

1 'Taxes,' in SDB, pp. 3183-85.

to demand further testimony than His own say so (John 5:31). They had already received *official* notification from John the Baptist, His accredited herald, for their official deputation had conveyed John's positive witness (John 1:19-28; see 5:33). They had the Father's testimony (John 5:36) in His now well-known miraculous works. As acknowledged by Nicodemus, one of their number, His works showed that He was sent of God (John 3:1, 2). More important than John's testimony or the miracles were the Old Testament Scriptures. But they disregarded them. Shortly Jesus would charge: 'Ye search the scriptures... and these are they which bear witness of me; and ye will not come to me, that ye may have life' (John 5:39, 40). Our Lord's actions that day laid claim on Old Testament prophecy: '... the Lord, whom ye seek, shall suddenly come to his temple...' (Mal. 3:1) being only one of many passages. All the prophecies of the Messiah's person and work and of the nation's duty to submit to and follow Him focused on Jesus that day when He first cleansed His Father's house, the Jerusalem temple.

Thus this first important public act of His career, transpiring at the very center of worldwide Jewry's national life, was not essentially a proof of messianic authority. It was rather a bold, forceful claim to that authority. He could not be ignored. The temple authorities were the first to be compelled to answer the question 'What will you do with Jesus which is called the Christ?' His assertion of messianic prerogatives and the patent rebuke of their false stewardship (He later said they had made His Father's house a den of thieves) were both rejected. Though they asked for a sign, Jesus gave *them* no further evidences except the veiled promise that when they had killed Him, He would rise from the dead: 'Destroy this temple and in three days I will raise it up.' Yet He did perform further miracles at the Passover. These miracles were convincing in a superficial way to 'many' but utterly without effect on the national leaders (John 2:18-20).

HE IS INTERVIEWED BY NICODEMUS

The language of John seems clearly to indicate that though 'many' were induced to believe by 'the signs which he did' at the Passover, these believers were not trusted by Jesus (John 2:23-25); but Nicodemus was an exception.[2] The word for 'man' in 3:1 ('a man of the Pharisees') and

John 2:23-3:21

---

2 RHG, p. 25.

for 'man' in the preceding verse ('he knew what was in man') are the same word. Further, the 'now' of 3:1 is frequently rendered 'but' and might be so rendered here. So we paraphrase, 'The public belief of the rabble, based on a carnal interpretation of Jesus' miracles, was insincere, *but* there was a man named Nicodemus who, knowing the testimony of the Baptist, knowing the Scriptures, and being a man of true faith, when he saw Jesus and witnessed His miracles, knew in his heart that Jesus had been sent to the Jewish people by God.' Jesus received Nicodemus as a sincere seeker.

Was Nicodemus also a deputy of the Sanhedrin sent to get information about Jesus by private interview? It has been seriously contended by able, reverent writers.[3] If they sent a delegation to John, why not one of their number known to be sympathetic to the mode of religion represented by Jesus?[4] It is a conjecture only, though not without some ground. Jesus, in any case, received the older man courteously and treated him with respect (John 7:50; 19:39). If he came secretly and wholly on his own initiative, as his coming by night seems to imply, there were great difficulties to overcome and not a little danger, for his colleagues were in deadly opposition to Jesus already, and their ruthlessness in gaining whatever ends they sought was well known.

John, who may have been present at, or in earshot of, the interview, brings to us, in his report of it, some of the truths at the very heart of Biblical religion: (1) The kingdom of God as Jesus then presented it has mainly spiritual dimensions. Without dashing Jewish hopes of national deliverance so brilliantly expressed in Old Testament prophecy, Jesus pointed out that the kingdom of God, being at root a spiritual reality, requires spiritual qualifications for entry. (2) A kingdom of God was present, taking shape under Jesus' immediate ministry, upon foundations laid by His herald, John, which to enter required a new birth. The words *born again* almost surely mean 'born from heaven,' for the word *again* *(anôthen)* is literally 'from above' and frequently is used in the sense of 'from heaven' (see John 3:27, and note the use of *anôthen* ['from above'] in John 19:15; James 1:17; 3:15, 17). It remained for Paul's epistles to spell out *why* the new birth is necessary for entering the kingdom of God.

---

3 SDHF, p. 63.
4 David Smith argued that "since Jesus was a man of the people, they [the rulers] deemed it expedient to entrust the errand to a representative of the popular party. And, moreover, there was a prominent Pharisee who seemed well suited for the delicate negotiation-one Nicodemus, a venerable rabbi and a member of the high court of the Sanhedrin." SDHF, pp. 63, 64.

Man is spiritually dead in trespasses and sins and without power to turn to God, having no interest in or discernment of his spiritual need (Eph. 2:1-3; 4:18, 19; I Cor. 2:14). Old Testament prophets discerned the need for divine initiative in their message of 'Turn to me,' and Jesus some months later would say by the shore of Galilee, 'No man can come to me, except the Father... draw him' (John 6:44). (3) God's Spirit is sovereign in His preparing the heart for, regeneration. To Nicodemus's misconceived questions (John 3:4, 9) — evidence that though he was a teacher, he had not dug deeply enough (Ezek. 11:17-20; John 3:10) — Jesus compared the Spirit's movements in the new birth to the wind (both the Greek and Hebrew words for wind and spirit are the same), even then perhaps whistling up the narrow streets of the suburb where Jesus lodged. There is a mysterious 'sovereignty' to the wind (John 3:8; cf. Rom. 9:16, 18; John 3:11-15). No one ever tells it where to blow. So it is with the divine Spirit. (4) The human means of salvation is faith and faith alone (John 3:16, 17), and (5) the basis is what God has done in Christ — 'God gave his only begotten Son,' He 'sent... his Son' (John 3:16, 17). (6) There is no other way (John 3:18), even though (7) men being evil at heart do not love either God's Son or the gospel about Him (John 3:19-21) — further evidence that God in grace must always seek and find and turn man, rather than the other way around. How much of the portion after verse 15 is Jesus' own words or John's enlargement on them cannot be known, but Jesus might have spoken it all.

HE JOINS FORCES WITH JOHN

It is very important that the interpreter of these verses hold distinctly John 3: before his mind that Matthew, Mark, and Luke report *nothing*, not a 22-36 syllable, of the larger part of a year after Jesus' temptation but before the opening of His ministry in Capernaum. All of John 2, 3, and 4 – 115 verses in all – falls in a hiatus between Matthew 4:11 and 4:12; between Mark 1:13 and 1:14; between Luke 4:13 and 4:14. One would assume, if Matthew, for example, were his only source (Matt. 4:18-20), that when the call to permanent association with Him, leaving their nets forever, came to Peter and Andrew and to James and John, Jesus had not met them before. Yet as a matter of fact we know from John that three of them at least, and probably all four (John 1:35-51), had been disciples for

---

5 John 4:1-3 suggests why Jesus spent those months in Judaea, viz., to win to Himself His forerunner's disciples.

about a year, and that a case could be made for rearranging the order of names to Andrew and Peter, John and James.

These men had been disciples of John.[5] Jesus had been baptized by John. For nearly a year John continued to minister in public. All the while the One he was still heralding was also quietly ministering in the same province. As already indicated, during this period Jesus' work was certainly not subordinate to John's but it was coordinate with it. The Synoptics do not start their report of Jesus' public ministry at all until that point when John's ministry ended. Matthew, for example, reports the end of the temptation, then without break, giving no indication whatsoever of Jesus' initial lengthy Judaean ministry, continues: 'Now when Jesus had heard that John was cast into prison, he departed into Galilee'; and there follows the bulk of Matthew's Gospel on the great Galilean ministry. Mark 1:14ff. presents the identical picture in this regard, and Luke 4:14ff. is the same except that Luke does not mention the imprisonment of John. So this first year of ministry (apparently all in Judaea, though He may have made visits back to Nazareth or Capernaum) is a total blank in the Synoptics. They must have regarded it, like His baptism and temptation, as preliminary to the real work of His itinerant ministry. That work is understood mainly as preparing the Apostles, in view of His certain rejection by Israel. This was a matter of history by the sixth or seventh decades, when the Synoptists wrote. The training of the Apostles was mainly to found a church after their Master's death (Matt. 16:18; cf. 16:20-23 and also Eph. 2:20). The key to Matthew's selection of materials, on these principles, is the last two verses of his book, in which Jesus gives the commission to disciple and instruct all the nations. A. T. Robertson's rubric for this section, then, seems very fitting: 'The Parallel Ministry of Jesus and John with John's Loyalty to Jesus.'[6] John's comparison of himself to the friend of the bridegroom, and of Jesus to the bridegroom who *alone will* carry away the bride (the church?) is very fitting.

John
4:1-42
Luke
3:19, 20
Mark
1:14
Matt.
4:12
Luke
4:14

HE LEAVES FOR GALILEE VIA SAMARIA

We know that Jesus did not depart Judaea until after Herod Antipas, tetrarch of Galilee and Peraea, had imprisoned John. The literary 'flashbacks' of Matthew 14:3-5 and parallels (Mark 6:17-20; Luke 3:19, 20) offer no hint of this fact, for it evidently did not suit the Synoptists'

6 RHG, p. 26.

purposes to report it. The Fourth Gospel makes a point of connecting Jesus' return to Galilee for the opening of His 'great ministry in Galilee' with the end of the Baptist's career. John therefore calls special attention to the fact that people now knew that Jesus was eclipsing His colleague and herald's success in winning disciples (John 4:1, 2).

The ministry in Samaria fits John's purpose to lead men to 'receive' Christ in faith for salvation (John 1:12; 4:39-42; 20:30, 31). That Jesus chose to travel through Samaria was a lesson in Christian principle. He also plainly told the woman that the Samaritan heresy was, indeed, a heresy (John 4:22). Jesus, not to be deterred from His mission as Messiah of Israel, gave the Samaritans only two days of His time (John 4:44), yet He showed that He would not let a case of bitter group social animosity provide any barrier to the proclaiming of the good news and the opening of fellowship based on gospel acceptance. The Jews, with good reasons (treachery [Neh. 4:1-23], apostasy [II Kings 17:24-41]) had shunned close connections with Samaritans for over five centuries, perhaps even seven. But that belonged to an epoch now ending. Jesus showed that in the epoch about to begin there are no political, racial, social groups who are outside the full privileges of the Christian association.

The spontaneous friendly response in Samaria contrasts greatly with the official response in Jerusalem at the previous Passover. Nor did the villagers of Capernaum, in the days ahead, receive Him well. Jesus enjoyed great popularity among the people of Galilee, especially outside of Capernaum, for about a year. Yet in a few days His home town of Nazareth would, by attempting, as a community, to murder Him, show how fully they deserved their evil reputation (John 1:46).

The Gospel of John abounds in stories of Jesus' personal encounters[7] with needy souls who respond to His ministry and preaching. But the story of the Samaritan woman at the well of Sychar is unique. The woman had no obvious need except forgiveness of sin, the conversation was fully personal and evidently private. The development is so circumstantial, detailed, and dramatic, and at the same time so timeless and universal in character and appeal, that it is selected here as a kind of supreme example of the Savior as evangelist and soul winner. He claimed to have come 'to call sinners to repentance,' to have been 'anointed... to preach good tidings" (Luke 4:18). Here He is on view at these self-assigned tasks.

---

7 Nicodemus, chap. 3; impotent man, chap. 4; blind man, chap. 9.

1. *The background* of the encounter is almost as significant as the event.

The episode with 'the woman at the well' is one that is 'in transit.' Jesus now closed His protracted ministry in Judaea and headed out for Galilee. That we shortly find Jesus again briefly in Jerusalem (chap. 5) means only that He still felt reasonably safe to participate in the national worship[8] at the temple. Jesus moved mainly only in the three acknowledged Jewish provinces – Judaea, 'beyond Jordan' (Josephus's Peraea), and Galilee. Why did He feel that 'He must needs go through Samaria' (John 4:4)? It might mean that He was planning to go to Aenon near the northern border of Samaria as directly as possible in order to gather and instruct the, disciples of the just-incarcerated Baptist .[9]

It might mean that He wanted to take the quickest route, but this is not likely in view of His two-day stopover at Sychar. The reason might have been the many spiritual-providential considerations (the value of the incident to all believers in all ages, the need of the woman, the entrance to Samaritan people for later evangelism [Acts 8:5-25], etc.). We would like to think the incident itself tips the scales toward the last and explains why the prescient Savior felt He had to go there (John 4:5).

The place is exceedingly interesting. Ebal and Gerizim (Deut. 11:29, 30; 27:4-28; Josh. 8:30-35), mounts of the cursing and blessing, are on either side. Old Testament Shechem,[10] Joseph's tomb (Josh. 24:32), and the well of Jacob – the latter with imponderable previous Biblical associations and today freighted with centuries of Christian sentimental attraction – are nearby.[11] Modern archaeology has uncovered portions of ancient buildings atop Mt. Gerizim bordering on the south of the pass in which the town of Shechem is situated. The ancient town of Shechem (that is, the significant parts of it) has been thoroughly excavated by the best scientific methods. Today one can walk, as the woman did, from Jacob's well to Sychar, about a half-mile north, at the foot of Mt. Ebal and then back a few hundred yards to the small, white, Muslim building housing the memorial of Joseph. Perhaps another five hundred yards farther is the edge of Tel *Balatah, the* Arabic name of the site of ancient Shechem. The distance from the well to the village of Askar (Sychar) is right for the story. It lies in plain view from Jacob's well. [Since the 1967 war this area has been one of intense hostility, not only against Jews but christian

---

8 The Law required that every adult Jewish male 'appear before the Lord' three times a year at the central sanctuary.

9 SDHF, p. 72.

10 Mentioned forty-three times in the Old Testament.

11 FANT treats the locality on pp. 34-42. See BA, 31:58-71; 32:80-103; BASOR, no. 180, pp. 740.

victims as well. As of 2002 the memorials at both the tomb of Joseph and the well of Jacob had been damaged or destroyed by local people.]

The circumstances – the weariness of a long day's travel (by the Roman reckoning, employed by John, the sixth hour is 6pm); a lonely, ostracized, vital woman at the more distant well, perhaps to avoid the more respectable wives and daughters who filled their jars at water sources in and nearer the village; the privacy provided by the absence of the disciples in 'the city' to buy supper provisions; the bold confrontation precipitated by the strange rabbi's request – all excite interest, both devout and curious.

2. The engagement (John 4:7-26) shows how the Lord led the woman step by step to confessing Him as Messiah and, through her, many more to faith in Him both as Christ and Savior of the world (John 4:29).

The woman, being a Samaritan, had many beliefs in common with Jesus and all other sincere Jews. The animosity of Jews toward Samaritans was partly based on race – the Samaritans were half Jewish-half Gentile in ancestry. Like Jews, the Samaritans accepted the Law of Moses (the Pentateuch), and in rejecting the rest of the Old Testament as Scripture, they were at least in agreement with the Jewish Sadducees who likewise received only the five books of Moses. They observed the Sabbath, practiced circumcision after the Mosaic teaching, observed some of the Levitical sacrifices (though at their own sanctuary on Mt. Gerizim), and celebrated the annual festivals of the Pentateuchal calendar. They claimed descent from Joseph, whose tomb was nearby, and called Jacob their father.[12] Certain writers have overdone the Jewish-Samaritan differences. Their roads, towns, and markets, for example, did not render Jews unclean according to Pharisaic rules, hence the disciples could buy 'clean' food and Jesus could take water from the woman's hand and pitcher (John 4:12).

Our Lord's first actions were directed toward *attracting the woman's attention.* Whether He deliberately chose the well-curb for His seat or not, if she was to let the pitcher down on a rope, she could hardly avoid proximity to Him. Though the Muslim religion has heightened the aloofness of women of the East, it appears always and everywhere to have been true that solitary women hardly accept conversational overtures from strange men.

Then He *engaged her in conversation* by a socially acceptable device-

12 Josephus, Antiquities 9.14.3; 11.12.5; 12.5.5.

breaking no social stricture – for, being thirsty and without means, He asked her to give Him to drink. This particular request (as the present writer has learned to sorrowful embarrassment not far from ancient Sychar) is joyfully granted by all decent people in that part of the world. There you do not hoard your water against the thirsty traveler. The woman was genuinely puzzled that One who was obviously Jewish[13] would ask favors of a Samaritan, and a woman at that!

He quickly *turned the conversation to spiritual and eternal things.* The woman, almost certainly of the lowest socioeconomic class, burdened with material cares, had perhaps never in her life thought more deeply than to join in the bare forms of her community religion. But Jesus compelled her to think of 'living water,' eternal life, inner health and peace. She had heard of Messiah, for Samaritans on the basis of the Pentateuch expected Him, but her ideas of Messiah would have been purely nationalistic and external.

Not only so, Jesus in saying 'Call your husband' (John 4:16) spoken words which pierced the conscience of the unfortunate woman. He had already *aroused curiosity* (John 4:12) about His teaching and a *desire to hear Him out* (John 4:15). At first unable to think in the language of symbols (e.g., living water is eternal life), still pondering if He might be greater than their common ancestor Jacob, in her simplicity (her words seem to carry no irony or sarcasm) she received a shock from the stranger when He said what He did (John 4:15, 16).

By that shock to her central being – where self-respect and moral consciousness reside – she was *driven to make several decisions: (I)* She was forced to admit her unhappy past and thus to drop the mask of respectability. One is tempted to read too much into Jesus' comment about her 'five husbands.' We are not at liberty to declare her an immoral woman, for we know nothing of the circumstances. The fact that she presently had a 'man' who was at least informally her husband assures us she was not promiscuous or a prostitute. The woman still had *some* standards to hide behind, though not many. (2) She also acknowledged Jesus to be a prophet. And it is probably accurate (certainly charitable) to regard her question about 'Jerusalem or this mountain' as a sincere question. As a fruit of our Lord's clear words on that subject, we know that the Samaritans were mistaken, 'for salvation is of the Jews,' and we have His jewel-like summary of the essence of true worship (John 4:24)

---

13 It seems likely that our Lord was recognized as Jewish by the color of the normal fringes on His garment (Num. 15:37-41), distinct from the color of the Samaritans'. Perhaps (surely our Lord wore no 'mazzuzoth') it was His 'Jewish' face. Yet the 'Jewish' look is really the Semitic countenance of Arabs and others, and Samaritans, apart from the high priestly family, are said not to have a 'Semitic' look.

– 'in spirit and in truth.' Furthermore, (3) the woman came to 'believe' (John 4:21; cf. vv. 29, 42) *Him* and to accept Him as the Messiah and Savior of the world.

3. *The sequel* (John 4:28-30) is unique in the Gospels.

The woman told the good news, via the 'men' – with whom, if not with the women of the village, she seems to have been on speaking terms – to the whole community. It is not purely speculative to wonder if our Lord's words about the whitened harvest were spoken to the amazed disciples just as the hurrying inhabitants moving down the slope from Sychar heaved into sight, seeking to meet and hear the stranger who still abode by Jacob's ancient well.

The Lord used the occasion to instruct His still uncomprehending disciples about the nature of evangelism. His own actions with the woman, which so amazed them, were a lesson in themselves (John 4:35-37), but He did not fail to drive the lesson home: (1) evangelism is always a matter of capturing the present opportunity (John 4:35); (2) sowing by some, reaping by others go on contemporaneously (John 4:36); (3) soul winning is not an individual assignment only but a corporate responsibility (John 4:37).

Further, the Lord's quiet declining of food for a little while, appetite taken by the joy of 'spiritual mastication' as in His immediately completed winning of the poor Samaritan woman's soul, will be forever the acme of teaching on the soul winner's joy. 'He that goeth forth and weepeth, bearing precious seed, shall doubtless come again with rejoicing, bringing his sheaves with him' (Ps. 126:6). It just may be that those next two days spent as guest of the villagers of Sychar, during which 'many more believed because of his own word,' were the most joyous of His entire public career.

Thus ends the first great epoch in our Lord's career. His many months in Judaea, first challenging the national leadership at the Passover when He drove the sellers of livestock and the money changers from the temple, thereby asserting messianic claims, then defending His action to 'the Jews' (in John, the Jerusalem leadership) but giving no 'sign,' instructing the seeker Nicodemus, working with John the Baptist until the latter's imprisonment, and finally preaching to the Samaritans en route to Galilee had been a mixed experience. The original five or six disciples whom He had received from the Baptist and who apparently were with Him throughout the period seem to have gone back to Capernaum and

Bethsaida near Capernaum. One of them, Nathanael, of Cana (John 21:2), scene of the Lord's first miracle, seems to have invited the Lord back to his home there. Perhaps Jesus was thinking now of gathering as many genuine disciples about Him as possible for instruction and hoped at Cana, the scene of His first success, to find a good place to make first consolidation of effort. Some weeks later Jesus would call all of the six to permanent association with Him and would to them add six more.

Excursus 2 – The Length of Jesus' Ministry

Except for the Gospel of John, almost nothing could be ascertained as to the precise length of our Lord's public career. On the basis of John's data, several chronologies of our Lord's ministry have been proposed.

There is an ancient one-year theory. A certain Ptolemy, disciple of the famous ancient Gnostic Valentinus, taught this theory, basing his argument probably on the silence of the three Synoptics and on a bizarre interpretation of Jesus' remark about 'the acceptable year of the Lord' (Luke 4:19).

There is also an ancient ten- to twenty-year theory. Irenaeus (second century) refuted Ptolemy, arguing from 'about thirty years of age' (Luke 3:23) and 'not yet fifty years old' (John 8:57) that Jesus' ministry lasted between ten and twenty years.[14]

On the basis of John's more complete data, in modern times the most generally accepted chronology takes as starting point Jesus' baptism by John a few months before Passover in March/April AD 27 and ends with His crucifixion on the day (by Jewish reckoning) of the 'last Passover' AD 30.

It is safe to affirm that Jesus' baptism took place within a year of the opening of John's ministry. John began his ministry 'in the fifteenth year of the reign of Tiberius Caesar' (Luke 3:1). According to the method of counting employed in the eastern provinces of the Empire, reckoning would start with Tiberius's brief coregency with Augustus, his fifteenth year being the calendar year (by modern reckoning) of AD 26.[15] Jesus came for baptism some weeks, at least, before the next following Passover. If He was baptized before January 1, then it was in AD 26; if in the month of January (as many scholars argue),[16]– then very early in AD 27. At this time He was 'about thirty years of age.' The December of His birth thirty

---

14 FHBC, p. 437.
15 ibid., p. 272, par. 423.
16 ALOL, p. xxi.

years before would have been in 5 BC (from I BC to AD I is only one year). Passover falls in the Jewish month Nisan (Exod. 12:6) (formerly called Abib), our March/April.

This first Passover of His public career is mentioned only at John 2:13-23. The second is unmentioned by John, but Jesus' reference to 'four months to harvest' in John 4:35 indicates clearly that the narrative has moved on to the month Shebat (January/ February) of AD 28.[17] The next feast mentioned simply as 'the feast' (John 5:1) was almost surely (as idiom indicates) Tabernacles,[18] celebrated in autumn (Tishri, September/ October). So though John does not mention the second Passover, he has rather clearly, if inadvertently, indicated its passing. Another close-to-certain indication of the passing of a second but (cf. Mark 2:23) unmentioned Passover is the incident of Luke 6, in which the disciples aroused the criticism of certain Pharisees by plucking ears of ripening grain. This would have to be shortly after Passover. The narrative does not appear to allow that Passover to be the one either of John 2 or of John 6:4. It has to fall between.[19]

The third Passover (AD 29) is distinctly mentioned (John 6:4). The following context of John 6 treats incidents of His pilgrimage to Jerusalem to attend this Passover. Six months later He was again at Jerusalem for the feast of Tabernacles (John 7:1, 14). Two months after that (Kislev, November/December) He was yet again in Jerusalem for the feast of Dedication (John 10:22). The narrative of events surrounding the last Passover, the fourth of His public career according to our reckoning, is the climax of each of the Gospels and provides the framework for the great bulk of the four accounts. They each trace the climactic development of events up to His death by crucifixion on the day before the evening when the whole of Jewry consumed their Paschal lambs 'without spot and without blemish.' This was in Nisan (March/April) AD 30.

The above is the most commonly received opinion - endorsed in a general way by the present author. It must be admitted that even aside from emphasis in the Gospels on the last week, there seems to be a disproportionate amount of narrative, sermons, and discourses crowded into the last year. Some remove the difficulty by postulating still another Passover between the third and the final one, placing it shortly after the

---

17 Ibid., pp. 178-89.
18 FHBC, p. 283.
19 On this reckoning, the theory that the mysterious reference to the 'second first Sabbath' (see NASB margin) could be the first of the seven Sabbaths between (Lev. 23:15-21). SLC, p. 234. Passover and Pentecost and the second such 'first Sabbath' of Jesus' career merit attention.

feeding of the five thousand in Galilee. This requires a ministry of over four years. In support it is noted that John does not refer to the second Passover, though we know it took place before the third of John 6:4, hence, no a priori objection to another unnoted Passover can be raised. In this way space is opened up for all the happenings from Mark 6:30, Luke 9:10, Matthew 14:13, and John 6:1 to the end of His ministry. Arguments are impressive but not compelling.[20] We shall follow the traditional view that the Lord's public career lasted three years and three or four months, from His baptism to the crucifixion, meanwhile acknowledging that we are dealing with possibilities and probabilities rather than certainties.

An excellent summary treatment, with full and significant bibliography, appears in a series of articles by Harold W. Hoehner. Part 3, 'The Duration of Christ's Ministry,' focuses on the duration and stages of His ministry. Hoehner favored the approximately three-and-a-half-year ministry, but he held the crucifixion to have occurred at Passover AD 32 rather than the more widely affirmed AD 30.[21] Jack Finegan furnished the data in succinct summary form and tended to support the AD 30[22] Among authors cited frequently in this volume, most accept the same. Exceptions are CJ Ellicott, who favored the shortest possible length, about one-and-a-half years;[23] and Johnson M. Cheney, who favored a four-and-a-half-year ministry.[24] The interested reader might do well to start with Finegan, then read Hoehner.

Excursus 3 – Why Only John Reports the First Year

Why does John alone tell us about that first year's ministry of Jesus? The first reason that comes to mind is that John may have been the only one of the four Gospel writers to have witnessed that year of ministry. Matthew did not become a disciple until later. The sources for Mark and Luke may not have contained the matter. But John, with the others of the original six, accompanied Him through those portions of this period reported in the Fourth Gospel as we know from John 2:22; 3:22; 4:2, 8, 27. If they did know about these months of ministry, it must not have suited the purposes of the three earlier Evangelists to report this material. Indeed

---

20 CLC, pp. 230-40.
21 'Chronological Aspects of the Life of Christ,' *Bibliotheca Sacra* 130 (1973): 338-51; 131 (1974): 41-54, 147-62, 241-64, 332-48.
22 FHBC.
23 EHL.
24 CLC.

they give scant attention to any of Jesus' visits to Jerusalem except the last. Jesus came as the Messiah of the Jewish nation to gather 'the lost sheep of the house of Israel.' It was His Father's will that Gentiles receive no more, during His natural life, than crumbs from the children's table (Matt. 15:21-28; Mark 7:24-30). It became clear very early, as early as the first Passover, that as far as the nation's leaders – priests, Levites, pontiffs, elders, and leading rabbis were concerned – He was nothing more than a powerful instrument of Beelzebub and nothing less than a dangerous and embarrassing challenge to their power. They immediately sought means to destroy Him. That this was the permanent state of mind of Israel's leaders is clear in the early chapters of Acts. So the Synoptists writing about twenty or thirty years later, when the first faltering steps were being taken through gospel preaching toward a worldwide extension of the present kingdom of Christ, they passed by the capital and the leaders, concentrating their attention on that period of His career when He was gathering believing men to form the core of the church He had foreseen and promised to build. Thus the Synoptists reported as little of His ministries in Jerusalem as was consistent with their narrative. Reflection on these truly impressive developments will bring sharply before the conscience that whether these inferences are correct or not, 'certainly at the close of the first year of the ministry of Jesus there fell already over Judaea and Jerusalem the shadow of the most frightful of all the national crimes [in the face of current prejudices, one hesitates even to quote this] which the world has ever witnessed, the rejection and crucifixion by the Jews of their Messiah.'[25]

Another fact may explain the paucity of information about this year. During a major part of it – the months between the interview with Nicodemus and the rising of a tide of opposition which drove Jesus out of Judaea (John 4:1-4) and brought about the imprisonment of John (Luke 3:19, 20) – Jesus joined rather closely with John the Baptist (John 3:22). The narrative suggests that for this limited time only, Jesus had His disciples baptize with the baptism of repentance (i.e., with John's baptism). Perhaps after the serious rebuffs at Jerusalem He decided to gain more followers, profiting especially from the previous work of John, though John the Baptist apparently continued some sort of ministry at Aenon near Salim for most of the year. Most geographers locate Salim a few miles west of Jordan, south of Scythopolis in the Plain of Jezreel, but there is no agreement whether the Decapolis or Samaria included

25 SLC, p. 53.

the area. In either case, Herod would have to extradite him. Jesus and His company apparently – if we may judge by His later custom – traveled about in the province of Judaea until January (the harvest, which occurred in May, was 'yet four months' away, according to John 4:35), when He left via Samaria. We know no incident, saying, parable, or miracle from that period of travel in Judaea. It must have extended from the previous April after the discourse with Nicodemus at the Passover season. The chapter division between John 2:23-25 and John 3:1 obscures the fact that the interview with Nicodemus was during the Passover festival. The Greek words *(en de)* with which John 3:1 begins definitely connect this interview with the Passover. It may be, therefore, that John, who certainly knew about those eight to ten months of activity in Judaea, regarded them as an interlude and, hence, unimportant to the main career of the Messiah, failing to fall under John's purpose laid out at John 20:30,31. Jesus was still associated with the herald, and His work was still preparatory to the main mission. Thus even John's report is sketchy and very selective.

Excursus 4 – Jewish National Responsibility for Jesus' Crucifixion

Some enlargement is here made of the point made in excursus 3 that the Jewish people *as a nation* did reject their Messiah and that the Bible teaches that God holds them responsible as a nation.

A spate of articles and books – not the least of these, the *Documents of Vatican II*, which has a section on it – have sought to absolve the Jews of any special *national* guilt for the death of Jesus. Almost everything current is bent to some degree away from the New Testament reports, and especially away from the very clear passages of the Book of Acts. There, while the guilty failures of Pontius Pilate and Herod and other Gentiles are not neglected (Acts 5:27), the crucifixion of Jesus is always a crime of the nation of Israel, acting representatively through their constituted civil and religious national rulers. The unpleasant (and presently neglected and unwelcome) recitation starts with the first sermon, 'Ye men of Israel, hear these words; Jesus of Nazareth, a man approved of God among you by miracles and wonders and signs, which God did by him in the midst of you, as ye yourselves also know: him, being delivered by the determinate counsel and foreknowledge of God, ye have taken, and by wicked hands have crucified and slain' (Acts 2:22, 23). Peter later said of them that 'ye [not Pilate] slew and hanged [Christ] on a tree' (Acts 5:30). Stephen charges that 'ye have been now the betrayers and murderers' (Acts 7:52; 10:39; 13:27). Nothing could be plainer than Paul's words to the Thessalonians a few years after the crucifixion, addressing them on the subject of religious persecution: 'For ye, brethren, became followers of the churches of God which in Judaea are in Christ Jesus: for ye also have suffered like things of your own countrymen, even as they have of the Jews: who both killed the Lord Jesus, and their own prophets, [he groups the contemporaries of Jesus with their ancestors] and have persecuted us (he groups them likewise with his own contemporaries a generation later); and they please not God, and are contrary to all men... for the wrath is come upon them to the uttermost' (I Thess. 2:14-16). In the last sentence Paul seems to indicate that the divine wrath executed by Titus on the people of Jerusalem of the generation of AD 70, when few, if any, of the persons of the Sanhedrin, personally responsible for the death of Jesus, were still living, was nevertheless a punishment on the nation. Jesus Himself forecast all this plainly in many statements, not the least being the parable of the king who made a marriage for his son (Matt. 22:2-10) and ended up 'wroth: and he sent forth his armies, and destroyed those murderers, and burned up their city' (Matt. 22:7).

It is a faulty inference, made all too frequently in Christendom, that this national crime is directly punishable by men or that living persons are *personally* guilty for the death of Jesus. But that God held and holds the nation guilty and has judicially blinded the nation (II Cor. 3:15, 16; Rom. 11:25) to the righteous, evident claims of His Son is a fact of Scripture. Meanwhile it is the Christian responsibility to respect the Jewish people for their history and accomplishments, to love them as beloved by God, and to preach the gospel to them.

Opening the Great Galilean Ministry: A Time of Growing Favor

The first year in Galilee was one of growing popularity[1] – always in spite of conflicts with the Jerusalem national leadership – to the point where the Galileans were ready to stage a march on the capital and to make Him king (John 6:15), so impressed were they with Him. At that point Jesus chose deliberately to wither that enthusiasm, and He withered it so thoroughly that within a few hours He was asking the Twelve, 'Will you also go away' (John 6:66, 67).

In chapter 5 we shall show the stages through which the Savior gained a central core of sincere followers and multitudes of fair-weather disciples – by what travels and stages, through what means, and in spite of growing opposition.

In chapter 6 we shall see how Jesus introduced some startling methods – especially His peculiar use of parables. We shall take note of growing

---

I As we already noted, Matthew, Mark, and Luke simply pass over the many months of Jesus' initial ministry in Judaea and Jerusalem. This is the period beginning with the first Passover up to His entrance upon the great Galilean ministry of eighteen months. After reporting that block of time (that is, the ministry in Galilee), Matthew and Mark hasten on to the passion. Luke gives a great deal on the ministry of that final six-and-a-half-months, with John supplementing and the other two supporting only at the end. But all three give large blocks of material on those eighteen months in Galilee now before us, while John adds several episodes regarding journeys to the festivals at Jerusalem during that time.

conflict with the leaders, how He employed bold strokes of logic and bolder demonstrations of His own authority in connection with the most obdurate, senseless attacks of His enemies. We shall see how at the end of a year in Galilee He brought His popularity with the lakeside crowds to flood tide and then deliberately destroyed it in a day by making clear the spiritual requirement of His kingdom which they carnally, mindlessly, and insistently refused to understand or to accept.

Chapter 7 will treat the special training of the Twelve during the next six months. They were often on the move, occasionally making a swift chassé back into the Capernaum area, but mostly on the borders, in Phoenicia or the tetrarchy of Philip.

Chapter 8 will trace our Lord's departure from Galilee and final six months of ministry in Judaea, Jerusalem, and Trans-Jordan.

LOCATING CAMPAIGN HEADQUARTERS

Luke 4:14-31
Matt. 4:13
John 4:46-54

Let us assume that Jesus had an invitation from Nathanael of Cana, who had probably been with Him in Judaea for the past several months, and that He resolved to begin the great efforts to win the less prejudiced citizens of the north at Cana, the very place where, at the wedding feast, He had made such a strong, favorable impression the year before (John 2:1-11).[2]

So the small band of seven men trudged on to Cana. Not many days later, at 7 pm, an officer of Herod, a resident of Capernaum nearly twenty miles to the east, arrived in town in anxious haste and inquired for Jesus. The noise of Jesus' miracles at the 'feast' at Jerusalem several months before had preceded Him. This man was seeking a cure for his son, sick to death. Our Lord was clearly piqued. Did the Messiah have no better standing in Galilee than a witch doctor with strong medicine? Jesus' probing questions, however, found faith, and the son was healed in a manner remarkably confirming the highest estimate of Jesus. John reports that the father 'believed, and his whole house' (4:53), language that pre-intimates the conversion of Lydia and the Philippian jailor (Acts 16:15, 31-34). The effect of this miracle, coupled with our Lord's preaching – evidently over a period of time and in several places – was electric. He was instantly famous everywhere He went in the province and beyond.

---

2 If 'the feast' of John 5:1 was Passover (RHG, p. 42; ALOL, pp. 189-98; SDHF, pp. 522, 523), the events of that chapter fall in this period (GJM, p. 78; ANT, pp. 502, 503). So argue many, though there are advocates of every Jewish feast and some authorities prefer to leave the question entirely open. Elsewhere in this book I have supported the view that the feast in question is Tabernacles.

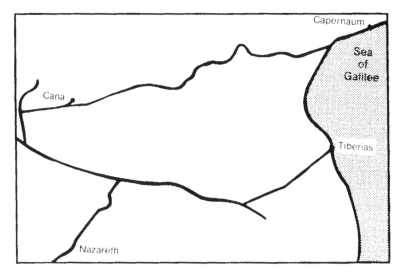

Map 3. Galilee

During this early period Jesus briefly visited Nazareth (Luke 4:16-31). The meaning of the events of that day is clear. The Lord in a very special way 'came unto his own, and his own received him not' (John 1:11).

Two matters, both of great interest and import, intrude upon the reader. The first is a question: Why did our Lord, in a direct affront, boldly antagonize the whole congregation? Answer: He did so because the very central error – or willful sin – of His people was clear to see and had to be attacked by Him whose name is both True and Holy. These villagers, gathered as one for Sabbath services at the synagogue to hear a now-famous son speak, were obviously assuming that their national election by God would save them individually. They drew all the unwarranted inferences from that false assumption. Though not learned, they themselves had adopted the life style of the learned Pharisee and scribe. Since they as a nation were God's people through Abraham, they expected to receive all God had promised to Abraham without Abraham's faith; since to them pertained the Law of Moses, they expected somehow to miss the curses of Moses' Law and to receive the marvelous rewards, but without any of Moses' endurance and loyalty, and certainly without the heart purity of that 'meekest man in all the earth' (Num. 12:3). So Jesus, without a single concession to their prejudice, yielding not an inch to considerations of winning an audience, let His message be (as the gospel always is) a savor of death (II Cor. 2:16; cf. Rom. 9:18) to those who seal their own doom by hardening their hearts. He would harden them still more. He pointed out that God had passed over all the widows of Israel during the famine in Elijah's time to sustain a believing heathen widow of nearby Sidon in Phoenicia (I Kings 17:8-16). God also had passed over the numerous lepers of Israel in Elisha's time to heal a believing heathen Syrian named Naaman (II Kings 5:1-14). It was all true and well known. Nothing so antagonizes men as an unanswerable argument. So they tried to kill Him. His countrymen would try to kill Him many times again in the next two years, finally with success and for the same set of reasons.

The second matter relates to the synagogue facilities[3] and practices of the time which provided a pulpit for the Lord, not only at Nazareth, but apparently several times a week for the coming year throughout Galilee. Coming into existence sometime after the destruction of Solomon's temple, by our Lord's time the synagogue was a universal means for gathering the Jews of every community together for regular worship and fellowship. Jews were under obligation, according to their rabbis, to form synagogues (i.e., both associations and buildings) wherever they might be. Wherever there were ten adult males qualified to supply the proper leadership, they were to form a synagogue. A special building – in shape, furnishings, and function not unlike a Protestant chapel – was preferred. There was special furniture to house the Torah and other Scriptural rolls, a lectern at which one stood to read, seats on the main floor where the men sat, a gallery for women, seats facing the assembly for elders and deacons. The congregation assembled on the forenoon of the Sabbath, again in the evening, and at stated hours on Monday and Thursday. Since the synagogue had certain civil functions, the leaders held court sessions too. The synagogue was also frequently the schoolhouse for the children. The schoolmaster was part of the synagogue staff. The Nazareth synagogue would have been the place where Jesus learned to read, as well as the place where, with the family of Joseph and Mary, He attended services.

Synagogue custom accounts for Jesus' being asked to read the Scriptures and to speak. Though it is very doubtful that every worshiper

---

3 Helpful and interesting discussion of the Jewish synagogue of Jesus' time will be found in ELTJM, 1:430-50; SHJP, 2:ii, 44-89. For those who read German, perhaps the most complete essay is 'Excurs, Der altjuedische Synagogeninstitut' and 'Excurs, Der altjuedische Synagogengottesdienst,' in SBCNT, 4.1, 115-188.

was eligible to be called to preach after readings from the Law and the Prophets,[4] it is agreed that whenever the ruler of the synagogue observed a qualified rabbi in the congregation, he was at liberty to call upon him for 'any word of exhortation' (Acts 13:14). This custom provided Paul frequent strategic opportunities in later years and was the instrument of our Lord's entrance to many communities, beginning with His sermon at Nazareth.

Since He was not welcome in Nazareth, He settled in Capernaum, commercial center of the eastern part of Galilee, located twenty miles northeast on the northwest shore of the Sea of Galilee. Matthew, who omits mention of the unhappy episode at Nazareth, calls attention to the fulfillment of Isaiah's prophecy that the Galilee lakeside would be the scene of the Messiah's special ministry (Matt. 4:13-16; cf. Isa. 8:23; 9:1, 2).

We are never told where He lodged in Capernaum. His family, who had visited there a year earlier, of course had not established residence there. Perhaps Jesus became a resident member of Peter's numerous household there (Luke 4:38). Though He was away from home much of the time, Capernaum is called hereafter 'His own city' (Matt. 9:1; cf. 2:1-12).

GATHERING DISCIPLES AND MINISTERING TO CROWDS

The crowds were now coming to hear Him.[5] Soon after settlement in Capernaum and already pressed by the multitudes, He came early one morning to the seashore. Seeing Peter and Andrew washing their nets near their fishing boats, He asked them to take Him aboard and push out a bit from shore. There He sat in the bow sheets and talked to the crowd already lining the shore, taking advantage of a slight distance from the crowd and the natural amplification of His voice. Shortly He asked the puzzled Peter to pull the boat out into deep water and let down the nets. It was the wrong time of day, and no doubt Peter, a fisherman, wondered about taking advice about fishing from a carpenter, but he obeyed. The draft of fishes taken was so great that Peter and Andrew summoned their partners James and John with their boat to save the catch. With Jesus' words, 'Come ye after me, and I will make you fishers of men,' ringing in their ears, these four Capernaum fishermen (four of the original six –

Mark
1:16-
2:22
Matt.
4:17-22
4:23-25
8:2-4
9:1-8
9::9-17
Luke
4:31-44
5:1-11
5:12-39

---

4 ELTJM, I:95.
5 Luke's purpose (I:3, 'in order') caused him to preserve approximate chronological connections where the other Gospel authors vary the order of events, or seem to do so. So Luke's order is usually to be regarded as chronological and will be followed mainly throughout the rest of this book.

Philip of Bethsaida and Nathanael of Cana not being present) now begin to company with the Lord day and night (Mark 1:14-20; Matt. 4:17-22; Luke 5:1-11). They will shortly be joined by Philip and Nathanael and six more – all of whom Jesus will ordain Apostles.

The people were greatly attracted to Jesus. He was now a locally acclaimed religious teacher and worker of wonders. This was acknowledged on the next Sabbath when the ruler of the synagogue – whether spontaneously or under pressure by the crowd, we do not know – invited Him to speak (Mark 1:20, 21). During the synagogue service occurred the first reported case of Jesus' curing demon possession – the strange, frightening features of demon possession (with which all readers of the Gospels are familiar) being highlighted.

It was also a new departure in Jewish preaching: 'And they were astonished at his teaching: for he taught them as having authority, and not as the scribes' (Mark 1:22 ASV). After services Jesus and the four disciples went to the house of Simon and Andrew ('Peter's house' in Matthew) where, finding Peter's mother-in-law ill 'of a fever' (an ailment common in the lowlands near the lake), Jesus 'touched her hand, and the fever left her' (Matt. 8:15). Then after the meal served by the restored lady, 'when the sun was setting,' multitudes of ill and demon-possessed were brought to the door (Mark 1:33), all of whom were made whole by Him (Matt. 8:16). Matthew, emphasizing the elements of fulfilled Old Testament prophecy, calls the healings and restoration a fulfillment of Isaiah's prophecy: 'Himself took our infirmities and bare our diseases' (Matt. 8:17; cf. Isa. 53:4). It is noteworthy that there was no local opposition to these Sabbath-day works of healing. Only later were the objections imported from Judaea. Our Lord gave His services to all who came.

Later, after the crowds had gone and after a short repose, 'a great while before day, he... departed into a desert place, and there prayed' (Mark 1:35 ASV). Somehow knowing where He had gone, the four followed. This sort of nocturnal retreat becomes standard for the rest of His career. The Mediterranean climate allows this at most seasons of the year. Frequently Jesus and His disciples slept as well as ate in the open.

Later in the day the crowds found Him, but without avail, for the Lord abruptly deserted Capernaum for a while, taking the four with Him. He had embarked on a preaching tour in towns 'throughout all Galilee' (Matt. 4:23; Mark 1:38, 39). He is said to have preached 'in their synagogues.' Since synagogue services were only on three days a week and travel was forbidden on the Sabbath, this first of His three main preaching circuits through Galilee may have consumed several weeks. The results were astounding. His fame spread so far that multitudes came not only from Galilee but from the Jewish provinces of Judaea and Trans-Jordan and from the heathen Decapolis as well. Matthew says they came from all Syria (Matt. 4:24), which as a geographical term includes all the Mediterranean littoral from Antioch on the north to the borders of Egypt on the south and from the Sea on the west to the desert of Arabia on the east. Only one notable incident of the circuit is mentioned – the first specifically mentioned healing of leprosy. Without noting the place where it occurred, all three Synoptics (Mark 1:44; Matt. 8:4; Luke 5:14) note that Jesus commanded the leper to observe the Mosaic ritual rules for certification of the cure and readmission to society. This involved a trip to the Jerusalem temple for ritual cleansings and priestly inspections (Lev. 13:40; 14:2ff.).

Back in Capernaum again – the circuit of Galilee having come to an end in a brief retreat in the rough hills east of the Lake of Galilee - the real battle with the Pharisees was joined (Luke 5:17). They had not seriously opposed Him in Galilee up to now because they were not numerous there. But when He returned with the four from the first circuit of Galilee, they were waiting for Him, ready to pounce. Far from avoiding conflict with them, the Lord tore into them, shattering their theological objections before they even had a chance to express them. Alfred Edersheim called attention to the anti-Jewish character the activity of Jesus now assumed.[6] (When the Gospels say 'the Jews' in this connection, they designate not the citizenry but the self-serving, apostate national civil-religious leaders.)

In Capernaum there occurred another striking incident. The extraordinary efforts of four friends of a paralytic lowered that poor man through the roof of a house where Jesus was ministering. They lowered the miserable body so that it lay immediately before Jesus. He, 'seeing their faith,' declared, 'thy sins are forgiven thee' (Mark 2:5; Matt. 9:2; Luke 5:20), knowing full well what the scribes and Pharisees present would think of that. And, quite unwittingly, they anticipated the fuller revelations to come of His full deity, reasoning silently, 'Who is this that speaketh blasphemies? Who can forgive sins but God alone?' Jesus directly attacked their unvoiced thoughts and laid down His challenge: '... is it

6 ELTJM, 1:499.

easier to say thy sins are forgiven thee; or to say, Arise... and walk?' Then, making bold claims to the divine power of forgiving sins, He healed the man and sent him on his way carrying his own litter! Amazement, fear of God, and honor to His name on the part of the populace, anger and bitter hatred on the part of the reprobate religionists from Jerusalem were the inevitable results.

This healing of a case of hopeless leprosy, against which rabbinic Judaism stood helpless, had been a blow to 'the Jews.' Forgiving *and* healing the paralytic was a second blow. Now in trip-hammer succession came a third: Jesus reached out and invited a hated Jewish tax-gatherer (Mark 2:13-17; Matt. 9:9-13; Luke 5:27-32) to the inner circle of His disciples. His Jewish name, Levi, betrays his origin. The name Jesus gave him, Matthew (equivalent to the Greek name *Theodore*, 'gift of God'), as he was always known afterward, is reported at this stage only by Matthew. Perhaps the other writers wished to spare him exposure by identifying Matthew as Levi, a former traitor to the interests of his nation. Capernaum was a crossroads of commerce and a port of entry to the dominions of Herod, hence Levi was out on the road at the toll stall (Mark 2:14; Matt. 9:9; cf. Luke 5:27). He gave up all his 'publican business' immediately and invited all his former associates – 'publicans and sinners' – to a feast at which Jesus and His disciples were honored guests. Not as guests but, after the custom of the time, as spectators, the Pharisees dared to complain to the four that contrary to rabbinic law they were eating and drinking with outcast publicans and sinners. Jesus, when He heard it, set forth two of His marvelous paradoxes, which have been both the joy of His friends and the consternation of His enemies ever since, challenging the Pharisees to go to their Scriptures (Matt. 9:13; cf. Hos. 6:6) instead of their traditions for guidance in matters of true religion. The situation was exacerbated by the fact that some Jewish fast, prescribed by tradition and observed by Pharisees, was being observed at that season. So the feast of Matthew was, as such, an affront to the Pharisees. They even managed to draw some of the Baptist's followers into the controversy. This was the occasion for Jesus to present three parables showing to all that He did, indeed, intend to bring about a complete break with the past in all outward ritual matters. This is the force of the illustration about the bridegroom and his friends, the impossibility of using unshrunk cloth to patch old clothes and of putting fermenting wine in used wineskins.

Pharisaic rabbinism now lay exposed for what it was – without power over the living death of leprosy, without any word of relief for the conscience stricken with guilt, and unable to extend any hand of welcome to the contrite. On the contrary, Christ, the Lord of the kingdom, whose good news He preached, had life for the dying (healing of the leper), forgiveness for the sinner (the paralytic), and hearty community of the heart with contrite, forgiven outcasts (Levi-Matthew and his friends).

ATTENDING A FEAST IN JERUSALEM

It is quite remarkable that the issues raised 'up there' at Jerusalem during 'a feast'[7] were the same as those just now observed at Capernaum. Some harmonists[8] argue that the trip to Jerusalem took place soon after our Lord's settlement at Capernaum or even a bit earlier, while others reverse the order of the fifth and sixth chapters of John.[9] However that may be, and no final harmonization appears possible, there are several points of contact between the healing of the paralytic by Jesus immediately after His settlement in Capernaum and the episode with the 'impotent man' at the pool of Bethesda. There is first the unspoken charge of blasphemy (John 5:18, when Jesus forgave the sins of the man 'borne of four'), for which the exact counterpart in John is Jesus' claim to a unique Father-Son relationship and the offense taken to that by 'the Jews.' This offense was so severe that it produced a determination to kill Him. Second, Jesus' claim to be God's minister of final judgment (John 5:22, 27) – of course involving final disposition of sins, as well as in the 'here and now' – was the counterpart of His forgiving the sins of the paralytic of Capernaum. Third, except for a kai ('and') Jesus' words to each of the two paralytics are precisely the same, to the very letter (John 5:8; cf. Matt. 9:6). Fourth, in both cases Jesus appealed to His works of divine power in the healing of hopeless cases as evidence of His being sent by the Father and of His participating in a unique relation to the Father (John 10:18; 5:19-30; cf. Matt. 9:6-8). Fifth, there is the objection to His ideas about Sabbath observance and the emphasis on that matter, which 'the Jews' kept harping on after His return to Galilee shortly thereafter (see below).

John 5:1-47

---

7 Examination of the evidence of textual criticism and the history of scholarly discussion leave the precise feast (as the author no doubt intended) unknown. As has been seen in excursus 2, the passage of a third Passover season during this epoch of our Lord's ministry is indicated by the approaching time of grain harvest-shortly after Passover in most of Palestine. It is certain that during this period of the Galilee ministry, this pilgrimage (reported only by John) 'up to Jerusalem' for 'a feast of the Jews' took place.

8 ELTJM, 1:460-71; ALOL, pp. xxii, 189-207.

9 See GJM, p. 78.

ENGAGING IN CONTROVERSY AND MINISTERING TO CROWDS

Mark Whether or not Jesus spent some time now at Capernaum cannot be
2:23-3:12 ascertained. Possibly on the journey home from the feast of John 5, a
Matt.
12:1-21 Sabbath found Jesus and His disciples somewhere in the open fields to
Luke
6:1-11 spend the day. Being apparently without provisions, the disciples – as
many a hungry farmer throughout the ages of man – began to pluck
heads of wheat on the wayside, rubbing and blowing away the chaff, and
then to eat. The heads could have been early green ears or late gleanings.
Now, rabbinic law had in no way added more grievously to the written
Word of God, making of it a burden which neither they 'nor their fathers
were able to bear' (Acts 15:10), than in respect to the Sabbath. They even
had a tradition against wearing false teeth (burden-bearing) and another
against covering spittle by scraping the shoe (ploughing). So of course
what the hungry disciples did, in the eyes of these gimlet-eyed monsters,
was reaping! Jesus answered with five strong arguments for a humane
interpretation of the Sabbath command: *first,* He cited the historical
precedent of David who even broke a ceremonial law in order to support
life (Lev. 24:9; cf. I Sam. 21:1-6); *second,* He cited another regular
precedent set by the serving priests who break general Sabbath law in
order to maintain the busy ritual routines on that day (Num. 28:9, 10);
third, and related to the second, He called their attention to the fact that
He is greater than the temple (Were His disciples shelling some corn for
Him?); *fourth,* as on an earlier occasion, He cited Scripture (Hos. 6:6)
to show that mercy is greater in God's sight than sacrifice; and *fifth,* He
claimed that the Son of man, obviously giving the name a divine
association, 'is Lord of the Sabbath.' This last was an oblique claim to
being Author of the Sabbath, as indeed He was.

About a week later, and probably in Capernaum, the Pharisees still
watching for Him to let down His guard, Jesus again challenged their
unexpressed criticism of His doing healing on the day of rest. He argued
from lesser to greater: anyone would act on the legal permission to
rescue a sheep fallen into a hole on the Sabbath; but a man is greater
than a sheep. He also charged that to forego offering help is an evil and
that to heal is a good; and since it is lawful only to do good, He *ought* to
heal. So the man's withered hand was restored, and the Pharisees, now
in unnatural alliance with Sadducean Herodians, 'took counsel how they
might destroy him' (Mark 3:6).

After this, perhaps for several days (the language suggests a continued observance), He took His disciples down to the Lake of Galilee (Mark 3:7-12; Matt. 12:15-21) and, employing the earlier means of a boat (that had been kept available), He continued an open-air ministry of speaking from the boat to the crowds on shore. He also carried on a ministry of healing diseases and of restoring the demon-possessed. Mark reports that people came from as far south as Idumaea, i.e., the neighborhood of Beer-sheba, from as far north as the Phoenician cities of Tyre and Sidon, from as far west as the Mediterranean Sea, and from as far east as the desert. Matthew, again identifying Jesus as the Coming One of Old Testament prophecy, sees Jesus' mild behavior, coupled with helpful ministry to Gentile as well as Jew (Tyre and Sidon were heathen lands inhabited by the remnant of ancient Canaanites), as the fulfillment of a prophecy of Isaiah concerning Jehovah's Servant (Matt. 12:17-21; Isa. 42:1-4).

INAUGURATING THE APOSTOLATE

Jesus brought this phase of ministry to an end by removal to the low hills west of Lake Galilee. There after a long night of prayer in His customary oratory – a mountain somewhere west of the lake – our Lord took that unique action which insured the continuation of His teaching and the effectuation of His redemptive work among all nations after His death, which He had come into the world to accomplish. Mark 3:13-19 Luke 6:12-16

Every good rabbi left behind him, at the end of life, at least a few who remembered him and tried to live by some of his teachings. This Rabbi left behind a group of men whom He called Apostles, who were empowered to speak and to act for Him and who after He was gone to heaven established that living organ, the church. The church rests today on the foundation, through Word and Spirit, of New Testament Apostles (Eph. 2:20). Using an old Hebrew and Aramaic word *shaliah*, in Greek, *apostolos*, meaning 'an authorized messenger,' Jesus gave this name the special meaning we find in the letters of Peter and Paul. Never since the passing of these apostles has there been such power in men on earth.

The calling of the Twelve had been postponed a good while, into the twelfth month of His ministry to the multitudes in Galilee. Very shortly thereafter He would make strenuous effort to evade the crowds in order to train the Twelve for their immediate mission to the lost sheep of the house of Israel (Matt. 10:5-7) and for their later worldwide mission (Matt. 28:19, 20). Further, the murderous opposition of the Jerusalem leadership was coming to fierce flood tide, and He foresaw the result. We can therefore be assured that He knew He must not delay longer the gathering of these men who were to be steadily 'with him' (Mark 3:14) to the very end. We can only guess the intensity of mental effort and fervor of prayer during that night on the mountain as He weighed His selections.

The Twelve are listed by Luke in a manner capable of interpretation as six pairs (Luke 6:12-16). Matthew, who postpones listing their names till the story of their preaching mission in Galilee, makes the pairing definite. Mark gives the distinct impression (Mark 6:7) that henceforth they were thus paired.

First, there are the two brothers, *Simon*, named Peter by Jesus, and *Andrew*, evidently the younger of the two. Peter is the only Apostle known to have been already married. He maintained a home at Capernaum, shared with his brother Andrew and Peter's mother-in-law, and perhaps also with his Master, Jesus. John's statement that their home was in Bethsaida (John 1:44) is one of the several hints that in addition to Bethsaida-Julias several miles northeast, near the east bank of Jordan where it enters Lake Galilee, there was a fisherman's quarter of Capernaum likewise called Bethsaida. Some see a bit of characteristic gentle humor in Jesus' calling the then veering and vacillating Simon Peter (*Cephas* in Aramaic, *Petros* in Greek), a stone. If John was 'the disciple whom Jesus loved,' Peter was the one who loved Jesus. His early weaknesses - he was impulsive, erring, too quick to speak, easily thrown into panic - are matched by lovable, equally human qualities - he was quick to repent, ardent in devotion, steady at last, faithful to death. Andrew, whose name is Greek and means 'manly,' is notable chiefly as the first Christian missionary (John 1:41). As his Lord predicted, Peter died a martyr's death by crucifixion. It was at Rome, late in the 60s, after nearly forty years in his Master's service.[10] Deeming himself unworthy to be crucified upright as his Lord, he was by his own request fastened to a cross head downward[11] (John 21:18). At about the same time Nero also caused Paul to be executed.[12] Both martyrdoms occurred at Rome and, in spite of the occasional sectarian opposition, are as well attested as any events of that epoch of Christian history. Of Andrew 'there is a steadfast and credible tradition that he was crucified at Patrae in Achaia; and it is said that he hung alive on the cross two days, teaching the people all the while.'[13]

---

10 'Peter,' in SDB.

11 SDHF, pp. 146, 147. See John 21:18.

12 So said Tertullian, ca. AD 200. Also FLAP, pp. 377-84.

13 SDHF, p. 146.

The second pair are *James* and *John*, two other brothers often called the sons of Zebedee and playfully (some say) nicknamed *Boanerges*, 'sons of thunder' (they actually appear *very* quiet), by Jesus. Certainly partners in fishing and presumably neighbors of Peter and Andrew, theirs appears to have been a fairly well-to-do family with servants – hired or otherwise (Mark 1:20). Their mother, Salome, overly ambitious for her sons, was otherwise of great strength of character and moral earnestness. There is strong indication, derived from comparison of the Gospel reports of the loyal women who remained at the crucifixion of the Lord, that this remarkable lady was a sister of Jesus' mother. If so, the two 'sons of Zebedee' were the first cousins of Jesus. (Some have sought, at least since Jerome's time, to interpret the same evidence to show that there were three, not four women present at the crucifixion, that one was Mary's sister, wife of Cleopas, and that this woman's children were Jesus' first cousins, called brothers and sisters in the Gospels).[14] These two sons of Zebedee and Salome, with Peter (and occasionally Andrew), formed an inner circle of the Lord's, sharing intimately some of the most important moments of His career – notably Gethsemane and the transfiguration. James was the first of the Apostles to die (Acts 12:2), setting the pattern of martyrdom which over the years they all followed. The single exception was John, who died last of all in ripe old age at Ephesus, to which, according to one line of tradition, he took the Lord's mother (John 19:26, 27) and where she died.

Philip (another Greek name) and *Bartholomew* (almost certainly the same as Nathanael) are the third pair. Philip was neighbor to the first four, being likewise of 'Bethsaida of Galilee' (John 12:21). (This phrase supports the assertion made earlier in this chapter that there were two cities called Bethsaida, one a suburb of Capernaum in Galilee and another, the well-known Bethsaida-Julias not far away in Gaulanitis, modern Golan, part of the tetrarchy of Philip.) He had been one of those recruited by Jesus at Bethabara when the Lord returned from the forty days of temptation. Without sufficient ground Philip has been said to be a

---

14 Cf. Matt. 27:56 and Mark 15:40 with John 19:25. John enumerates four women at the cross: (1) the mother of Jesus, (2) her sister, (3) Mary the wife of Cleopas, and (4) Mary Magdalene. Perhaps modesty kept him from saying the second was his own mother, Salome (as passages above make certain). Jerome, in support of a doctrinal interest (i.e., the perpetual virginity of Jesus' mother), held that only three women are enumerated by John, the second being 'the sister of Jesus' mother,' viz., Mary the wife of Cleopas (Alphaeus), and that it is her children (Mark 15:40 and Matt. 27:56), really His cousins, that are called "the Lord's brethren.'" But (1) it is unlikely that two sisters were called Mary, and (2) James the Little (Mark 15:40) was an Apostle, and none of 'the Lord's brethren' were Apostles (cf. Acts 1:13, 14).

reluctant disciple, even being identified with the disciple who wanted to stay home until after his parents' decease (Matt. 8:21, 22). On the contrary, he was excited enough to fetch Nathanael (John 1:45) and talented enough at other procurement tasks to be put in charge of food supply to the apostolic band. (That he was in charge of food supply is an inference based on our Lord's question to him before feeding the five thousand [John 6:5-7].) He must have been friendly to strangers and approachable by them (John 12:21, 22). Nathanael was originally brought to Jesus by Philip and is, like him, rather obscure in the New Testament, except for that first incident when he showed himself quite a discerner of men as well as a student of Scripture (John 1:45-51). He is named as one of the six who went fishing with Peter after Jesus' crucifixion and thus was privileged to witness a post-resurrection miracle, the draft of 153 'great fishes,' and to enjoy an extended ministry of Jesus to the happy but dumbfounded group of men (John 21:21-23). Most scholars feel the identification is certain of the one the Synoptics always call Bartholomew (Bar-Talmai, 'son of Talmai,' like Bar-Jona, 'son of John') with the one John always calls Nathanael. Philip is always coupled with Nathanael under the designation of Bartholomew in the lists of Apostles in the New Testament. He may have been responsible in some way for both of the visits to Cana by Jesus (John 21:2; 2:1; 4:46), for Cana was his home.

Next are *Thomas* and *Matthew*. Thomas (*Thoma* in Aramaic), like the Greek equivalent *Didymos*, is not a name but an epithet meaning 'twin.' Eusebius, the great fourth century church historian, said his name was Judas.[15] Since two others of the Twelve bore that name, he was designated 'Twin' by the writers, who had some difficulty with a superfluity of Judases, to distinguish him. Except for John's Gospel (14:22), we would know almost nothing of this skeptical and gloomy man who could also manifest great loyalty and spontaneous, sincere devotion. Evidently when this Judas-Thomas-Didymus spoke, as contrasted with the more prominent early Simon Peter, he could be counted on to have thought his words over and to mean them with mind and heart. Tradition credits him falsely with authorship of a Gospel. Martyrdom in Persia or India was also in the ancient tradition about him. The Church of Malabar (India) still claims him (probably through confusion with a later Thomas) as founder. About Matthew we know little except that he was a tax collector at Capernaum when Jesus called him; that his Jewish name, *Levi*, was

---

15 Ecclesiastical History I.13.

supplanted by *Matthew* ('God's gift'), apparently by Jesus, who liked to give new names to His followers; and that he wrote the first book of the New Testament. Of the disciples who became Apostles, his is the only 'recruitment' reported after those two wonderful days when Jesus recruited the first five (Andrew, John, Peter, Philip, and Nathanael) at or near Bethabara.

The ninth and tenth are *James*, son of Alphaeus, and one variously called *Judas* the son of James, *Lebbaeus*, or *Thaddeus*. Once he is called 'Judas... not Iscariot.' (At Luke 6:16 and Acts 1:13 the rendering should by all means be 'son of James,' not 'brother of James.') It has been contended that Alphaeus, the father of this 'James the Little,' is the same as Cleopas (both are traceable to the Aramaic word *halpai*). If so, and if he is the same Alphaeus as the father of Levi (Matthew), then their mother Mary stood at the cross and we have another large family group in that first circle of loyal believers. John Chrysostom wrote that this James was also, like Matthew, a tax gatherer.[16] Of this Judas we can say that his name *Thaddeus* (*Libbai* in Aramaic) means 'courageous, hearty.' Besides this, about all we know of him is that he once asked Jesus a question (John 14:22).

The other *Simon* and *Judas Iscariot* are the sixth and last pair. Simon is called 'the zealot' by Luke and 'the Canaanite' by Matthew and Mark. That *Zealot* implied anything more at the time of Jesus than one fired by earnest religious zeal is pure assumption. The 'zeal' of recent writers to make him a political radical is probably incorrect.[17] *Canaanite* of the King James Version (better *Cananaean*) is almost certainly from neither the town Cana nor the Old Testament Canaan, but from the Aramaic word for zealot, and Luke has so translated it. The word *Zélôtés* (i.e., zealot) bears the same relation to *Cananean* that *Peter* does to *Cephas*. In each case the former is a New Testament Greek translation of the Aramaic spoken by Jesus and His disciples. We know almost nothing of him. That strange man Judas Iscariot (Luke 6:15; Acts 1:13; Matt. 10:4; Mark 3:15), 'which also became the traitor,' the mystery of why Jesus chose him at all and why, having chosen Judas, the Lord seemed deliberately to lay his greatest weakness, an inordinate love for money, wide open to temptation by making him the company treasurer, we will consider later.

---

16 See SDHF, p. 151.

17 'Since the name zealot was not used to describe a sect or party earlier than AD 66, Lake and Jackson think the title may describe not his politics but his character, i.e., ... zealous... enthusiast.' HWWJ, p. 62.

PREACHING THE SERMON ON THE MOUNT

Matt. In some not-clearly-specified way, but by some means, Jesus dismissed
5-7 – or escaped – the miracle-hungry crowd. When He addressed His
Luke
6:17-49 disciples alone (Matt. 5:1, 2), it was 'up into the mountain' (Matt. 5:1).
Later He gave a shorter version of those remarks to the multitudes from
everywhere 'on a level place' (Luke 6:17). This, at least, if not
demonstrable, is a feasible explanation of the circumstances of this
longest recorded address (the sermon on the mount) of Jesus. Many of
Jesus' remarks in this sermon He repeated later on several other
occasions[18] (Luke 11:1-4; 12:22-31). This sermon is an extended exposition
of the true Biblical morality which Jesus' contemporaries should have
found in their Scriptures. In large part it is Old Testament religion
raised high and placed in full spiritual perspective. Jesus also added
some important truth as well as corrected many current misapprehensions
of Biblical revelation, misapprehensions cultivated by rabbinic learning
gone astray.

---

18 An extended examination of the content and doctrine of this famous sermon, so plain and yet so
puzzling, belongs in a work of exposition or doctrine rather than a work on the career of Jesus

CHAPTER 6

Completing the Great Galilean Ministry:
A Time of Great Popularity

After concluding the sermon on the mount, Jesus apparently presented a shorter version of His remarks to a mixed group from everywhere, someplace below the mountain.[1] When this was finished, He quickly moved on back to 'headquarters' at Capernaum. The mixed multitude of the curious, the thrill seekers and the miracle mongers as well as some genuine seekers after the kingdom of God, followed in the wake (Matt. 8:1, 5; Luke 7:1) of the official party composed of Jesus Himself, His disciples, and the faithful ministering women (Luke 8:3).

RENEWED CONFLICT WITH 'THE JEWS'

If Jesus hoped for some respite at home, He was disappointed, for no sooner had He entered Capernaum than a delegation of elders from the local synagogue were found waiting to confer with Him. A Roman army officer (centurion) permanently stationed there, a generous man who had paid for construction of the synagogue building, so they said, had persuaded these synagogue officials to intercede with Jesus, begging Him to come heal a favorite servant.

Matt.'
8:5-13
11:2-30
Luke
7:1-50

---

1 Contrast 'up into the mountain... sat down' (Matt. 5:1 ASV) with – 'came down... and stood on a level place' (Luke 6:17 ASV).

There is a background to this incident. Though a Jewish city, both the Romans and the Romanizing Herod were important at Capernaum. Tiberias, where Herod's court was located and whence a royal official had sent to Jesus at Cana to solicit healing for his son, was only twelve miles to the south. Herod, though Jewish in religion, was Roman in his sympathies and dependent upon the Romans for his power. That a Roman army officer should have furnished money to build a Jewish synagogue is surprising, but it further demonstrates the strength of Roman influence in this corner of Galilee. The synagogue elders, whom we may safely suppose had no relish for their mission, having accepted the centurion's largess, were in no position to refuse the errand. Furthermore, the spectacular initial miracle in their town the healing of the nobleman's son many months before together with the widely publicized miracles since that time, would have given the non-Jewish centurion great hope for his servant, provided only that a Messiah for Israel could be persuaded to help a Gentile. Thus there was urgency in the elders' embarrassed request. The precedent set by the earlier healing of the nobleman's son suggested to the centurion that a personal visit by the Savior was unnecessary. This pious centurion's genuine faith was the cause of great amazement to Jesus, and it provided occasion for Him to rebuke the already marvelous unbelief of His own people and to prophesy the preponderance of Gentile faces in the throng of the saved with Abraham, Isaac, and Jacob in the coming kingdom of God.

This prophecy embodied the promise of God's coming blessings on Gentiles which had so antagonized the synagogue crowd of Nazareth several months before and which would repeatedly cause even His own disciples to stumble in the months leading up to Calvary.

Of course 'the servant was healed in that hour.'

Jesus had no quiet for relaxation during the following days. Soon afterwards (the KJV following many ancient manuscripts, has 'the day after') the Lord and His party are found far out in the Plain of Esdraelon at Nain, more than twenty miles south-southwest of Capernaum. There occurred the first recorded restoration of life to a deceased person in His ministry. He actually broke up a funeral cortege as it moved along, carrying the dead son of a widow to the place of burial (Luke 7:11-17). We are not surprised to read that people there 'glorified God, saying, A great prophet is arisen among us: and, God hath visited. his people' (Luke 7:16 ASV).

From the first day of His ministry, the Lord demonstrated by word and deed that He was indeed the long-promised Coming One, the Messiah. Andrew had exclaimed to Peter, 'We have found the Messiah' (John 1:41 ASV). Philip told Nathanael that the prophet whom Moses promised, 'one like unto me,' had come to them (John 1:45; cf. Deut. 18:15ff.). He had acclaimed the 'Lamb of God' (John 1:29), 'the Messiah, the Savior of the world' (John 4:42). Yet He had not spoken of Himself directly in these terms. The nearest He came to that was in response to an official inquiry from John the Baptist. This incident, recorded in Matthew 11:1-19, must have occurred at this period of His career. John, now in prison, may have wondered why Jesus was not acting more energetically to inaugurate the promised hegemony of Israel over its enemies. 'Art thou he that cometh, or look we for another?' (Matt. 11:3 ASV). Even in response to this, though clearly indicating that He was indeed the Messiah, He called attention to His works and words, fulfillment of the Old Testament promises, and let them speak for Him (see excursus 5, pp. 127, 128).

During this period He must have visited most of the towns within a few hours' walk of Capernaum. Matthew, for instance, at this point refers to 'the cities where most of his mighty works were done.'

That the pressure of spiritual conflict was rising is clearly indicated by the furious tone of the words with which He verbally lashed some of those hardened communities (Matt. 11:20-24). Chorazin and Bethsaida nearby are both mentioned in His fierce denunciation.

The mystery of the hardening of sin and the sovereign grace of God, in election and calling, shouts out of the text here (Matt. 11:20-30). God lavished messengers and miracles on those towns. They did not repent. If Tyre and Sidon had received the same benefits, they would have repented long ago. Yet when our Lord moved on to the area of Tyre and Sidon in a few months, He only very reluctantly performed but one recorded miracle there. He did not enter the two towns to preach, and of course there was no general repentance. Yet Jesus goes on to pray and thank God for sovereignly enlightening the babes, presumably the disciples, and He issued the most gentle invitation to the overwrought multitude to 'come unto me.' People will never cease to argue these matters; may they likewise never blame God for their own or other's unbelief nor charge God falsely because He does not save all (John 3:36). The wonder always is, that He saves any!

This excursion ended with a very strange episode (Luke 7:36-50). There was developing a kind of crescendo of devotion from Jesus' new disciples, coupled with a persistence of stiff-necked spiritual nonperception on the part of the Pharisees. We are indebted to Luke for the story. Not all the Pharisees were His enemies, for He was dinner guest at the house of a Pharisee named Simon, though we are not sure where – almost certainly not in Capernaum. As the members of the dinner party reclined at table, feet extended outward, an unnamed woman from among observers and listeners came forward, knelt at His feet, wet His feet with her tears, dried them with her hair, and began to anoint them with precious ointment brought in an alabaster box. While Jesus calmly accepted the display as quite proper (evidently there were social precedents for what appears today as an extravagant demonstration), the Pharisee host felt it showed up Jesus as a false prophet. No genuine prophet, thought he, would accept these attentions from a sinful woman (a harlot?). Jesus, again using the unspoken thoughts of an objector as an opportunity to teach, showed that greater love was to be expected from one who had sinned much than from one who supposed he had sinned little. We may hope that as Simon the Pharisee thought about this, he came to wonder just who the greater sinner was – he or the sinful woman.

This episode – and two others, all reported only by Luke (11:37; cf. 14:1ff.), in which Jesus was dinner guest at the home of a Pharisee – preserve a valuable facet of Jesus' ministry which otherwise we would not have. He was very sociably inclined, perfectly natural and composed in every situation, never shocked, always genteel, sometimes sharp, frequently witty, always the gentleman but nevertheless standing His ground where the pursuit of His ministry was concerned.

There has been from very earliest times in the West a general identification of this sinful woman with Mary Magdalene, and she in turn with Mary of Bethany. David Smith, among many others, argued very convincingly for this threefold identification[2] If he is correct, then Jesus received this amazing tribute from Mary twice (Luke 7:36-50; cf. Mark 14:3-9; Matt. 26:6-13; John 12:2-8). And mainly on the basis of this identification, it is thought that Simon the Pharisee's home was in Magdala, thought to be on the shore of Galilee at about its westernmost protrusion.

---

2 SDHF, pp. 206, 211

THE SECOND TOUR THROUGH GALILEE

About a year passed after our Lord's entrance upon the great Galilee ministry before He gave up on the general populace. He then began about six months of ministry aimed at the Twelve primarily and conducted as privately as possible. During that year of intentionally general ministry (though the crowds interfered with privacy during the last six months and got a lot of His attention in spite of His desires), the writers mention that He made three main 'circuits' of Galilee. All three Synoptists mention the first (Mark 1:38; Matt. 4:23; Luke 4:44), but only Luke mentions the second[3] (Luke 8:1-3).

Luke 8:1-3

Luke's summary statement relates to a period when the populace was friendly and Jesus was proceeding at full tilt in this His major campaign to win a following which, after His rejection by the nation, would furnish seed for the church. In this He was successful. He commanded the Twelve, on the eve of His passion, to go before Him to Galilee where, after His resurrection, He would meet them. At one of His last resurrection appearances, no less than five hundred brethren in Galilee met Him there on a mountain (I Cor. 15:6ff.; Matt. 28:16-20).

How did He go about enlisting this seminal group? 'And it came to pass soon afterwards, that he went about through cities and villages, preaching and bringing the good tidings of the kingdom of God, and with him the twelve, and certain women who had been healed of evil spirits and infirmities: Mary that was called Magdalene, from whom seven demons had gone out, and Joanna the wife of Chuza (Herod's steward), and Susanna, and many others, who ministered unto them of their substance' (Luke 8:1-3 ASV). The sense of the passage, especially of the verb, he went ('he was going' in Greek), is clearly that this was His procedure for some time, consuming weeks or even months. Since time for the Savior's work was short (John 9:4,5), we find Him journeying quickly from place to place. He would always, as a herald, announce the

---

3 Though Mark and Luke mention the third tour or circuit, it features very largely in Matthew's account, for in that connection he gives a very large section-forty-seven verses (Matt. 9:35-11:1; cf. Mark 6:6-13 and Luke 9:1-6)-to details of instruction by the Master to the Twelve. Luke's declared intention to relate all matters in order practically insures a careful chronological order for his narrative except where some principle calls for a diversion. Matthew does not follow the chronological order very closely in this section, and Mark is brief and sketchy. Most scholars therefore follow Luke's order in the Galilee ministry. We have been doing the same. We therefore have employed Luke's references to the three circuits of Galilee as kind of a framework on which to group the various elements of the story.

presence of the kingdom, say something of its nature and requirements, and move on. Until the last circuit the Apostles did not preach. On His first limited tour He had only 'the four' and no attendants. Now He goes as head of a large entourage on a formal campaign. His twelve Apostles, chosen to be 'with him,' are there for basic training. On a later Galilee circuit, going two by two, they proclaimed Messiah's advent, yet they were still, even then, far from being competent teachers – no sub-rabbis. At this stage they were mainly Apostles by appointment and in preparation only. The material welfare of Jesus and the Twelve was cared for by grateful women of means, some of whose names are given. Presumably they bought food in the towns and villages of the area, prepared and served it wherever local hospitality was not sufficient. On these journeys adequate changes of clothing and items of personal care were taken along.

Jesus' usual procedure, as indicated by the Gospel narratives and the researches of scholars of ancient Jewish customs, was about as follows: He would preach and heal on the streets and ways if no building was available. Ordinarily, however, He availed Himself of the privileges which His fame as a rabbi gave Him, to enter the local synagogue to preach and teach at the regular services.[4] These services occurred twice on the Sabbath, once on Monday, and once on Thursday. These two days, since they were 'market days,' brought the farm people to town for buying and selling as well as worship. The synagogue would have been open on other days for informal meetings. His fame as a healer brought crowds of people bringing their sick. Many followed Him from town to town just to watch and listen. Others, knowing that His home was in Capernaum, would wait there for Him.

A specimen day of His activity when He was, so to speak, 'at home' in Capernaum is that first Sabbath at Capernaum (Mark 1:21-39; Luke 4:31-44). 'He enters upon the Sabbath into the synagogue and teaches, filling all His hearers with astonishment at his words. He there heals a demoniac, probably immediately after the discourse. Leaving the synagogue, He enters Peter's house and heals a sick woman [Peter's mother-in-law], and crowds coming to Him at evening, He heals many others. Next morning, after a time of meditation and prayer, He departs...' (John 9:4, 5).[5]

---

4 ELTJM, I:432; ALOL, p. 241.
5 ALOL, p. 242.

A BUSY DAY AT THE END OF THE TOUR

Luke's narrative furnishes the framework (Luke 8:1-39), with the other Synoptists filling in details (Mark 3:19-5:20; Matt. 12:22-13:53; 8:18, 23-34).[6]

Here is how the day began. After His customary time of prayer and meditation somewhere out under the open sky, Jesus came midmorning 'into a house'[7] (Mark 3:19) for the usual Jewish breakfast – one of the two meals of the day.[8] But such a multitude gathered into and about the house from the countryside and nearby villages that He could not even eat (Mark 3:19, 20).

Jesus' enormous popularity with Galileans was matched by now marvelous, bitter enmity from the national leaders at Jerusalem. Sensing His purposes in Galilee and greatly fearing them, embittered by His miracle at the pool of Bethesda and His utter rout of their best arguments against Him at that time (John 5), they had sent emissaries to Galilee who were now dogging His steps. 'They watched Him with jealous and malignant eyes, angry at the enthusiasm of the multitude and eager to find occasion against Him.'[9] They launched their attack early on this busy day.

For a starter Jesus restored a blind and dumb man 'possessed with a devil' (Matt. 12:22). The multitude, greatly impressed, asked among themselves, 'Is this the son of David?' (Matt. 12:23) – i.e., Is this the Messiah of Old Testament prophecy? The Pharisees, spoiling for trouble and in great discomfiture, desperate for a credible argument against Him, charged, 'This man doth not cast out demons, but by Beelzebub the prince of the demons' (Matt. 12:24 asv; Luke 11:14-36; Matt. 9:27-34; cf. John 7:20; 8:48, 52; 10:20). The miracle was indisputably real, but they felt they had to say something to discredit Jesus and thus to stem

---

6 I assume the chronology and arrangement of RHG for the materials in the Gospels regarding this remarkable day.

7 The expression 'into a house' - like the German zu Hause - may mean He came home, back to Capernaum. But it seems preferable to understand His home en route, where He was being entertained.

8 SBCNT comments on Luke 14:1 that the Hebrew word of which to ariston is the Greek transliteration, 'among the Rabbinical writings often designates the morning meal, the prandium of the Romans. In general among the Jews in the course of the day two mealtimes were taken, only on the Sabbath were there three designated necessary mealtimes... to deipnon =Sec Adah signified chiefly the main mealtime, which on the week days was taken in the later afternoon hours and on the Sabbath after the conclusion of divine services .... When there were also guests who had been invited to take part, [Sec Adah] ... became the designation for any optional guest meal.' 2:204-6 (my translation).

9 SDHF, p. 176.

the tide of enthusiasm. Their charge was simply: He is in league with Satan.

Jesus' answer was indignant, defiant, and contemptuous, turning the pharisaic charge to their further discredit and His own acclaim. He first showed the manifest absurdity of the charge. For the devil to cast out devils were to bring disunity to his own cause and further his own defeat. Just as a house divided or a city divided tends to destroy itself, so Satan would be destroying his own kingdom if he should cast out his own devils. Since this was absurd, it followed that Satan's house was being plundered by Jesus' miracles of goodness and that the promised kingdom of God had come among them in His miraculous works. Though He did not expressly say so – to do so might prematurely have precipitated the crisis which came after the feeding of the five thousand – the crowd was left to infer that the Messiah is here in the person of Jesus of Nazareth.

In this connection Jesus retorted their accusation against them: '... if I by Beelzebub cast out demons, by whom do your sons [disciples] cast them out? therefore shall they be your judges' (Matt. 12:27 ASV). He then countered their wicked and malign charge with a truly terrific charge: There is a sin which because of its very nature can never be forgiven, and they had just now committed it. In assigning the works of the Spirit-endued Son of God to Satan, they were (Heb. 10:26-31) blaspheming God's Spirit. Their hearts were now hopelessly hardened – now calling good evil and evil good[10] (Isa. 5:20). The bitter, cutting invective with which Jesus now proceeded to dissect His opponents is almost unique in our language, except for later occasions when He directed more of the same against these same blind guides. It needs no defense; the Pharisees deserved it and, as Jesus proceeded to say, their evil hearts were the fountain (Matt. 12:33-37) of their blasphemous words. Furthermore, they were assaying to be the means whereby the whole Jewish nation should be led to hard-hearted rejection of their Messiah, the Savior of His people from their sins.

As soon as Jesus stopped for breath, the scribes and Pharisees, having just rejected a marvelous miraculous sign, asked for another, just as if they had not seen one already. Jesus' response (Matt. 12:39-45) was as fierce as His interrupted previous speech. They are an evil and morally perverted group. Obliquely referring to Jonah's experiences as a sort of type of His coming resurrection and the sole 'sign' to be 'given' them,

---

10 SLC, pp. 41, 42.

He drew another damning lesson for them from Jonah. Nineveh believed Jonah without any miraculous signs. Likewise the Queen of Sheba obeyed the divine wisdom of Solomon. But One who is greater than Jonah or Solomon is now present, and these vile reprobates will do nothing but reject Him. Their corruption is manifold, their doom certain and not far off!

'While he was yet speaking,' His family,[II] including His mother, who had set out several hours – perhaps a day – earlier, arrived in the unnamed town of this crucial, fierce verbal battle (Mark 3:31-45; Matt. 12:46-50; Luke 8:19, 20). Being unable to get to Him on account of the crowd, certain of His family called to Him from the edge of the throng (Mark 3:20, 21). Someone else conveyed the message to Him that His mother and other kinsmen were there to confer with Him. It was their purpose to get Him under their control and compel Him to return to Nazareth with them.

Sometime earlier, news of the frantic crowds and of Jesus' unrelenting efforts to heal men and to win their hearts had come to Nazareth. His family – brothers and sisters – all except His mother, were still unbelieving. They had no vision of His mission and therefore failed to understand the purpose of His extraordinary activity. Perhaps they were unable actually to believe it, knowing Him only as a quiet, tending-to-business carpenter and an older brother. Perhaps, supposing He had taken leave of His senses and rejecting the Pharisees' charge that 'he hath Beelzebub' (Mark 3:22), they set out from Nazareth to take Him in charge and to bring Him home. If so, they did their best according to their lights, and this is to their credit.

The texts are plain enough that Jesus both rejected and denounced their mission and purpose. What mystifies the reader is, Why? What were the motives of His 'brethren'? And above all, what was Mary's understanding of His present activities, and to what extent had she joined in the plan of action adopted by her other sons?

Jesus' earthly family were humble, unlettered folk; their guides and models were the leaders of the pharisaic party. These jealous hypocrites had not demurred to attempt subversion of the disciples' loyalty to their Master (Matt. 9:11) and probably had tried to sow discord between John's disciples and Jesus. They did not now shrink from using their social

---

II The language quite clearly designates His kinsmen rather than His "friends" or disciples. See Mark 3:21 NASH margin.

position and moral influence to subvert the meagre support Jesus' unbelieving brothers rendered Him. They had seen to it that exaggerated, misconstrued reports of His recent 'carrying on' at Jerusalem (John 5) reached them. The brothers may have been led to fear even for their own safety if they did not 'stop Him.' This may have been mixed, as we have suggested above, with genuine concern which they in their uncomprehending,[12] incredulous state of limited vision had for Jesus' own welfare. They are not represented as hardened, unrighteous men. Several of them later gave their lives for Jesus' sake. Upon reflection, their reasons for coming to take charge of Him and force Him to come home do not seem obscure or wholly unworthy.

But how about Mary? She was with them, but knowing the marvel of His conception and the events surrounding His birth, she did not share His brothers' opinions of Him. Yet, being a widowed mother, she had to live with both them and their opinions. Mothers have a way of being honestly but inconsistently loyal to all their sons! Her reason for accompanying them may have been just to see Him, perhaps – like every mother – to get Him to ease up in His energetic efforts. She was certainly being used (as perhaps the Pharisees had designed) to attempt deflection of her Son from His mission. 'Whatever her motive, Mary's conduct betrayed an utter misapprehension of His Messianic vocation and a culpable distrust of Him who, while her son after the flesh, was yet, as she knew, her Lord.'[13]

As to Jesus' words, sharp as they were, they were not improper even for a son to his mother. He properly assessed the situation and responded appropriately. 'Without going so far [as]... to see pride or ostentation in this, that she... summoned Jesus to her outside the house, since the opposite might as well have been her motive, we cannot but regard the words of Christ as the sternest prophetic rebuke of all Mariolatry, prayer for the virgin's intercession and, still more, of the strange doctrines about her freedom from actual and original sin, up to their prurient sequence in the dogma of the "Immaculate Conception."'[14]

One would think the day had furnished enough crises for the Master now to seek repose – as He sometimes did after rough encounters. But for Him, the day had just begun. Since the crowds were not to be avoided

---

12 Many months later they were still cold toward Him and very sarcastic in their remarks to Him (John 7:2-5).
13 SDHF, p. 182.
14 ELTJM, 1:577.

in Galilee and it did not yet suit His purpose to depart from Galilee, on this very day He introduced the new method whereby He might present as much truth to the crowds as they could bear while at the same time deepening His Apostles' and close disciples' understanding of the truth of which they were shortly to be bearers to the world. This method was the very special use He made of the familiar pedagogical device known as the *parable* (see excursus 8, pp. 130-31).

The parable or similitude is essentially a laying side by side of earthly, material things and heavenly, spiritual things in order that upon sincere, sober reflection the earthly and material may contribute to understanding the spiritual and heavenly. Since the earthly side of the comparison is familiar to the hearer, there is danger that he may rest content that he knows what the speaker means simply because he knows about seeds or pearls or fishing or mustard or whatever, and, not being willing to ponder or ask for explanation of the spiritual meaning, he may remain satisfied with the entertainment aspect of the story. Thus the parable is a form of judgment (Matt. 13:9-15) on his shallow hardness of heart. On the other hand, the spiritually minded will learn much spiritual truth by reflection and even more by asking the Teacher to explain – which is exactly what the disciples did. So on that day Jesus spoke parables by the seaside to the multitudes (Mark 4:1, 2; Matt. 13:1-3; Luke 8:4). After discoursing at some length, Jesus left the multitudes and went 'into the house' (Matt. 13:36-40) where He explained the parables to certain disciples and even spoke additional parables.

Late in the same day, at evening, Jesus made a sudden effort (Mark 4:36-41) to get away from the pressing crowds. The close disciples and He, without taking food or other raiment, took to a boat for the eastern shore of the lake. On the way, in the falling darkness, a sudden storm overtook them and the accompanying boats as the exhausted Lord slept in the stern, head resting on the pilot's pillow. Upon being awakened, He miraculously stilled the storm to the astonishment of all, for no storm ordinarily becomes calm in a moment. Nor was there rest on shore. There followed a terrifying meeting of the two demoniacs of Gerasa[15] who came out of the tombs near the town (Mark 5:1-20; Matt.

---

15 Mark says (5:1) this incident took place 'in the country of the Gerasenes' (the environs of Gerasa), as does Luke (8:26). But Matthew calls it (8:28) 'the country of the Gadarenes' (the environs of Gadara). These reflect what scholars today regard as the 'best text.' But a well attested reading of Matthew 8:28, followed by the KJV, has 'Gergesenes' - from the name of a town, Gergesa. Gerasa is known in Arabic, and hence in modern nomenclature, as Jerash. It is on the modern road from

8:28-30; Luke 8:26-29). The Lord healed them but failed to gain relief from crowds and again crossed the lake back to Capernaum that night. Thus Jesus found Himself compelled to go at least twenty-four hours without rest except for the nap in the boat. Another busy day awaited Him in Capernaum, including the raising from the dead of the daughter of a synagogue official named Jairus and several lesser healings (Mark 5:21-43; Matt. 9:18-34: Luke 8:40-56).

A LAST VISIT TO NAZARETH AND A THIRD TOUR

Mark 6:1-29
Matt. 13:54-58 9:35-11:1 14:1-12
Luke 9:1-7

It was quite in keeping with Jesus' feelings and mode of acting that He should make one last effort to win some from 'His own' community of Nazareth (Mark 6:1-6: Matt. 13:54-58). So, this time accompanied by the Twelve, He returned to Nazareth for a visit, and 'when the Sabbath was come,' He again taught in the synagogue. Though no vicious effort to kill Him occurred, as on the visit a year earlier, the response was wholly negative. One may guess that His 'wisdom and mighty works' of which they had heard, and now in a meager way witnessed, only brought inferiority feelings to them. They were both 'astonished' and 'offended.' He quickly left and continued on His way.

The third and final tour to proclaim the presence of the kingdom of God immediately followed (Luke 8:56; cf. 9:1, 2). We might regard the Nazareth visit as the first stage of it except that Luke's orderly narrative places the third tour immediately after the raising of Jairus's daughter and omits mention of the second Nazareth visit. 'And he called the twelve together, and gave them power and authority over all demons, and to cure diseases. And he sent them forth to preach the kingdom of God, and to heal the sick' (Luke 9:1, 2 ASV).

Without doubt the greatest significance of this part of the account to readers today lies in the comprehensive instructions Jesus gave the Twelve

---

Damascus to Amman, about eighteen miles east of the Jordan from a point twenty-five miles south of the Sea of Galilee. Gadara was a town about six miles southeast from the place where the Jordan River flows out of the Sea of Galilee. Until recent times no one knew where the long-forgotten Gergesa was. W. M. Thomson gave a fascinating discussion of its discovery and location at a point midway on the east shore of Galilee. It was a ruin in Thomson's time, called Kersa or Gersa by local bedouin Arabs. Whatever one may think about the manuscript evidence and whatever explanation is preferred for the three names – Gerasenes, Gadarenes, Gergesenes – the only location for the incident so far proposed which fits the narrative must be the ruined Kersa. *The Land and the Book,* 3 vols. (New York: Harper, 1876), 2:33-38; (Reprinted-Grand Rapids: Baker, 1945), pp. 333-38, 353, 359. Also see J. C. DeYoung, 'Gerasa, Gerasenes,' in Merrill C. Tenney, ed., Zondervan Pictorial Bible Encyclopedia, 5 vols. (Grand Rapids: Zondervan, 1975), 2:698-701.

(Matt. 10:5-42). Jesus was compelled to give many instructions for the church on mission through the coming centuries, months before His listening Apostles had the faintest glimmer that there would ever be a 'church,' when they had not the slightest notion of the long ages to separate their short lives from the true consummation of the age in a second advent of the Messiah. They expected the visible, external consummation of the kingdom of God in a few months or years at most.[16] Jesus at this time nevertheless skillfully lay before them instruction for three stages of their future witness, beginning with the preparatory stage in which they, before Calvary, Easter, and Pentecost, were so very quickly to pass (vv. 5-15). The second (vv. 16-23) emphasizes the period after Jesus' ascension and on past the destruction of Jerusalem to the end of the Apostolic age. The third (vv. 24-42) is directed mainly to all Jesus' disciples on through the present age to the second advent of Christ. Only Matthew has preserved a lengthy and detailed report of the instructions, devoting all of chapter 10 to it. It is at this point, where the beginning of their distinctly apostolic ministry occurs, that Matthew first lists the names of the Twelve. (See excursus 6, pp. 128-29.)

In the portion related to the immediate mission of the Apostles (Matt. 10:5-15), He commands the utmost in unencumbered movement – no spare clothing, no provision for emergency. Jesus planned to finish quickly His work of announcing to Galilee the kingdom of God. Instructions for later journeys (Luke 10:1-16) allowed many material provisions and supplies forbidden on this single preaching mission.

There is no reason to doubt that Jesus saw clearly all the future, not only of His earthly career, but of all that flowed out of it unto His second advent. When we read His disclosures of it, however, not only here but at various junctures, especially in His great Olivet discourse, the disclosures are immediately addressed to fledgling Apostles. The standpoint bears much more similarity in the mixture of figurative and literal, near and far, plain and obscure, especially lack of time perspective, to the forecasts of the future in Old Testament prophecy than to the lucid descriptions of the future in some of Paul's epistles or even the Apocalypse of John.

The above remarks are not a digression. The Lord's ministry is coming to a climax. He is about to disabuse – unmistakably and forever – His

---

16 Up to the very end of His life with them, they 'supposed that the kingdom of God was immediately to appear' (Luke 19:11 ASV). Even after His resurrection this opinion persisted (Acts 1:6).

large fair-weather following of the false notion that their kingdom-of-God expectations were about to be fulfilled by some *tour de force* to Jerusalem and resultant expulsion of Roman overlords. Jesus never negated their hopes – not even when the Apostles, still not quite comprehending, expressed them again during His forty days with them after His resurrection (Acts 1:6, 7). Yet He continued to emphasize, as He had done much earlier to Nicodemus (John 3:1 ff.), that the kingdom of God can never be entered except by spiritual regeneration; nor can its visible, final manifestation on earth come except by Israel's national spiritual renovation. These matters were all a matter of prominent prophetic record, but neither the common people nor their leaders were paying attention to the record. They were too busy glorying in their historic national excellencies and in hating the Herods and the Romans.

THE COLLAPSE OF THE GALILEAN CAMPAIGN

The Apostles returned to Jesus at Capernaum exulting in their successes in duplicating the miraculous signs of the presence of the kingdom of God, signs previously wrought only by their Master (Mark 6:30; Luke 9:10). How little they understood of their Lord and His ways! Within forty-eight hours He would dissipate all the superficial popularity in a single sermon to the multitude. Here is how He did it. (See excursus 7, p. 130, for discussion of the murder of John the Baptist at about this time.)

The effort of Jesus and the Twelve to escape the crowds by fleeing across the head of the lake to the hills near Bethsaida (Luke 9:10b, 11) and the successful effort of the crowds to find Him there, the ensuing astounding miracle of feeding the five thousand – all this is well known and requires no special explanation. All four Gospels report this in detail (Mark 6:30-44; Matt. 14:13-21; Luke 9:10-20; John 6:1-13).

The immediate sequel is of utmost importance. In response to the miracle of the loaves and fishes on the green hillsides (John 6:10) near Bethsaida-Julias in the tetrarchy of Philip, ecstatic nationalistic enthusiasm for Jesus as Messiah reached its peak in Galilee, where up to now His most concentrated labors had been devoted. John writes that Jesus now perceived 'they were about to come and take him by force, to make him king' (John 6:15). Jesus resolved to end a popularity based on a false understanding of a whole range of things – the spiritual aspect of God's kingdom, the spiritual regeneration necessary to enter God's spiritual kingdom, His own purposes and work as Redeemer of men. He could not save men who had no heart appreciation of their lostness. This He proceeded to show them.

So He dismissed the crowds (i.e., He tried to dismiss them), then commanded the Apostles to row back to Capernaum while He Himself successfully sought brief solitude up in the heights of the Golan. The Apostles, late in the night, beset by a stormy crossing, were startled to see their Lord overtake them by walking on the water. Peter tried to walk across the water to meet Him and got a lesson in faith (Mark 6:47-52; Matt. 14:24-33; John 6:16-21). Dawn found them in a fertile country district, the Plain of Gennesaret, south of Capernaum. Before many hours had passed, portions of the frantic multitude had made their way by foot or by ship to the west side of the lake. Jesus meanwhile had walked back to town where the waiting crowd confronted Him again.

Then in the synagogue where he addressed them (John 6:59), that crowd got the surprise of their lives. The man who had compassionately healed and fed them now accused them all of loving only His gift of food (John 6:26). Then He discoursed at length (John 6:26-65), not, as many say, on the purely spiritual nature of God's kingdom as such, but on the nature of eternal life. He spoke of Himself, the only source of this life, of faith alone as the human mode of receiving it. As he had earlier taught Nicodemus, He insisted on the invincible necessity of special divine enlightenment and enablement for a man to exercise saving faith. He really said nothing directly about the nature of the kingdom of God. He rather spoke of the present necessity of genuine faith in Christ to enter it. This debate-discourse has no value at all for interpreting the Lord's Supper (or Eucharist). In the language of Jewish rabbis, to eat and drink the flesh and blood of the teacher was to give attention to the rabbi and to heed as well as obey what he said both outwardly and inwardly.[17] John 6 is not a displaced 'communion meditation' as both liberal critics and Roman sacramentalists would have it.[18]

By quick stages the crowds fell away. As obdurately stupid in spiritual matters as the Pharisees, like them they ask for a 'sign' (John 6:30; cf. vv. 49, 58) – something like the giving of manna by Moses (Exod. 16:21; Num. 11:8) so many generations before – apparently oblivious to the similarity of the feeding of their crowd of five thousand only a day earlier.

---

17 See Stock-Billerbeck II. 485 Alford ANT 525
18 See Raymond E Brown, *The Gospel According to John* (i-ixii), New York: Doubleday 1966, pp 282-294.

At this Jesus asserted that the 'true bread' had already come down from heaven. Then asserting Himself to be that bread, He spoke of their already apparent rejection of Him and the reason why: 'But I said unto you, that ye have seen me, and yet believe not. All that which the Father giveth me shall come unto me; and him that cometh to me I will in no wise cast out' (ASV). The saying includes another appeal to believe, coupled with strong assurance of acceptance (John 6:36, 37). Again He affirmed that only those 'given me' would ultimately be saved (John 6:39). In response, says John, 'the Jews therefore murmured' (6:41 ASV), i.e., gave audible signs of strong displeasure with Him. Shortly Jesus responded with another affirmation of His doctrine of grace: 'Murmur not among yourselves. No man can come to me, except the Father that sent me draw him' (6:43, 44) – to be saved one must learn directly from the Father. After this, employing 'bread' as a familiar rabbinic figure for a rabbi's words or teaching and the figure of eating for belief,[19] Jesus spoke of His flesh as the divine bread given for the life of the world. The crowd of Jews with whom He had been so amazingly popular the day before got to quarreling about Him among themselves, and they apparently left the synagogue.

Not only the Jews but 'his disciples,' apparently followers of a long time, were offended 'when they heard this' and said, 'This is a hard saying; who can hear it?' Not to let the matter rest, for the time had come to winnow away the chaff, the Master reaffirmed the spiritual nature of salvation, repeating thereby the assertion of the movement of God in election and grace prior to human faith: 'For Jesus knew from the beginning who they were that believed not, and who it was that should betray him. And he said, For this cause have I said unto you, that no man can come unto me, except it be given unto him of the Father' (John 6:64, 65 ASV).

The dismal end of the campaign for Galilee and the sad desolation of Jesus are evident: 'Upon this many of his disciples went back, and walked no more with him' (John 6:66 ASV). But the Twelve held firm, Peter being their spokesman. 'Do you also want to leave me?' asked Jesus. Simon Peter answered Him, 'Lord, to whom shall we go? Your words are words of eternal life. We have faith, and we know that you are the Holy One of God' (John 6:68, 69 NEB).

---

19 'Such language would sound less strange in Jewish than in modern ears, since, alike in the Scriptures and in the rabbinical literature, instruction is called bread and those who absorb it are said to eat it.' SDHF, p. 241; cf. ELTJM, 2:25-36 and SBCNT, 2:484, 485.

On this dismal note the campaign for the minds of men in Galilee came to an abrupt end.

From now on, though Jesus spent considerable time with the crowds, He no longer sought the synagogue audiences. He would now devote six months almost exclusively to the Twelve, moving from place to place in the northern Jewish provinces, and after that, another six months traveling with them in eastern and southern parts of Palestine, land of the Jews.

Excursus 5 – The Messengers from John the Baptist

About this time Jesus first disclosed – albeit somewhat indirectly - His claim to be the Messiah promised by the Old Testament (Matt. 11:2-30). Over eighteen months before, at the baptism, John had proclaimed Him the Lamb of God (John 1:29, 36), the Son of God (John 1:34), which the first disciples understood to mean the Messiah (John 1:41). Nathanael had then proclaimed Him the Son of God and King of Israel (John 1:49), while Jesus used language of Himself suggesting fulfillment of one of Daniel's prophecies of Israel's messianic King (Dan. 7:13; cf. John 1:51). But Jesus always, except for that initial day, had spoken of Himself in such a way as to direct His disciples' attention away from His being the fulfillment of all the Old Testament promises about a glorious national deliverer for Israel. He never told them they were wrong to expect such a deliverer. But Jesus knew that such hopes were ill-timed for them. His first advent was to secure redemption. He was, at His first advent, to be the slain Lamb so clearly foreseen in the prophecy of Isaiah 52:13-53:12. But these matters cause great controversy among sincere and well-informed disciples even today – the twentieth century of the Christian era. The disciples, certainly less so the crowds, were then in no position either to desire to hear or to understand the distinction between His two advents. That John the Baptist would send two disciples from his lonely prison cell in (according to Josephus) faraway Machaerus, located in a rugged area overlooking the Dead Sea east of the sea's northeastern shore, clearly shows that His cures of disease and plagues; casting out of demons; restoring the lame, deaf, blind; preaching good tidings to 'the poor'; even recently raising the dead, were His credentials, as indeed, 'he that should come' (Matt. 11:3) in fulfillment of Old Testament prophecies of the Messiah (see Isa. 29:18, 19; 35:5, 6; 61:1ff.). This identification was not explicit but was unquestionably implicit and plain for all to see. We may be certain that John the Baptist, at least, was fully reassured.

It is too bad the messengers already returning could not report to their master John the magnificent eulogy Jesus gave of him as soon as their footsteps could no longer be heard. The crowds – on this point sadly including also all the Twelve – were unable to put it all together. They wanted the Son of man of Daniel 7, the Son of David of Ezekiel 34, not the Suffering Servant of the Lord of Isaiah 42-53. They wanted the fruits of suffering but no suffering, a crown but no cross. And so the matter was to stay throughout our Lord's earthly life down to the very last day.

Excursus 6 – Jesus' Instructions in Matthew 10:5-42a

These instructions and their interpretation are critical to understanding the unfolding mission of Christ. The *'primary reference is to the then mission of the Apostles to prepare His way,* but it includes, in the germ, instructions prophetically delivered for the ministers and missionaries of the Gospel to the end of time. It may be divided into THREE GREAT PORTIONS, in each of which different departments of the subject are treated, but which follow in natural sequence on one another. In the FIRST of these (vv. 5-15), our Lord, takes up the position of the messengers whom He sends from the declaration with which the Baptist and He Himself began their ministry, 'The Kingdom of heaven is at hand.' He gives them commands, *mostly literal, related primarily only to that first mission of the twelve to the cities of Israel.* This portion concludes with a denunciation of judgment against that unbelief which should reject their preaching. The SECOND (vv. 16-23) refers to the general mission of the Apostles *as it developed itself, after the Lord should be taken from them, when they would be preaching both to Jews and Gentiles* (vv. 17, 18), and subject to persecutions (vv. 21, 22). This portion ends with the end of the apostolic period properly so-called, verse 23 referring primarily to the destruction of Jerusalem. In this portion there is a foreshadowing of what shall be the lot and duty of the teachers of the Gospel to the end, inasmuch as the 'coming of the Son of Man' is ever typical of His final coming in judgment. Still the direct reference is to the Apostles and their mission. and the other only by inference. The THIRD (vv. 24-42), the longest and weightiest portion, is spoken directly (with occasional reference only to the Apostles and their mission, v. 40) *of all disciples of the Lord,–* their position – their encouragements, – their duties, – and finally concludes with the last great reward (v. 42).'[20]

---

20 The present discussion, including Henry Alford's unmatched comments, is difficult, but it is

One mysterious sentence in the second section is an important hinge by which to hang interpretation of gospel history: 'Ye shall not have gone over the cities of Israel, till the Son of man be come' (Matt. 10:23). This is preceded by prediction which fits only apostolic history in the period immediately following the ascension of our Lord – 'hated of all men... he that endureth to the end,' etc. Henry Alford went on to say, 'In order to understand these words it is necessary to enter into the character of our Lord's prophecies respecting His coming, as having an *immediate literal*, and a *distant foreshadowed fulfillment*. Throughout this discourse and the great prophecy in ch. xxiv we find the first apostolic period used as a type of whole ages of the Church; and the vengeance on Jerusalem, which historically put an end to the old dispensation, and was in its place with reference to that order of things, the coming of the Son of Man, as a type of the final coming of the Lord. These two subjects accompany and interpenetrate one another in a manner wholly inexplicable to those who are unaccustomed to the wide import of Scripture prophecy, which speaks very generally not so much of events themselves, points of time, – as of processions of events, all ranging under one great description. Thus in the present case there is certainly direct reference to the destruction of Jerusalem; the end directly spoken of is that event, and the *shall be saved* the preservation provided by the warning afterwards given in ch. 24:15-18. And the next verse directly refers to the journeys of the Apostles over the actual cities of Israel, territorial, or where Jews were located. But as certainly do all these expressions look onwards to the great final coming of the Lord, the end of all prophecy; as certainly the shall be saved here bears its full scripture meaning, of everlasting salvation; and the endurance to the end is the finished course of the Christian; and the prospect in the next verse is to apply to the conduct of Christians of all ages with reference to persecution, and the announcement that hardly will the Gospel have been fully preached to all nations (or, to all the Jewish nation, i.e., effectually) when the Son of Man shall come. It is important to keep in mind the great prophetic parallels which run through our Lord's discourses, and are sometimes separately, sometimes simultaneously, presented to us by Him.'[21]

---

rendered necessary by the very materials of Matthew's tenth chapter. Alford leads the way, and I have sought to distill his guidance. ANT, pp. 68, 69. I have slightly modified Alford's sentences for clarification.

21 ibid., pp. 71, 72.

Excursus 7 – The Murder of John the Baptist

At about this time Herod Antipas, tetrarch of Galilee and Trans-Jordan, heard of Jesus' marvelous words and deeds, and perhaps also of what the Apostles were doing, for Mark and Luke note the same immediately after the story of the Apostles' mission in such a manner as to indicate that he was aware of their exploits, too. The Synoptic Gospels report that this gave that guilty monarch considerable anxiety, perhaps even pangs of conscience (Mark 6:14-29; Matt. 14:1-12; Luke 9:7-9), for he wondered, they say, if Jesus might be John the Baptist, whom he had murdered at the whimsical suggestion of his wife, risen from the dead. Josephus, reporting the murder of John from the standpoint of public policy, asserted that it was to forestall any future political difficulties which John might cause.[22]

Excursus 8 – Jesus' Use of Parables

In His own time, Jesus was not thought to be doing anything unusual when, as a Jewish rabbi, He employed many parables in His discourses. The Old Testament itself furnishes a good many literary pieces which would fall into that category. If we regard the parable as an extended figure of speech, we may rightly say it is part of the genius of the Old Testament poets and prophets. The rabbis of Jesus' time were adept in the use of parables. The folklore of the Near East to the present time, as well as the common speech of the people, is strikingly full of parable, allegory, metaphor, simile, hyperbole, and every form of figurative language to a degree that our Western speech usually is not. Perhaps the greatest beauty of the Jewish Talmud lies in this same genius for figure of speech.

A treatment such as the present one, aiming to treat in brief scope the life of Christ, has no place for an extended treatment of Jesus' parables. Teachers and students using this book, however, may wish to study Jesus' parables at greater length and depth. I therefore furnish immediately following, in somewhat modified form, the list of parables and related materials in the Gospels furnished by a writer famous for his illuminating guide to the several parts of the Bible (see Table 3).[23] This is followed immediately by Excursus 9 'On Interpretation of Jesus' Parables'. At the

---

22 Antiquities 18.5.2.
23 SGG, pp. 549-51.

end of this book, an Appendix, 'A Preamble to Modern Criticism of the Parables of Jesus' will introduce the reader to the rather fruitless efforts of modern critics to set aside the canon of the New testament Gospels but use them as a resource to get back to the *ipsissima verba* (very words) of Jesus.

Excursus 9 – On Interpretation of Jesus' Parables

A biblical parable is generally understood as a story told to teach some moral, lesson, or doctrine. Usually one idea is the burden of each parable. The prophet Nathan's apparently fictitious story of the little ewe sheep and his point, 'you are the man' (II Sam. 12:7, see also vv 1-5) is an example. It is worth noting, however, that though the lesson was very simple, Nathan used many more words to elaborate the point and to drive it home to David than he employed in the parable itself. It was all so very realistic that David at first thought it was a true report of injustice in his kingdom and he was bout to put judicial process in motion.

Jotham's parable of the bramble (Judges 9: 7-15), however, is not a believable story. It is not only fictitious but fabulous. The trees go out to make a king over themselves. The olive tree, the fig tree, the grape vine and the bramble speak as if human. There is a central thrust, 'Get rid of Abimelech,' but almost everything the trees say and do has rather specific parallel and application to affairs in the ancient city of Shechem. The story is part fable (speaking animals and plants) and part allegory (a story in which the various elements each stand for something).

The pithy comparisons of the book of Proverbs are called parables, too (Prov. 1:6), and the strange taunting song against the king of Babylon, in which the earth sings, trees talk and shades in the realm of the dead make speeches, is also called a parable (Isa. 14:3-11). Further, while the Hebrew Bible uses a variety of terms for these things, the Septuagint (ancient Greek translation) often employs *parabole* (parable), as the foregoing references from Proverbs and Isaiah show. Each of these passages comes across in the Greek New testament allusions and quotations as a *parabole*, transliterated rather than translated as 'parable'. So in sober reality our word parable becomes an indefinite designation of several different kinds of stories, riddles similitudes, and the like.

There is therefore no strict basis in the language of scripture to classify all the parables of Jesus under any common technical term (*genus* or *genre*). Jesus' parables are, however, much closer to the single-idea type (Nathan's parable) than the allegory-fable type of Jotham or the complex imagery of the taunt song of Isaiah 14.

As far as can be determined, there is little, if any, disagreement about the above-mentioned assertations among New Testament scholars today. Until the Protestant Reformers, the parables were commonly expounded as allegories. Calvin was the first important teacher to break severely from that habit of interpretation and truly sought the lesson or doctrine Jesus was teaching by looking steadfastly at the parable in its context. His comments are still valuable today.

The great scholarly expositors of the nineteenth and twentieth centuries treat Jesus' parables as similtudes - a certain truth corresponds to a point made by a story – not some part of the story but the whole of it. This is the general rule. Sometimes more that one truth might be taught, but if so it is plain. There may be other elements of instruction present but they are subsidiary to the main lesson.

Some parables are very simple – a seed that grows to harvest wholly by 'automatic' powers and processes. There is nothing the farmer can do but wait. The lesson is *patience* (Mark 4:26-29). There is apparently no other lesson, though patience is much more than a word and I have written several paragraphs about it in another book. But some parables have several parts and if the parable teaches one truth, that truth has 'parts' or 'features'. Such is the similitude of the seed and the four soils. Several parables predict the course of future events – the rejection of the Savior by His people, the gathering of Gentiles into the church and even the destruction of Jerusalem by the Romans. These are close to outright allegory. Two of these follow one another on the narrative of the Passion Week: the householder and the faithless husbandmen (Matt. 21:33-46); the king and the reluctant wedding guests (22:1-4). Of course, liberal scholars will employ their critical tools to expunge any such future plans of Jesus from the 'authentic tradition.' Joachim Jeremias has 'discovered' ten ways by which the 'creative church' and the 'redactors' are said to have modified and embellished the original parables and sayings of Jesus. (Joachim Jeremias, *The Parables of Jesus*, 2nd Ed. Rev., New York: Scribners, 1972). These modifications and embellishments may be detected, he says, by finding any parts identical to distinct features of either the Judaism or the church of about AD 60. What is left is said to be authentic. Other criteria are employed but this is the chief one.

Yet the more moderate of the liberal critics acknowledge that the 'authentic kernel' sometimes contains allegorical elements. A. M. Hunter, who is certainly moderate and generally helpful, commented:

We are asserting that no aesthetic scruple would have prevented Jesus [from] using allegory if and when it suited his purpose... A good working rule would be this. When interpreting, don't try to eliminate everything allegorical... and so trim them into pure parables. On the other hand, never allegorize to the point which mars the one lesson, or warning, or challenge, which the parable was meant to convey.[24]

The parables are not mere pleasant tales to illustrate sermons or to cultivated audiences. They were delivered in an atmosphere of sharp conflict. After one of them one segment of the crowd was so incensed they sought to have Jesus arrested (Matt. 21:45-46).

However much or little the disciples understood, Jesus clearly declared to them that His words would be fully understood only after the effusion of the Spirit upon them. The apostles were supposed to explain them further to us and we are therefore in a much better position than the first audiences. Some principles that good interpreters use are as follows:

1. Expect to find the unknown conveyed by the known. This is true of all communication to some degree. All abstract ideas are conveyed by use of language figures of one sort or another. Think, for example of how the words *image, imagine* and *imagination* are used. An *image* is a physical object shaped to be like something else. To imagine is to form an object in the mind and *imagination* is the faculty or process of forming mental images.

2. The chief point of comparison is to the whole parable. The point cannot be understood until the end. When Jesus says, 'The kingdom of heaven is like,' the comparison (similitude) is not simply a net or leaven or a grain of mustard seed but the whole story of a net, of leaven, or of a grain of mustard seed. Hear Jesus out before you make up your mind.

3. Expect the point of the parable to be a truth that challenges the reader to some change of life, some act of repentance or faith. The people of Jesus' day, who were amused or entertained but not challenged, missed the point. Some who did see the point were only angered. Only a few truly understood and believed. Jesus' parables were not democratic media of mass appeal. He never got elected to anything except a cross!

4. Do not expect every detail to have specific meaning. Most details serve only as vehicles for the story. There may be elements of allegory

24 A. M. Hunter, *The Parables Then and Now*, Philadelphia: Westminster, 1971.

(multiple symbolism), but most of Jesus' parables convey a single idea (again think of Nathan's parable). In a true allegory such as Bunyan's *The Pilgrim's Progress* every detail such as the 'Slough of Despond' has a precise and obvious counterpart in the Christian's life. None of Jesus' parables is quite like that.

5. Even in parables which border on allegory, expect that often the main point will be spelled out plainly by the Gospel author. Luke, for example, informed his readers clearly that Jesus spoke the parable of the pounds in order to correct the notion 'that the kingdom of God should immediately appear' (Luke 19:11, KJV). If the scripture speaks with authority, Luke can hardly be set aside for the learned opinions of Dodd, Jeremias, or Bultmann.

6. Sometimes the main point is clearly conveyed by the historical setting. Both scribes and Pharisees, Luke says, had grumbled becase Jesus warmly welcomed tax-gatherers and sinners to hear him (Luke 15:1-2). Immediately Jesus spoke three parables (the lost sheep, the lost coin, and the prodigal son) comparing joy on earth over finding lost things to the joy of heavenly beings 'over one sinner who repents' (vv7,10). The father's words to the brother of the prodigal son convey the same lesson: 'But we had to be merry and rejoice, for this brother of yours was dead and has begun to live, and was lost and has been found' (v32). The lesson is plainly *joy*, not forgiveness, as the nearly uniform exegesis of liberal Protestant theologians would have it.

7. Like Paul Harvey's famous *The Rest of the Story* and good yarns everywhere, the point of the parable usually comes at or near the end. Look for 'the punch line'. Think of the three parables that the scribes and Pharisees missed and which God, heaven and the angels have over sinners who repent comes at the very end of the parable.

8. Sometimes Jesus rather clearly explained what certain parables meant and expected the disciples to gain sufficient insight to interpret similar parables on occasion (see Matt. 13:51-52; cf vv 18-23 and 36-43).

Table 3. The recorded parables

Parables in One Gospel

	Matt.	Mark	Luke	John
Wheat and tares	13:24-30			
	13:36-43			
Hidden Treasure	13:44			
Pearl of great price	13:45, 46			
Fish net	13:47-50			
Householder	13:51, 52			
Unmerciful servant	18:23-35			
Laborers in vineyard	20:1-16			
Two sons called to work	21:28-32			
Marriage of king's son	22:1-14			
Ten virgins	25:1-13			
Talents	25:14-30			
Sheep and goats	25:31-46			
Seed growing secretly		4:26-29		
Householder and porter		13:34-37		
Two debtors			7:41-43	
Good Samaritan			10:30-37	
Friend at midnight			11:5-8	
Rich fool			12:16-21	
Waiting, watching servants			12:35-38	
Barren fig tree			13:6-9	
Great supper			14:16-24	
Unfinished tower			14:28-30	
Unwaged war			14:31, 32	
Lost bit of silver			15:8-10	
Prodigal son			15:11-32	
Unrighteous steward			16:1-13	
Rich man and Lazarus			16:19-31	
Unprofitable servants			17:7-10	
Unjust judge			18:1-8	
Pharisee and publican			18:9-14	
Pounds			19:11-27	
Door of the sheep				10:1-10
Good shepherd				10:11-18
				10:25-30
Vine and branches				15:1-6

Parables in Two Gospels

	Matt.	Mark	Luke	John
Inward light	6:22, 23		11:34-36	
Two builders	7:24-27		6:46-49	
Unclean spirit	12:43-45		11:24-26	
Leaven in meal	13:33		13:20, 21	
Master and thief	24:43, 44		12:39, 40	
Faithful and evil servant	24:45-51		12:42-46	
Lost sheep	18:12-14		15:3-7	

Parables in Three Gospels

	Matt.	Mark	Luke	John
Savorless salt	5:13	9:50	14:34, 35	
Lighted Lamp	5:15	4:21	8:16, 17	
			11:33	
Bride and Bridegroom	9:14, 15	2:19, 20	5:34, 35	
New cloth on old garment	9:16	2:21	5:36	
New wine in old wineskins	9:17	2:22	5:37-39	
Sower and soils	13:3-9	4:1-9	8:4-8	
	13:18-23			
Mustard seed	13:31, 32	4:30-32	13:18, 19	
Wicked husbandmen	21:33-41	12:1-9	20:9-16	
Rejected stone	21:42-46	12:10, 11	20:17-19	
Sprouting fig tree	24:32-35	13:28-31	21:29-33	

Illustrations Similar to Parables

	Matt.	Mark	Luke	John
Fishers of men	4:19	1:16, 17	5:10	
Salt of the earth	5:13			
Light of the world	5:14-16		11:34-36	
Dogs and swine	7:6			
Doomed plants	15:13			
Strait gate and shut door			13:23-30	
Mote and beam	7:1-5		6:41, 42	
Broad and narrow ways	7:13, 14			
Good and bad fruit trees	7:16-20		6:43-45	
Physician and the sick	9:12, 13	2:17	5:31, 32	
Offending members	5:29, 30	9:43-47		
Birds and flowers	6:25-34		12:22-31	
Of Satan's kingdom	12:24-28	3:23-26		
Strong man	12:29, 30	3:27	11:17-22	
Good and bad treasures	12:34-37			
Blind guiding the blind	15:14		6:39	
Chief seats at feasts			14:7-11	
Harvest field				4:35-38
Grain of wheat				12:23-26
Defilement	15:10, 11	7:14-23		
	15:15-20			

CHAPTER 7

Special Training for the Twelve: Out of Favor and on the Move In and About Galilee

The period of Jesus' ministry now before us is distinct from all which preceded, in many ways. During the first four to six months, just previous to that first Passover, He was finding and shaping Himself for the coming struggle. It consisted of His baptism, temptation, calling five or six disciples from among John's followers, a short return to His home by way of Cana (where He performed the first miracle), then, just before Passover, transfer – evidently with His family – to Capernaum. This is where four of those first six disciples lived.

The second period, about a year, beginning with the first Passover of His ministry and on to the season of the second Passover, was spent in Judaea. All we know of it is found in the second, third, and fourth chapters of John. Since the area of Samaria (John 4) was joined to the Roman province of Judaea, His two days there may be subsumed under the Judaean ministry. During this year, though Jesus and the Baptist worked harmoniously, it was John's portion to 'decrease' and Jesus' to 'increase.' The six initial Galilean disciples (Andrew, Peter, John, James, Philip, and Nathanael) were with Him at least part of the time.

The third period, falling between that second (but unnamed) Passover and the third (John 6:4), was one of vigorous ministry in all parts of Galilee, a time of appointing Apostles, attracting disciples, initial opposition from Jerusalem Pharisees growing to fierce hatred, climaxed by a crescendo of popular acclaim at the miracle of feeding the five thousand. It closed with the appalling rejection of the Lord after His sermon next day in the Capernaum synagogue.

Our Lord passed the six months to follow, the period now to be considered, exclusively in the company of the Twelve, as far as possible. He avoided the people of the lands where they came as much as was consistent with His heart of compassion for those who discovered Him in His various places of retreat. He no longer dwelt among or consorted with very many Jews. The land of Phoenicia where He first went was almost entirely heathen, while the Decapolis where He next sojourned was in large part heathen. Nor do we have any evidence that the faithful women of means who accompanied, supported, and ministered to the Lord and the Twelve, accompanied them on these journeys.

There are several reasons, some stated, others clearly to be inferred why the Lord sought these times and places of retreat from His own people, Israel, even though He had clearly stated that He was sent to the lost sheep of the house of Israel (Matt. 15:24; cf. 10:6) and had commanded the Twelve (Matt. 10:5) on their first mission not to go into any way of the Gentiles:

1. A very serious danger to Jesus' person and to His ministry had developed in the person of the tetrarch Herod Antipas. The third tour of Galilee, the Twelve proclaiming 'everywhere' the presence of the kingdom of God and manifesting its power, had mightily impressed the whole province (Luke 9:1-6). The noise thereof reached even to Herod's palace at Tiberias, the lakeside capital city only a few miles south of Capernaum. The three Synoptic Gospels all report (Mark 6:14-29; Matt. 14:1-12; Luke 9:7-9) Herod's perplexity over Jesus at that time. Being almost as depraved as his father, though not as intelligent or resolute, he had allowed himself to be tricked by his vengeful wife, Herodias, into a civil lynching of John the Baptist. She could not bear John's rebuke of her open adultery. Herod now pondered what to do. Being an irresolute, feckless prince, had Jesus' popularity or influence continued to rise, he would probably have followed out whatever the strongest influence on him might be, either to incarcerate and execute Jesus as he had John, or to praise and support Him. Most of the time now, Jesus was careful to avoid the neighborhood of Tiberias, capital of Herod's dominions in Galilee,[1] and Herodian Galilee in general, until He left the area for good.

---

1 Herod had dominions east of Jordan and south of the Sea of Galilee, designated indefinitely as 'beyond Jordan' in the Gospels but called *Peraea* by Josephus.

2. The Pharisees and their scribes, angry with Jesus from the moment of His appearance at that first Passover (John 2:13-21), were now furious with Him and sought ways to discredit or kill Him. They were coming down from Jerusalem to Galilee in larger numbers with the express purpose of opposing Jesus. They were ubiquitously present wherever He spoke in Galilee. When He first preached in the Capernaum synagogue on the first Sabbath of His residence there and, when after the sermon He cured a spectacular case of demon possession, there was no opposition. No one present saw anything wrong with such a deed of compassion and deliverance on the Sabbath. Later when He forgave a man's sins as He healed him, there were local scribes and Pharisees on hand to question His authority and to accuse Him of blasphemy (Luke 5:21). Then the same parties raised objections to His disciples' mingling with 'publicans and sinners' (Luke 5:30) and to their apparent neglect of traditional (not Mosaic) fasts (Luke 5:33). Shortly after this Jesus was verbally attacked by these same people when He healed a lame man at the pool of Bethesda while He attended one of the Jewish feasts there (John 5:1-16). At that time He defended Himself against the charge of Sabbath breaking (John 5:17ff.), as He did several times later (e.g., Luke 6:1-11), always very effectively, publicly showing up the hypocrisy of His accusers. His sermon on the mount eloquently condemned their showy self-righteousness (Matt. 6:1-18). He condemned them for their rejection of John the Baptist's message, calling them childish play-actors whom no genuine honest man could please (Luke 7:28-35). So we should not be surprised that they soon accused Him of being in league with the devil (Matt. 9:34; 12:22-37).

Just as the action of the present chapter begins, the scene opens on a fierce exchange: a delegation of Pharisees and their scribes from the Jerusalem Sanhedrin arrive in Capernaum and criticize Jesus for allowing His disciples to break a truly stupid non-Mosaic law about washing the hands (Mark 7:1-23; Matt. 15:1-20). Jesus countered their charge with a fierce denunciation, charging them with hypocrisy in employing false piety as a means of defrauding parents and thereby of breaking the fifth commandment (Mark 7:1-23). Even the disciples were shocked by the devastating fury of Jesus' reply to the Pharisees (Matt. 15:12). They even misunderstood it as a parable (Matt. 15:15), unable to believe He meant literally what He said. But the hatred of the scribes and Pharisees was now implacable. Jesus wanted no final collision with them until the time was right. He knew it was the Father's purpose that they should kill Him, but not then. It was time for Jesus and His circle of Apostles to leave the territory.

3. Some, emphasizing that the new ministry would be in heathen territory, hold that a chief purpose of the move was to help break the anti-Gentile biases of the Apostles.[2] No doubt this may have figured in Jesus' mind.

4. Above all, however, aside from the matter of sheer physical safety for Jesus from Herod on the one hand and the Sanhedrin Jews on the other, Jesus wanted a time to instruct privately the Twelve. Few outstanding miracles, therefore, belong to this period; they did not tend to promote privacy for teaching. Apparently assured that the disciples accepted Him as *King* of Israel, He now concentrated more on the *kingdom*.[3] The feeding of the five thousand was an indirect result of Jesus' first, abrupt attempt (unsuccessful) to find retreat from Jewry outside the country. The Twelve were far from ready for the climax when He would be betrayed, falsely tried, and crucified. They must be as ready as, before the resurrection, ascension, and Pentecost, as they could be made. Even on the night of the Last Supper, Jesus felt compelled to say, 'I have yet many things to say unto you, but ye cannot bear them now' (John 16:12 ASV). Hence, 'the time had come when He could not wait longer. The shadow of the cross was coming rapidly towards Him. The total eclipse would find the Twelve wholly unprepared for the catastrophe... At any rate they must be told the truth.'[4]

RETREAT TO PHOENICIA

Mark 7:24-8:10

Matt. 15:21-38

At different times the old Canaanite nation of Phoenicia, whose chief cities were Tyre (nearest Israel) and Sidon farther north, had figured in Jewish history. Phoenicians appear in favorable light in the times of David and Solomon when their kings had aided in supply of materials and craftsmen to build the first temple; in the time of Ahab, in unfavorable light, for the royal house of Tyre had furnished the king of Israel with Jezebel, his wife. Their offspring blighted several generations of the royal houses of Israel and Judah. The people of Phoenicia were northwestern Canaanites, of the same depraved religion in former times as the Canaanites of Palestine, upon whom the sentence of extermination

2 EHL, pp. 199, 200.
3 ibid., pp. 204, 205.
4 RHG, p. 99.

fell in Joshua's time. It was an 'unclean' land. Ordinarily no Jew would go there. A grave problem for itinerants like Jesus and the Twelve would have been procurement of kosher food, for they could not carry several weeks' supply of food.[5]

But the reasons for Jesus and the Twelve to go to Phoenicia were sufficient. Many years later, no doubt at Peter's word, Mark included in his Gospel, at a point only five verses earlier than this story of ministry in Phoenicia, this parenthetical remark: 'This he said, making all meats clean' (Mark 7:19 ASV). A new dispensation was dawning in which Gentiles would associate without distinction with the sons of Abraham, Isaac, and Jacob (Gal. 2:11-14). Peter, of course, at this time had a lot more to learn about that (Acts 10:9-16).

Many writers, until fairly recent times,[6] have questioned if Jesus went beyond the border clear into Phoenicia, for Mark 7:24 seemed unclear. But Matthew plainly says, 'Jesus... withdrew into the parts [*eis to merē*] of Tyre and Sidon' (Matt. 15:21 ASV), while the now-corrected text of Mark 7:31 (ASV) clearly says, 'he went out from the borders of Tyre, and came through Sidon...'

Only one incident – quite unique in the Lord's career is reported. We would like to know how long He sojourned in that well-favored land of swelling sea, fruited slopes, and snow-capped mountains. What did the Savior of the world do? How was He treated and how did those parochial Apostles respond in the remnant of world-renowned Tyre, the 'mart of nations' (Isa. 23:3), the 'merchant of the people for many isles' (Ezek. 27:3), the 'joyous city, whose antiquity is of ancient days' (Isa. 23:7); and in her mother, Sidon (Isa. 23:7, 12)? Why did not one of them tell us? 'Was it distasteful to the Jewish evangelists that the Lord showed such grace to the Gentiles? [Luke omits the whole tour.] Or were they so distraught by the unfamiliar scenes [in coming years they would travel to many] that they retained no distinct remembrance...?'[7] Whatever the reason, Jesus was impressed by the openness of the Phoenicians to Him and later pointed up the damning contrast with the hardhearted response of the cities of Galilee (Luke 10:13, 14).

There is no evidence, however, that His journey through Phoenicia became a preaching mission. Though He could not be hid entirely – people had come from those areas to hear Him during the time of His

---

5 SDHF, p. 235.
6 See note on text in EHL, pp. 218, 219, 232, 233.
7 SDHF, p. 253.

popularity in Galilee – He did take residence in a private house (Mark 7:24) to instruct the Twelve. We read of no throngs attending His passage from place to place until after He departed Tyre 'and came through Sidon' and came nigh 'unto the sea of Galilee... through the borders of Decapolis' (Mark 7:31 ASV; cf. Matt. 15:29).

What shall we say about our Lord's seeming unfeeling churlishness with the 'Syrophoenician' Canaanitish woman who with great passion, feminine charm, and sharp wit, but with difficulty, got help from Him for her demon-possessed daughter (Mark 7:25-30; cf. Matt. 15:22-28)? The reason why He tried to avoid another great public healing is plain enough – He was there precisely to fulfill an infinitely greater need, necessary instruction of the future foundation stones of the edifice called the church. We can really rule out any objection to the mother's Gentileness. He had made exceptions before to the rule about going 'only to the lost sheep of the house of Israel,' and He had previously poured water on the wheel of his mission out of Elijah's mission to Gentiles of the very same region long before (Luke 4:26; cf. I Kings 17:9) (Sarepta, or Zarephath, is not far from Tyre). The real mystery is His harsh-sounding language – so utterly strange to Him in speaking to the humble needy.

Many different considerations have been offered through the ages, from John Chrysostom to the latest writer on the subject, which taken together relieve the matter of serious difficulty.[8] (1) His harshness may have been merely assumed, merely a mask. If so, the woman's faith was tested by difficulty and strengthened by success while the disciples' prejudices were somewhat reduced. Though it tends to envelop the incident with a theatrical air, it is not thereby to be ruled out. (2) Perhaps His words as understood then and there did not really sound insolent. In styling the heathen, 'dogs,' He used a diminutive form of the word (as 'doggie'), possibly indicating endearment. Unfortunately this cannot be certain, for the diminutive of *dog* was also used to indicate contempt. (3) It may be that in Greek-speaking territory and addressing the woman in Greek, He cited a familiar Greek proverb, something like 'You starve yourself to feed dogs.' Hence Jesus was saying: 'People too poor to feed their own kids shouldn't own expensive pets and affect stylish manners.' There are many such proverbs in all languages. (4) Perhaps a proverb was cited, but it warned against wasting charity in a quarter whence no good is to be gained in return. (5) The most interesting suggestion

---

8 ibid., pp. 249-52.

connects the idea of a proverb with straight-faced, twinkle-in-the-eye humor. This was advocated long ago by David Smith and recently by Elton Trueblood.[9] Smith found a very convincing, nearly exact verbal Greek parallel to Jesus' sharp-sounding words and the mother's witty reply in Philostratus's *Life of Appolonitts of Tyana.*[10]

But would Jesus engage in banter? Would raillery fit Him? Let us judge yes on both counts. The girl's case, while serious, was not desperate. Her mother was not a super-pious, frowning, hyper-orthodox Jew but a 'Greek, nimble of fancy and keen of wit, delighting in quips and cranks, and responding, even in the midst of sorrow, to a playful assault. Our Lord's treatment of her is an instance of His wondrous insight into human character. He perceived at a glance what was in everyone with whom He had to do, and knew exactly how to handle him.'[11]

He, now that He was a public figure, even in a foreign land, quickly moved up the coast to Sidon and then, striking south of south-east, crossed the lower southern end of the Lebanon Range and the valley of the Litani River to the slopes of Gaulanitis (modern Golan Heights) in the Decapolis (Mark 7:31), not far from Bethsaida-Julias where He had performed the miracle of feeding the five thousand a few weeks before. He again sought solitude for Himself and the Apostles in a mountain, and again solitude was stolen from them by the sick and the curious. Another spectacular healing brought more sick people and their friends which, in turn, led to many miracles of healing and large crowds. Even though His desire for privacy with the Twelve was frustrated, there was some gain. The people in this half-heathen land 'glorified the God of Israel' (Matt. 15:31) and were thereby brought closer to a believing response when Christians evangelized the area a few years later. But Jesus knew that He must somehow rid Himself of the crowds embarrassing Him in the time set aside for more special training of the Twelve. So as in a similar situation earlier, He miraculously fed the four thousand hungry people, then 'straightway he entered into the boat [presumably in attendance for this purpose] with his disciples' and departed in a manner which prevented the curious crowd from following.

---

9 *The Humor of Christ* (New York: Harper and Row, 1964), pp. 116-25.
10 SDHF, p. 251.
11 ibid., p. 252.

BRIEF FORAY BACK INTO GALILEE

Mark 8:10-23
Matt. 15:39-16:12 The place called *Dalmanutha* and *Magadan (Magdala* in the KJV)[12] to which the Lord and the Twelve went by boat was somewhere on the western shore, but far enough from Capernaum to hope for brief respite from crowds. But right away, almost as if they had an appointment with Him, 'as if they missed Him and were glad to see Him back,'[13] His old adversaries the Pharisees showed up to challenge Him. They had witnessed many of His signs and did not challenge their reality, but now asked for something more meaningful - a 'sign from heaven,' perhaps like stopping the sun and moon on the 'long day of Joshua.' Jesus was greatly distressed with them. Galilee and its acknowledged leaders were as hopeless as everI He gave them a short answer and quickly took to the boat and headed back for heathen ground.

This was the third time His enemies had asked for a sign. Some two years earlier, during the Passover (John 2:18, 19) at the beginning of His ministry in Judaea, He acknowledged some legitimacy to their demand,[14] saying enigmatically that His resurrection would be the sign. The second time they asked, He manifested great indignation, but then later He seemed to refer again to His resurrection as the sign. On that occasion He also sarcastically treated their now-amazing unbelief as itself a sign, in contrast to ancient Nineveh's faith (Matt. 12:38-42). Their third demand He turned away with contempt, heaping scorn on the willful stupidity of 'wise' men who could read the signs of nature but had no regard for the very Son of God from heaven.

This incident is noteworthy in that here the Sadducees, usual adversaries of the Pharisees, are mentioned for the first time (Mark 8:15; cf. Matt. 16:6) in the Gospels and never again until the last week. They appear to have been associated, in Jesus' mind, with the Herodians. The Herodians had a good while before taken sides with the Pharisees against Jesus (Mark 3:6). Christ had now put all His enemies in bed together! On the last day of His public ministry, they would appear together against Him. They would be soundly trounced, one after another, in public debate, and thoroughly discredited by Him.

So Jesus and His disciples put to sea again, heading northward for

---

12 Perhaps copyists put a familiar place name *(Magdala)* for an unfamiliar one. If it is not the same as Magdala, about four miles northward from Tiberias, it is unknown. FANT, pp. 45, 46.
13 RHG, p. 104.
14 SBCNT cites Dent. 13:2; Matt. 12:38-42; Luke 11:16, 29-31.

the long pull to the head of the lake. As the knocking of the oars mixed with the gentle splash of the waves, Jesus pointedly warned, 'Beware of the leaven of the Pharisees [narrow religious bigotry] and of the Sadducees[15] [worldliness]. Now the disciples were doubly 'at sea,' physically and mentally (Mark 8:16). Though Jesus' metaphor was simple enough, they were too sluggish of wit just then (Mark 8:14-16; Matt. 16:5-7) to catch the figure. Both Gospels note that in haste to be shed of Magadan and the Jewish religious pirates there, they all forgot to take along sufficient food, and the destination was many hours away. So they thought Jesus might be gently reproving them for their thoughtless omission. After all, they had nothing else to do just then but care for such matters. The reader wonders why they thought the way they did. If they had no bread at all with them, then why 'beware' of any kind of bread. How could they be so dull? Jesus proceeded sharply (and not very patiently) to rebuke both their little faith (Had He not recently fed five thousand and four thousand with much left over each time?) and their dullness. Finally the point soaked in. He was warning against the *teachings* of their noted enemies! Impatience with disciples is not always blameworthy. A student needs to be set on his ear once in a while. Every conscientious teacher of responsible adults will truly sympathize with Jesus on that long afternoon ship ride.

RETREAT TO CAESAREA PHILIPPI

The party put ashore at a point just east of the mouth of the upper Jordan and started to hike northward toward the slopes of Mt. Hermon through Bethsaida. Recognizing Jesus, someone brought a blind man to Him (Mark 8:22-26). Rather than risk the gathering of another crowd, Jesus swiftly seized the blind man by the hand, led him quickly outside the border of the town, and there, employing a mode of working (He spat in the man's eyes and laid hands on him) evidently designed to arouse believing expectancy, partially restored the man's sight ('I behold men as trees walking'). Then He repeated part of the procedure, with complete restoration following. The man must not have resided in the town, for Jesus commanded him to go straight home, not even to set foot in the town. So the Lord, while not neglecting compassion, nevertheless successfully prevented the gathering of a curious following. After this

Mark
8:22-
9:32
Matt.
16:5-
17:23
Luke
9:18-45

---

15 Though Jesus' actual words were 'of Herod,' He seems to have been thinking of the Sadducees as allied with and supporting Herod

He and His band spent a long time among 'the villages of Caesarea Philippi'[16] (Mark 8:27).

During this last extended retreat many very important developments took place. Of these, Peter's confession and the transfiguration are of utmost significance, matched by the grandeur of the simple narratives. Of equal import were the three distinct occasions (Mark 8:34-37, cf. Matt. 16:22-26 and Luke 9:22-25; Mark 9:9-13, cf. Matt. 17:9-13 and Luke 9:36; Mark 9:30-32, cf. Matt. 17:22, 23 and Luke 9:43-45) during this period when the Lord plainly told the disciples of His death and resurrection soon to be effected at Jerusalem.

We may suppose that they required the better part of two days for the hike from Bethsaida-Julias (Philip's winter residence) to the neighborhood of Caesarea Philippi (his summer residence). The route was uphill all the way and about forty miles long by the road. The road leads up the east side of Jordan about twelve miles, then about fifteen miles to the right toward Damascus as far as *el Quneitra,* high in the Golan, then ten miles northwest along the heights to the outer slopes of Mt. Hermon, until from the high plateau the road descends another eight or ten miles to Philip's then-new city of Caesarea. One of the headwaters of the Jordan issued from a cavern nearby, sacred to the pagan god Pan. We may imagine the famous conversation between Jesus and His disciples (Mark 8:27-30; Matt. 16:13-20; Luke 8: 19-21), Peter being their spokesman, as taking place about mid-day on the third day of travel from Magadan. (They would have been late disembarking down at Bethsaida and would have scarcely cleared the town by nightfall.)

We dare not pause long to comment on the words of Christ (Matt. 16:13-20) – that belongs to a study of His teachings. But they do represent a crisis in His career. Some of the Twelve have now been with Him over two-and-a-half-years. All have been with Him continually for more than a year. Do they apprehend His person? Do they understand anything vital to His mission? Jesus knows what the people are saying and draws that out of them first. And He would not have forgotten that on the day of that first meeting, Andrew had called Him the Messiah (John 1:41) and that the next day Nathanael had called Him the *Son of* God and the *King of Israel* (John 1:49). Did they – now that He had showed plainly that He

---

16 'Jesus goes on to the region of Caesarea Philippi on Mt. Hermon, where no hostility had been aroused, and he could quietly instruct the Twelve. He probably remained in that vicinity several months, as this whole period of retirement lasted six months... Each of the... retirements is into heathen territory (Ituraea [part of the tetrarchy of Philip]... Phoenicia, Decapolis) where Greek influence prevails, and where the Greek language is dominant.' RHG, p. 98.

contemplated no military campaign immediately to expel the Romans and then set up a renewed Davidic monarchy in Jerusalem – still regard Him as the Christ and the Son of God? Peter's hearty response showed Jesus that indeed they did, however vague their understanding of that affirmation. Natural man never gains this insight (I Cor. 2:14) to Jesus' character and universal saviorhood apart from especial divine enlightenment, and Peter was no exception.

That Peter is called a rock, that the church was to be founded on 'this rock,' has had various explanation. The one which seems correct is that in a literal sense the church was to be founded upon Apostles. Paul distinctly says so (Eph. 2:20-22): the church's foundation is the Apostles, and Christ is the cornerstone. Of greater value than settling this controversial question is to observe this very first clear announcement of the future building of the church of Jesus Christ and this pointed allusion to its nature. The actual formation of this body of saved men, joined in vital unity by the new special ministry of the Holy Spirit, would take place in less than a year (I Cor. 12:13; cf. Acts 2:1ff.). In a few weeks Jesus talked about the church again (Matt. 18: 17). The binding and loosing power - that is, the pronouncement of forgiveness of sins - was later extended to all the Apostles (John 20:23) and after that to all the churches.

All three Synoptics carefully specify that on this very day when so much joy came to the Savior from their clear, loyal expression, He made the sad announcement that 'he must go unto Jerusalem, and suffer many things of the elders and chief priests and scribes, and be killed, and the third day be raised up' (Matt. 16:21 ASV; *cf.* Mark 8:31; Luke 19:21, 22). He had intimated as much several times before. But even now the Apostles neither understood nor accepted it. They never did until the contest was all over. Peter even tried to talk Him out of it and got the most severe rebuke the Lord ever gave him for his thoughtless impulses (Mark 8:32, 33; Matt. 16:22, 23).

Jesus closed His discourses (Luke suggests that the incidents of Peter's confession and Peter's rebuke occurred on the same occasion [Luke 9:20-22], and the Synoptics all connect the latter with the matter now to follow) with a severe warning (Mark 8:38; Matt. 16:27; Luke 9:26) and an enigmatic promise: 'Verily I say unto you, There be some here of them that stand by, who shall in no wise taste of death, till they see the kingdom of God come with power' (Mark 9:1 ASV; cf. Matt. 16:28 and Luke 9:27).

A certain school of interpreters looks beyond the following context for an answer. They believe in no future *mani*fest kingdom of God on earth (no millennium). Hence the prophecy was fulfilled on earth in the church, a wholly spiritual kingdom. Others see the church as indeed the present form of the reign of God in Christ on earth yet look for a visible manifestation of God's sovereign rule on earth after the second advent. The latter group of interpreters think the prophecy was fulfilled in the transfiguration.

We judge that however men choose to regard the idea of a future visible reign of Christ, there is a clear grammatical connection of Jesus' promise with the transfiguration narrative. This is true of all three accounts. Furthermore, the promise is that 'some' (only three, not all twelve), standing there were to 'see the kingdom of God come with power' (Mark 9:1 ASV). Then the accounts continue, 'and after six days' (Mark), 'and after six days' (Matthew), 'and... about eight days [Luke counts the termini] after these sayings... he took with Him Peter and John and James...' (ASV). Let the reader judge if the connection is not close to unmistakable between the promise and fulfillment in the transfiguration.

There on the mountain the incarnate Christ, in His future glory (not the pre-incarnate Logos), was seen with glorified men (Moses and Elijah), while worshipful men in the flesh 'saw the Son of man coming in his kingdom' 'with power' (Mark 9:2-8; Matt. 17:1-8; Luke 9:28-36), and we judge that it is precisely what Jesus was talking about when he said some standing there would 'see the kingdom of God come with power.'

There is another side to the incident. The close of the earthly lives of Moses and Elijah and their departures for heaven were both very unusual. Of Moses it is said, 'and he [the Lord] buried him... but no man knoweth of his sepulchre' (Deut. 34:6 ASV); and of Elijah, he 'went up by a whirlwind into heaven' (II Kings 2:11 ASV). The former stood for Law, the latter for Prophecy. Both spoke with Him of His coming 'exodus'[17] – passion, death, resurrection, ascension – indicating that in Christ's career the Law and the Prophets find their fulfillment. Hence there is a pedagogical purpose for us all in this part of the career of Jesus. We ought to think of it in connection with Peter's later reference (II Peter 1:19, 20) to it and his statement of how even the angels and ancient prophets were interested in how Christ would fulfill the Old Testament histories and predictions (I Peter 1:9-12).

---

17 Greek for 'decease' is *exodus*, 'way out.'

There are two other clear purposes of the transfiguration event. Moses and Elijah understood divine purposes in the death of Jesus, even if no other men on earth did. In terrible need of human comfort and the solace of sympathetic conversation in His 'hour of darkness,' the Father graciously dispatched Moses and Elijah to fill the need. Further, the inner circle of the Apostles, especially Peter, needed to appreciate the death of the Redeemer from heaven's standpoint rather than Satan's.

Yet, in spite of the glimpse of heaven, Peter blundered again (Matt. 16:22, 23). He wanted to stay right there and build three memorials and – his tongue engaged before his mind was in gear – said so out loud. Then the cloud of the divine presence overshadowed them. God's voice addressed them: 'This is my beloved Son. *Listen* to him!' How much they needed really to listen in this brief season of special experience and sequestered instruction!

Shortly after the transfiguration, the party of four walked down the mountain. We may imagine Christ as breaking a profound silence, saying, 'Tell the vision to no man, until the Son of man be risen from the dead.' After that they could share it, but meanwhile it would be for their own comfort and strength. Yet the three disciples missed the point. As they lagged behind their preoccupied Master, they asked one another what the rising from the dead might mean, perhaps wondering if He were referring to the 'last day.' And, relapsing into confusion, they got up nerve to ask about the advent of Elijah but not about the question topmost in their minds (Mark 9:10-13).

Meanwhile at the foot of the mountain, the scribes had discovered the band of nine apostles and were badgering them in the presence of a crowd. Jesus then performed a healing no more remarkable than many others of His, rescuing the nine from the jeering scribes and teaching a lesson in prayer and dependence on God - 'Without me you can do nothing' (Mark 9:14-29; Matt. 17:14-20; Luke 9:37-43).

They then headed back for Capernaum. Along the way Jesus spoke to them all of His coming passion, death, and resurrection; but they simply were unable to understand (Matt. 9:30, 32; 17:22, 23; Luke 9:43-45). Only months later, after the crucifixion and on Easter evening, were they able.

LAST EFFORTS IN GALILEE

Matt. Once again in Capernaum, a bit of interesting minor disturbance of
17:24-
18:35 their peace came from a different quarter – the collector of the annual
Mark poll tax for support of the temple, who evidently called at Peter's house
9:33-50
Luke where the Lord was now known to be lodging. Significantly, only Matthew
9:46-62 the collector of Roman taxes, reports this dunning of Jesus for a Jewish
tax (Matt. 17:24-27). This tax of half a shekel, authorized by Moses
(Exod. 30:13; cf. II King 12:2; II Chron. 24:6-9; Neh. 10:32), "was to be
paid every year for the service of the sanctuary... by every male who had
attained the age of twenty... and as we learn from the Mishnah[18] ... was
levied in the month Adar [March]."[19] Why Jesus had not, by late August,
paid the tax is to be accounted for by His being out of the city of
Capernaum, evidently His legal residence, when six months before, the
local collectors had set up their booths for a day. Now they meant to nail
Him. The careful reader will perceive what must surely have been Jesus'
amusement at Peter's quick answer to the collector, before he really
knew for sure what the Lord had done about the tax. When Jesus answered
Peter's never-voiced question by sending him out to get the coin from a
fish's mouth, it was surely meant as a little joke on Peter to help him
stop blurting out nonsense words before his mind was engaged to his
tongue. We may nevertheless be sure that Jesus greatly appreciated his
impulsive Apostle's instant loyalty.

In the following fortnight or so, before they departed from Galilee,
two more minor but important (for the lessons taught) incidents occurred.
In one the Apostles received a much-needed lesson in the importance of
childlike humility (Matt. 18:1-5; Mark 9:33-37; Luke 9:46-48), and in the
other John got a severe rebuke to his developing (and surprising, in this
gentle youth) sectarian zeal (Mark 9:39-50; Matt. 18:6-8; Luke 9:49,
50).

Perhaps the bit of teaching from this quiet period that is most
meaningful to us today is the formula for settling one class of disputes
among members of a local church (Matt. 18:15-35). Students of the growth
of doctrines in the New Testament are grateful for the first two references
to the church in the New Testament, both coming from this period of
retirement and special instruction of the Twelve, and reported only by
Matthew. The former (Matt. 16:18) contains the promise of the church

---

18 Shekalim 1.3.
19 EHL, p. 229.

universal, and the latter (Matt. 18:17) a procedure of discipline in the church local.

One gains the impression from reading this part of the Gospels, especially Luke (9:57-62), that Jesus is fully aware, even if the Twelve are not, of the growing power of darkness about to envelop them all and to kill Him; that as He now sets out for the feast of Tabernacles, He will not have even a certain roof (Luke 9:58) or a pillow for His head to sleep. The disciples who look back disqualify themselves for the kingdom of God (Luke 9:62). As He steadfastly set His face to go to Jerusalem (Luke 9:51) to die, He must have felt that He too, now having put His hand to the plough, must never look back. The purpose of Christ, formed in eternity, enforced and rendered explicit at the baptism and through the temptation, would be sorely tested, but He would not fail nor be discouraged till He had set righteousness in the earth (Isa. 42:4).

CHAPTER 8

Training the Twelve and Preaching: The Last Six Months (In Judaea and Trans-Jordan)

For this part of Jesus' career, it is necessary to piece together all four Gospels, for not one of them provides a continuous narrative. The chronological framework seems to be a series of three forays to Jerusalem or its environs (Bethany), with various ministries between and afterward. This is all before the fourth (and final) trip at the time of the Passover when our Lord was crucified.

TRAVELING TO JERUSALEM

It seems that Luke (who wrote long before John did) was opening three spaces in his narrative in which to place the materials from John; for three times in the narrative, he speaks of Jesus at that time as making a journey to Jerusalem, though only after the last does he carry the narrative immediately on to Jerusalem.[1] Luke is thinking of all of this part of Jesus'

---

1 'According to John's chronology, Jesus was in Jerusalem at the Feast of Tabernacles (7:2), at the Feast of Dedication (10:22), and at the Passover (12:1). Just after the Feast of Dedication we find him abiding beyond Jordan, where John had baptized (10:40). From this point he comes to Bethany near Jerusalem at the raising of Lazarus (11:17), whence he withdraws to a little town called Ephraim in the hills north of Jerusalem (11:54). Here he abides a while with his disciples away from his enemies till he goes to the Passover. Such is John's outline of these last six months of the Saviour's life.' RHG, p. 276.

life as a movement on to when the Son of man should be 'glorified,' lifted up on a cross, at Jerusalem, for it is not possible, Jesus Himself says with telling irony in this section, that a prophet perish outside of Jerusalem.

The first of Luke's openings for John's narrative of a trip to Jerusalem, which appears after Jesus and the three disciples had returned from the transfiguration to Capernaum (Mark 9:2, 33; 10:1; cf. Luke 9:28, 29, 51), reads: 'And it came to pass, when the days were well-nigh come that he should be received up, he steadfastly set his face to go to Jerusalem.' Immediately Luke's text finds them moving south. At this point we should insert John's story of Jesus' journey (about the first of October) to arrive late at the feast of Tabernacles. This Jerusalem ministry of John 7:14a-10:21 was during the last days of the feast and as He lingered on a few days afterward.

A second reference by Luke to a trip to Jerusalem by Jesus and His disciples reads: 'And he went on his way through cities and villages, teaching and journeying on unto Jerusalem' (Luke 13:22). If Luke's and John's narratives complement one another, then at this place Luke might be accounting for our Lord's presence there and ministry at Jerusalem at the time of the feast of Dedication (in late December) set forth in John 10:22-39. If so, then there is no extended reference to a Peraean ministry in Luke 13:22-17:10 but these chapters belong to the late Judaean ministry. It seems better therefore to relate Luke 13:22 to the journey to Bethany near Jerusalem for the raising of Lazarus, and to suppose that He had been in Judaea before the feast of Dedication and had returned to Jerusalem without any mention of the trip. After this we know He returned to Trans-Jordan (John 10:39-41).

So, though we find no reference to it anywhere else, Jesus journeyed from Trans-Jordan to Bethany, a town less than two miles from Jerusalem, for the raising of Lazarus (John 11:1-53), but quickly retired to a town of northern Judaea called Ephraim (John 11:54). He must have remained there through January and much of February, on spiritual retreat with His own.

At this point Luke, for the third time, mentions a journey to Jerusalem

---

In favor of combining Luke's narrative with that of John, A. T. Robertson wrote: 'John gives us three journeys, - the Feast of Tabernacles (John 7:2ff.), the journey to Bethany at the raising of Lazarus (John 11:17f.), the final Passover (John 12:1). Luke likewise three times in this section speaks of Jesus going to Jerusalem, 9:51; 13:22; 17:11. Hence it would seem possible, even probable, that their journeys corresponded. If so, then John 7:2-11:54 is to be taken as parallel to Luke 9:51-18:14. This plan is followed by various modern scholars.' ibid., p. 278.

from a point near both Galilee and Samaria (to which John's mention of Ephraim neatly fits): 'And it came to pass, as they were on their way to Jerusalem, that He was passing through the midst of Samaria and Galilee' (Luke 17:11 ASV marg.). Soon after this, Mark and Matthew again furnish parallel accounts (Mark 10:1; Matt. 19:1) to Luke's, though John does not until the arrival at Bethany (John 12:12).

Each time He entered or approached Jerusalem during this period, He aroused fierce opposition, at least two efforts being made to stone Him (John 8:59; 10:31). Always He retired to minister in the countryside of Judaea or in the Trans-Jordan.

The above is, I judge, the most commonly accepted opinion regarding the framework of the Gospel reports of the last six or six-and-a-half-months of our Lord's ministry. I think the more one reverently reads the narratives, the more amply justified it seems to be.[2]

IN JERUSALEM AT THE FEAST OF TABERNACLES

This brief episode opens with both His friends and His enemies in a tizzy of excitement at Jerusalem over the possibility that He might come to the feast of Tabernacles (John 7:11, 12). That amazing year in Galilee had made His name a household word from one end of the country to the other. He had not attended a single feast for at least one-and-a-half-years, counting it better to improve His time up in the north without unnecessary controversy. Now, somehow the word had got around that He might come. Perhaps the words 'not... yet' are indeed the true text of John 7:8, and His brothers, discerning a purpose to arrive late, had planted the idea; or He may have traveled slowly; and Galileans moving past His party had spread the word.

John 7:1-10:21

A year before, the Galileans had all been for Him. Now opinion is divided. 'The Jews' – i.e., the patrician leadership[3] – are uniformly and strongly against Him (John 5:15, 16; cf. Matt. 12:14; Mark 9:6; Luke 6:11), the Sanhedrin two years earlier pledged to kill Him. As a result the plebian multitudes speak nothing openly for or against Him, being afraid to open their mouths. But among themselves some whisper, 'Even if He is not the Messiah, He is a good man.' Others denounce Him as a demagogue (John 7:12, 13).

---

2 SGG, pp. 500, 501; RHG, pp. 276-79; John W. Shepard, *The Christ of the* Gospels: An *Exegetical Study* (Grand Rapids: Eerdmans, 1939), p. 343; and many others.

3. 'The Jews' in John is quite uniformly 'the unbelieving section of the nation especially the rulers, in contrast to the friendly multitude.' RHG, p. 49(n); cf. SDHF, p. 62(n).

Then suddenly in the midst of the week of Tabernacles, Jesus appeared in the outer court of the temple teaching the people. Not everyone recognized Him, but as the light began to dawn, men wondered in public how He managed to stay free and alive, for it was well known that the leaders wanted Him dead. No one seemed to be sure He was there, or if so, who He was or what He claimed for Himself (John 7:25-27). Meanwhile Jesus maintained His cause and preached His message. Something He said about His leaving the world made them wonder if He might be about to leave Palestine to spread His message personally in the Jewish Dispersion. The leaders were puzzled, now that most of them were hearing Him directly for the first time, that without benefit of learning (John 7:14, 15) – i.e., training in their theological academies – He spoke so well.

On the seventh day of the feast, the Sanhedrin authorized their police to take Him in custody (John 7:32). But next day, a now-traditional extra 'last day, the great day of the feast,' Jesus marvelously proclaimed the great events of redemption soon to come. This was the day when a priest brought water in a silver pitcher from the pool of Siloam for a beautiful ceremony in the temple. Jesus appropriately spoke of Himself as 'living water,' and in symbolical language He spoke of the pentecostal outpouring of the Holy Spirit. Such grandeur was too much for the police. To their superiors' discomfiture they returned without Him.

For several days after that, Jesus lingered – spending nights at the Mount of Olives and days teaching in the city (John 7:53). His audience was now the Jerusalem populace (John 8:21-59), for, the feast being over, the visitors had gone. After a particularly heated exchange – in the course of which Jesus charged both His fair-weather friends and outspoken enemies with being lustful children of the devil, and claimed that He Himself was Abraham's Lord and the eternal 'I Am' they attempted to stone Him. They would have done so except that He lost Himself in the crowd of listeners and got away (John 8:59). There was another now-familiar scrape with the Pharisees over healing a blind man on the Sabbath (John 9:1-41). There soon followed His great allegorical address on the shepherd, the sheep, and the one fold, intimating that shortly multitudes of non-Jews would be brought into God's fold (John 10:1-21). This, of course, greatly distracted many of His Jewish audience, and we are not surprised that they became fiercely divided over Him. Some thought Him a demoniacal, mad man (John 10:20), while others asked how a demoniac could heal blindness (John 10:21).

CAMPAIGNING IN JUDAEA OUTSIDE JERUSALEM

Again in the countryside, He chose seventy disciples other than the Luke 10:1 -13:21 Twelve, gave them instructions and powers similar to those previously granted the Twelve just before the third tour of Galilee, and sent them on as heralds into 'every city and place, whither he himself was about to come.' The number seventy may be seen as another symbolic prophecy of an impending extension of the kingdom of God to the Gentiles. Jesus came to be the Savior of the whole world, and gradually that universal mission was coming out. The Jews (and the Bible itself) to the present day employ numbers symbolically, and the Jews regarded mankind as composed of seventy nations, basing their reckoning on Genesis 10.

Luke's narrative indicates that Jesus waited, probably somewhere in Judaean countryside, for the return of the seventy before moving on Himself. If, as some think, the thirty-five pairs went only to thirty-five villages,[4] the wait was not long. Their return, reporting that even the devils were subject to them, led Jesus to prophesy the future, complete victory of His work over Satan (Luke 10:17-20). Their success and joy brought Him great joy in the Spirit (Luke 10:21-24).

The villages visited, first by thirty-five pairs of heralds and then by Jesus, are left unnamed. We know that in one of them a lawyer, bold enough to stand before the man who had put the Jerusalem doctors to flight, was thoroughly trounced in a discussion about eternal life and about 'who is my neighbor?' (Luke 10:25-37). During this time Jesus visited Bethany (unnamed) and was received into a home whose mistress was a woman named Martha and who had a sister named Mary (Luke 10:38-42). This is the first clear mention of any association with this home. Their brother, Lazarus, is not mentioned at this stage. During this epoch Jesus says many things which are similar to sayings earlier in Galilee (Luke 11:1-13; 12:1). Charges against Him, as that He is in league with Satan, and His responses, are likewise familiar ones (Luke 11:14-54; 13:10-21). Jesus found that generation similar to the generations of prophet-murderers of all generations past, only more consummately murderous (Luke 11:51, 52). We find Him now more pointedly condemning the Pharisees, calling them fools and accusing them of hypocrisy (Luke 11:37-54). His sermons also take an eschatological turn, often speaking of hell and especially of His (from our perspective) second advent, urging

---

4 E.g., CLC, pp. 110, 111.

spiritual preparedness and repentance (Luke 12:13-43; 13:1-9; cf. 16:19-31). He also alludes to a future time when His followers will be persecuted, not only by Jewish leaders, but by Gentile magistrates (Luke 12:49-53).

Jesus was clearly becoming more eager to have it all over (Luke 12:49-53). 'He longs to see the fire blaze, to receive His baptism of blood. One cannot wonder at this when he recalls what the Master has already undergone and how hopeless the task seems. So few understand... This outburst is not impatience, but it helps us catch a glimpse of the volcano of emotion locked in the Savior's heart.'[5]

BACK IN JERUSALEM AT THE FEAST OF DEDICATION

John 10:22-39 This visit was to be the last one before the end. The time was at about our Christmas time. To this day in our land in cities where there are concentrations of Jews, as the decorations go up, children at school ask, 'Christmas or Hanukkah?' The festival commemorates the rededication[6] of the second temple in the second century BC, after its desecration by Antiochus Epiphanes.[7]

One day Jesus quietly reappeared at Jerusalem in the portion of temple precincts known as Solomon's porch, thought to be a surviving part of the temple built by Solomon and destroyed by Nebuchadnezzar. The hostile rulers soon reappeared, too. Now they want to know if He claims to be Christ, the Messiah. 'Tell us plainly,' they demand. It was a legitimate demand. The idea had been floating around throughout His ministry, and He had never quite said 'I am Messiah' before a public meeting, even though many times He had used names of similar but more ambiguous meaning. Even now they do not get the word *messiah* out of Him. To have yielded the point might greatly have agitated the common people and precipitated the climax before the time. So as before, He pointed to His works, implying that they spoke plainly enough. Then He added the claims that He conferred eternal life and was one with the Father. Again we are not surprised that they charged Him with blasphemy. He answered by arguing *(ad hominem)* that their Law sometimes calls men, 'gods.'

---

5 RELJ, p. 127.

6 I Maccabees speaks of the *restoration of the altar,* but II Maccabees 10:5 of *cleansing of the sanctuary.* John 10 refers to the memorial festival as the *feast of Dedication,* borrowing language from I Maccabees 4:59 and numerous Old Testament references to various dedications of the sanctuary (Num. 7:10, 11, 84, 88; II Chron. 7:9; Neh. 12:27; Ezra 6:16, 17). The word *dedication (hanukkah) is* used by Jews today for the feast. Also, following Josephus, it may be called 'feast of lights.' *Antiquities* 12.7.7.

7 I Macc. 4:52-59; II Macc. 1:1-64, esp. v. 57.

The report ends with mention of another unsuccessful effort to take Him into custody. Jesus led a charmed life until the Father's time came for Him to die.

This was the end of His final campaign of ministry in the land of Judaea.

MINISTERING IN THE TRANS-JORDAN

Jesus did not stop in Judaea when He ended this last brief ministry in Jerusalem, but descended to the Jordan, crossed over to the east side and thence north to Bethany (Bethabara), where John had baptized Him about three years before (John 10:40-42). Here He received a fine reception, the local people being convinced that everything John had said of Him was true.

John 10:40 -42
Luke 13:22 -19:28
Mark 10:1-52
Matt. 19:1- 20:34

The ministry there and elsewhere in the Trans-Jordan must have lasted for several weeks. It ended when He left for Bethany on the occasion of Lazarus's death. Except for John 10:40-42, Luke alone provides any report of these weeks in the Trans-Jordan (Luke 13:22-17:10). Luke 13:22 introduces all of this material with a statement which suggests that all of it was spoken as He journeyed 'unto Jerusalem.' Perhaps Luke is thinking of all the period after Jesus' final departure from Galilee for Tabernacles as a journey to Jerusalem. It may, however, relate to the first stages of the journey to Bethany, near Jerusalem, for the raising of Lazarus.

Many things appearing in the discourses are, as in the case of the late Judaean ministry, reminiscent of the Galilean work.

We are not provided an extensive setting for the discourses,[8] parables, and miracles, as was provided in the story of the ministry in northern regions. Somewhere a man wanted to know if only a few were to be saved – a perennial question. Jesus told the listeners to be more concerned rather that they themselves were entering the narrow door (Luke 13: 23-30). He used the occasion again to predict the presence of unnumbered Gentiles with the Jewish patriarchs in the final kingdom of God, and the absence of many Jews.

Some Pharisees showed unaccounted-for concern lest, since He was back in Peraea (Trans-Jordan), part of Herod's dominions, Herod might try to kill Him (Luke 13:31-35) as he had the Baptist. Were they genuinely concerned? Were they stooges for Herod to get Jesus to move on? Or were they stooges for the Sanhedrin to get Him back in Judaea and hence

---

8 See excursus 10, pp. 189-92.

in their clutches? Who can say? At any rate, Jesus in effect dared them to report Him to Herod[9] He also affirmed that He would be at His work only a short time longer and would certainly finish it.

Jesus improved on His time of waiting for the climax at Jerusalem by teaching and warning. On a certain day a leading Pharisee invited Him home for a Sabbath-day breakfast (Luke 14:1-24). Jesus used the occasion to heal a dropsical man and appealed to the guests' own kindness to animals in similar distress (dropsy suggests being in a well of water) as ample justification for the Sabbath healing. He spoke a parable to the invited guests. It was about seeking chief seats at feasts. He addressed another to His host about the blessing of inviting the poor and unfortunate, and still another – to a guest – about who would enter the final kingdom of God. With the denouement drawing near, Jesus issued several pungent warnings about conditions and costs of discipleship (Luke 14:25-45).

At this point Luke introduces several of Jesus' choice parables (Luke 15:1-32). To correct the Pharisees' objection to His welcoming those whom they regarded as sinners, Jesus spoke the parables of the lost sheep, the lost coin, and (perhaps most-loved of all Jesus' parables) the lost, or prodigal, son. These were to the Pharisees. Then He taught stewardship to the disciples (Luke 16:1-13) – though not in private, for the Pharisees heard (Luke 16:14) – by the parable of the unjust steward. He also warned the Pharisees of the deceitfulness of money and condemned their loving money too much by the frightening story of the rich man who went to hell and the poor man who went to heaven (Luke 16:14-31) neither condemning riches nor praising poverty but showing the invincible necessity of righteous living and holy character. These parables are the most impressive for teaching true religion that mankind shall ever hear or read.

This portion of Luke's narrative ends with special lessons for the disciples on offending the weak, on forgiving their brethren, on faith and doing one's duty (Luke 17:1-10).

---

9 The sedate language of our English versions of the Lord's reply to 'concerned' Pharisees, 'It cannot be that a prophet perish out of Jerusalem,' followed by His lament over Jerusalem, obscures what is one of the funniest 'one-liners' in all literature. Here He was in a remote country district where the only Jerusalem-oriented people around were some 'creepy' characters who dogged His steps 'for kicks' and to gather evidence against Him. When they expressed concern that the king (Herod) of Galilee and Trans-Jordan (where they then were) might kill Him, Jesus answered, to put the sentence in our idiom, 'Oh, don't worry about my coming to a violent end here. I'm a prophet, you know, and Jewish prophets are supposed to be lynched in Jerusalem.'

RAISING LAZARUS IN BETHANY

The incident of the raising from the dead of Lazarus of Bethany and its John 11:1-53 peculiar aftermath belong wholly to John's Gospel. Jesus, who more than once saw special divine purposes in physical evils (John 9:3), declared that Lazarus's sickness was not for death but (in God's providence) 'for the glory of God, that the Son of God may be glorified thereby' (John 11:4 ASV). It is the only case in the entire gospel story where Jesus ever did anything deliberately to set up a situation whereby a miracle would create some special public impression (John 11:6ff.). Lazarus's resurrection was a deliberate challenge from Jesus' personal power and divine Sonship, thrown fiercely in the face of His now marvelously malevolent enemies, the Pharisee-Sadducee alliance in Jerusalem. This explains His seeming lack of sympathy with the faithful sisters who supposed that a simple notification of Lazarus's condition would bring Jesus swiftly to their aid (John 11:21, 32). It also explains what seemed to Thomas a reckless decision to return to the environs of Jerusalem. The charming simplicity and loving words of Martha and Mary, coupled with their rocklike faith, have made them examples to all men since. Martha's confession, much like Peter's, goes a small step further in verbal exactness ('I believe that thou art the Christ, the Son of God, which should come into the world'). It is a jewel of Christian expression (John 11:27). The combination of anger over stupid custom (the florid Jewish mourning John 11:33, grief over His own and the sisters' loss, and disappointment at the general lack of understanding brought our Lord to genuine tears of weeping, giving an insight to His humanity found nowhere else. On the other hand, the serene dignity of His own Lordship is on supreme display as He caused the stone to be removed and, in full confidence, commanded, 'Lazarus, come forth!'

The Jerusalem Jews responded quickly and monstrously (John 11:45-53). They did not rejoice that a prominent, pious neighbor had been restored to his loving family. They were simply exasperated that more people were now acknowledging Jesus' claims. A meeting of the Sanhedrin was convened to fashion some response in order to overthrow Jesus Himself since they could not overthrow His words and deeds. They expected to lose their place as leaders and their country as a nation, for they expected Jesus now to make a play for national political leadership after which the Romans would come and beat them all down by military force. Caiaphas, the high priest of the time, spoke more prophetically than he knew when he asserted that the death (by their hand) of Jesus was now necessary to save the nation, as the Fourth Gospel explains (John 11:49-52). Once more the Gospel writer foresees and calls attention to the worldwide significance of Jesus' life and redemptive work. The Sanhedrin now took official counsel how they might put Jesus to death (John 11:53).

RETREATING TO EPHRAIM

John 11:54 Galilee had finally decided that Jesus was not their Messiah, but no one there outside His hometown (Luke 4:28-30) had tried to kill Him. Jerusalem, however, had now twice tried to kill Him by stoning and was now pledged to kill Him.

Though not mentioned by name, the Sadducees, being dominant in the priestly leadership of the Sanhedrin, were now more committed to His destruction than the Pharisees, among whom He apparently still had some friends. So Jesus, while remaining in the province, betook Himself to 'a city called Ephraim,' said to be in countryside near the wilderness. Information later in the story indicates a place to the north. It must have been one of the numerous villages on the break of the Judaean plateau where it drops off toward the Ghor.[10] The area is rough, wild, and not largely inhabited. Anathoth, Bethel, and Ai, villages of Biblical story, and one called by today's Arabs *et Taiyibeh* are near this line. The last, *et Taiyibeh* – about fifteen miles from Jerusalem – is plainly visible, just a few miles to the north from the modern road which passes the site of ancient Bethel. It is thought by many qualified scholars, on what looks like sufficient evidence, to be the Ephraim of John 11:54.[11] 'It is a very secluded neighborhood... close to the wilderness [the barren gorges leading down to the Jordan Valley].'[12] The Samaritans (John 4) had shown themselves friendly (when He approached *from*, not *toward*, Jerusalem). Since their border was near, He may have chosen Ephraim in order to have a place of escape in case any probing Sanhedrin police should

---

10 Ghor is the name, in modern Arabic, for the low-lying plain of the Jordan Valley from the southern end of the Sea of Galilee to the northern end of the Dead Sea. Brush and trees grow in this area, as well as cultivated crops, grass, and flowers, in their season, toward the north, but toward the south it falls off to barren desert. Nearer the river itself is a 'badlands' area, but the actual narrow flood plain, 150 feet lower down, is called the *Zor*. This is a dense thicket of tropical woodland, still today the range of wild animals.

11 HDB, 1:728; KBA, p. 394.

12 KBA, p. 394.

come looking for Him. 'Moreover, Ephraim was nigh to the wilderness where at the outset of His ministry He had been tempted of the Devil; and it may be that during His sojourn there He would revisit the scene of His early conflict, fortifying Himself by remembrance of His triumph for the last dread ordeal.'[13] The devil would very much have liked for Jesus, even at this late moment, to have allowed him to make matters up with the Sanhedrin, a place where Satan's influence was great.

With the retirement of Jesus and His close followers to Ephraim for a kind of final spiritual retreat, the travels of Jesus, except for a last pilgrimage to death at Jerusalem, were at an end. Some conclusions on the travels and their meaning for the present are in order.

In the first place it must be acknowledged, much as we might wish it were otherwise, that we know the actual sites of very few of the events of His life. We know the geographical framework well enough – mountains, rivers, plains, Nazareth, Bethlehem, Capernaum, and a few other places – but almost nothing more. Most of the words and deeds of Jesus are not connected in the Gospels with any particular place, even though we generally are told what province of Palestine He was in at the time. When some town or other place is mentioned in a nearby paragraph, it is usually a mistake to connect the discourse or miracle under discussion with it. It is thought by many – and it sometimes appears in print – that Jesus was in Tyre or Sidon or Caesarea Philippi, but upon examination the cited texts usually only say He was in the 'parts' or neighborhood of those places. We know that He visited many villages in a land of villages. Once He sent seventy messengers on ahead to announce His coming to certain villages, but the names of all save about a dozen of the towns and villages He ever visited escapes us. We may be fairly sure only of Nazareth, Bethlehem, Jerusalem, Bethany near Jerusalem, Bethabara (Bethany beyond Jordan), Cana, Capernaum, Jacob's well (possibly also the neighboring town of Sychar), Bethsaida-Julias, Nain, Magadan (Magdala?), Ephraim, and apparently Emmaus. Further, inasmuch as Near Eastern people name parts of geographical eminences rather than the whole of them, there is doubt as to the precise location of things as, for example, in and about the Mount of Olives. Who can say just how much of the ridge with several peaks, lying to the east of Jerusalem, was known *then* as the mount of Olives? The mountain, like the valley which runs between it and the eastern side of Jerusalem, is even today known by segments. The upper part of this valley, north and east of Jerusalem, is

---

13 SDHF, p. 377.

Wadi Joz (Valley of Walnuts), to the east is *Wadi Sit Miryam* (Valley of Lady Mary), and to the southeast is *Wadi Nahr* (Valley of Fire). This is not the way we in America, at least, usually assign names, but it will be a mistake to think the ancient Jews followed our custom. Palestine is, therefore, at present, hardly the place to go if one wants to be absolutely sure of following very many of 'the footsteps of Jesus.'

We have anticipated another conclusion several times: Jesus moved only in the stream of Jewish life in Palestine. He largely ignored the Hellenistic (Greek) and Roman populace. His itineraries show it, as does also His ministry. There were many centers of Hellenistic culture in Palestine and several Herodian and Roman capitals, but we have no record that Jesus ever visited even one of them except on His way somewhere else. Sepphoris and Tiberias (Hellenistic cities of Galilee) were not far from Nazareth and Capernaum, but Jesus avoided them. Current journals of archaeology report and illustrate a thriving Gentile culture at Sepphoris, but Jewish participation in that culture at that place occurred much later where it became a leading centre of Jewish scholarship.[14] When He visited the vicinity of cities of Phoenicia and of the Decapolis, He stayed out of those cities. He was there for rural retirement, to get away for awhile from the quarrelsome and curious crowds of the Jewish centers. It is a mistake to think of Jesus as a cosmopolitan person. 'Had the writers of the Gospels, who were providing writings intended in part at least to appeal to Gentiles, been able to tell that Jesus ministered freely to Gentiles in Galilee and elsewhere, they would certainly have done so. The conclusion is clear. The ministry of Jesus was deliberately limited to Jews, and was confined almost entirely to centers free from Gentile influence. There is no trace of a planned effort to reach the Gentiles who were all about Him. The mission to Gentiles has its roots in the teaching and miracles of Jesus [and in His work of redemption] but its actual inauguration waited until the Apostolic age.'[15]

These facts lead on to another important conclusion. The story of our Lord's redemptive mission and career is indeed found only in the Gospels, but the meaning of it, just as He Himself said on that last, sad night with the Eleven (Judas had left), is interpreted for us mainly in the epistolary portions of the New Testament. Said He: 'I have yet many things to say unto you, but ye cannot bear them now. Howbeit when he, the Spirit of truth, is come... he shall receive of mine, and shall shew it unto you...' (John 16:12-14).

---

14 See BA 60.1, Mar., '97, p54
15 WFHAB, p. 94.

Excursus 10 – The Chronology of Jesus' Last Six Months:
Harmonizing the Four Accounts

The student of the life of Christ will find considerable variation among the scholars in their manner of understanding the arrangement of the materials in the Gospels now before us. Mark (10:1) and Matthew (19:1) are almost completely silent, reporting scarcely more than the departure from Galilee and the initial extended ministry down in Judaea. Luke's narrative starts with Galilee and ends with the final journey from Jericho to Jerusalem, mentioning many events but no intervening arrivals at Jerusalem. All of John 7-11 falls in this period. In fact John mentions at least three journeys to Jerusalem during the last six months and another journey, between the second and third, to Bethany (raising Lazarus). Luke devotes about nine chapters (9:51–18:34) to this period, filling in what Mark and Matthew omit but scarcely at all duplicating John. It is not hard to accept as fact that Luke deliberately set out to supplement Mark and Matthew, while John at a much later date, from his own eyewitness knowledge of events in and near Jerusalem in the period, determined to supplement all three. Samuel J. Andrews[16] put John 7:2–10:21 back in an earlier period between the healing of the blind man of Bethsaida and Peter's confession at Caesarea Philippi. A recent writer,[17] having surveyed the problem, rather gives up on an effort at harmonizing the materials except in a very general way and follows a recitation more topical than chronological for this period. Others[18] attempt to put it all in harmony - and, I judge, with considerable success. Those who grant that there are many incidents and teachings of the ministry in Galilee, now closed, which are similar to those now reported as occurring in Judaea or Trans-Jordan are more disposed to feel a harmony can be successfully constructed. A. T. Robertson observed that any traveling religious teacher meets similar questions in similar situations, giving similar answers in different places.[19] This principle results in a 'harmony' such as Robertson's, which accepts Luke's narrative as truly consecutive, as Luke seems to claim, and which weaves in the material from John 7-11, rather than a very arbitrary, subjectively arranged one such as that of Ernest D. Burton and Edgar J. Goodspeed.[20] There will be disagreement on some details.

16 ALOL, pp. xxiv, xxv.
17 GSLC, pp. 103-48.
18 RHFG, pp. 74-95; RHG, pp. 95-125; CLC, pp. 109-38; RHS, pp. 114-50.
19 RHG, pp. 124, 125.
20 BGHSG, pp. 103-224.

For example, Andrews and Robertson, who worked on similar principles, disagreed as to where the visit of Jesus to the feast of Tabernacles (John 7:1-10:21) belongs. Otherwise their principles lead to nearly identical results for this section of the life of Jesus.

Without going further into technical matters, we shall accept the arrangement of Robertson's *Harmony*. It is essentially the same as others just cited and is at least a feasible framework on which to discuss this last great epoch of His ministry. This allows us to consider Luke's narrative from 9:51 to 18:15 (after which Mark and Luke again are usually parallel) to be, as Luke claims for his Gospel in general, in approximate consecutive order; we need not consider it a mixed collection of material from the whole period of Jesus' ministry.

Excursus II – Local Human Culture in Jesus' Discourses

The largest single block of Jesus' teaching reported anywhere in the Gospels is in Luke 9:51-19:27. This belongs chronologically in the last six months. Most of this time was spent in Trans-Jordan (Peraea), though Luke's report is singularly free of geographical and chronological details. He is plainly interested in giving his readers extensive knowledge of typical and significant examples of Jesus' teaching.

Here as nowhere else we meet the human mind of Jesus, as well as the ancient, Palestinian, Jewish world in which His thoughts moved. These chapters furnish likewise the cultural patterns of the people, even for the casual reader.

They also show how fully Jesus was a part of that particular local culture. When the woman at the well exclaimed 'How is it that thou being a Jew?', she too was thinking and speaking out of a very localized culture. She saw Him as the Gospels reveal Him and as we must see Him, not as a great cosmopolitan character, but as a Palestinian Jew. In fact, His culture may be described as that of a rural Galilean Jew.

It is precisely because of this that His teachings are timeless. They are truly set in a single culture. The authors of the Gospels do not try to make of Jesus a sophisticated, urbane man of universal culture. There really can be no such person. Each of us also is a creature of a local culture. To the degree we are not, we tend to be disoriented and even deracinated. By incarnation He became *man*, yet to do so He had to become a *man*. It is as such that He is the cosmic Christ, Savior of the world.

Across the distance of two millennia and the barriers between ancient Oriental and modern Western culture, to say nothing of the distance between twentieth-century urban life and ancient rural village life, the themes plainly come through.

From this block of Jesus' teaching, I have arranged in tabular form (see table 4) some of the items which one meets there. They fall into six categories: places, persons, cultural items, natural history, customs, and ideas. The places mentioned are all local; the persons are mainly Biblical or contemporaries of Jesus. The ideas are distinctive to people who grew up in the atmosphere of the Old Testament. (The wordings and spellings in table 4 are in the main drawn from the KJV.)

Table 4. Local culture in Jesus' teaching

Cultural Items		Natural History	Customs	Persons
Flocks	piece of ground	foxes, dens	journeying	Elias
prophets	yoke of oxen	birds, nests	putting children to bed	Mary
kings	streets, lane	lambs, wolves	arming oneself	Martha
lawyers	highways, hedges	serpents, scorpions	plowing	Beelzebub
neighbours	disciple	babes	two men sleeping in bed	Abel
priests	parable	lilies	grinding together	Zacharias
Levites	salt	grass	begging	Pilate
oil	savor (noun)	egg (hen's)	trading	Herod (called a fox)
wine	Scribes	ravens	kissing	Zacchaeus
beast	sinner	sparrows	marrying a wife	Lazarus
raiment	piece of silver	hairs	inheriting	rich man (Dives)
Samaritan	two sons	ground	spinning	Noah
twopence	portion of goods	cloud	eating	Lot
three loaves	living (money)	shower	drinking	
ovens	journey	south wind	burying a father	Places
bags	riotous living	heat (weather)	bidding farewell	
flesh (to eat)	hired servant	sky	praying	Jerusalem
pharisee	robe	fig tree	sweeping, garnishing	village of Samaritans
seats in synagogue	fatted calf	vineyard	sucking the paps	another village
synagogues	music, dancing	ox	girding the loins	Chorazin
markets	rich man	grain of mustard seed	waiting for lord	Capernaum
burning lights	steward	gardens	knocking (for entrance)	Jericho
cup	debtor	hen	standing watch	Bethphage
platter	nobleman	brood	being drunken	Bethany
graves	far country	wings	receiving stripes	Mount of Olives
magistrate	kingdom	ass	taking the lowest room	Samaria
judge	hundred measures	sheep	making a great supper	Galilee

168

				Ideas
palace	unrighteous mammon	famine	bidding to supper	finer of God
goods	beggar	swine	carrying on the shoulder	seventy
thieves	sores	husks	putting away a wife	seven spirits
enemy	purple	oil (olive)	being buried	fire (as judgment)
purse	bank	wheat	feeding cattle	baptism (as experience)
script	usury	crumbs	eating supper	written in heaven
shoes	millstone	dogs	selling	written in the law
house	housetop	sea	planting	hypocrisy
candle	field	little ones (infants)	building	spirit of infirmity
bushel	judge	sycamine tree	putting an ox in a stall	east, west, north, south
leaven	widow	lepers	smiting the breast	dropsy
farthings	publican	lightning	writing fifty	three measures
barns	needle's eye	camel	writing eighty	
storehouses	citizens	sycamore tree		
adversary	napkin	colt		
officer	laborers			
prison	harvest			
sacrifices	sepulchres			
vinedresser	wedding			
Sabbath	menservants			
synagogue ruler	maidservants			
gate	rich neighbour			
meal	daughter-in-law			
pit	lame			
feast	blind			
poor	maimed			

Part 3

'I am leaving the world'

CHAPTER 9

His Last Journey to Jerusalem

THE JOURNEY TO JERICHO

John's narrative suggests that Jesus did not break off the retreat at Ephraim until 'the passover of the Jews was at hand' (John 11:55 ASV). Shortly after this in his narrative, John lets us know that Jesus arrived at Bethany, Lazarus's hometown, only 'six days before the passover' (John 12:1). But John tells nothing of the lengthy circuitous route He walked as a Passover pilgrim with the Twelve.

John 11:45-54

Luke 17:11-19:28

Mark 10:1-52

Matt. 19:1-20:34

This part of the Gospel narrative, at first carried only by Luke (17:11-18:14), then briefly only by Mark (10:1-12) and Matthew (19:1-12), after that most of the way by all three Synoptics, is finally carried by all four Gospels (Mark 10:18-11:11; Matt. 19:13-21:11, 14-17; Luke 18:15-19:44; John 12:12-19). The narrative is sparse at first, devoted mainly to Jesus' sermons to the disciples and the gathering crowds. Then the story picks up speed, and we are brought quickly to Bethany on Friday evening and on Sunday to the temple in the city.

At first the apostolic band and their Lord walked northward 'through the midst of Samaria [since the fact that He was moving from south to north Samaria is mentioned first] and Galilee' (Luke 17:11). Only a slight penetration of Galilee would have brought them into conjunction with the large pilgrim caravans of Galileans, who, like themselves, were going up to the Passover. His previous entrances to the city had all been private. This time, as His brothers had suggested a good while before, He would go as a King attended by His own entourage (John 7:1-6).

A strange atmosphere of expectancy prevailed, both in Jerusalem and among the pilgrims. Will He come? What do you think? the early arrivals were asking as they mingled at the temple (John 11:55, 56). Even the Pharisees, as they travelled together with Him, sensed something unusual in the offing, asking Him when the kingdom of God should come (Luke 17:20, 21). To them Jesus responded, 'The kingdom of God is *among you* and will not be observed by searching.' This surely refers to the presence of the King Himself who had long since brought the kingdom in His person, for there is no way whereby the kingdom could be 'within you,' that is, in the hearts of the legalistic Pharisees. The King they sought stood before them! In Him was the promised kingdom.

At this time Jesus spoke much of His second advent and of conditions to prevail at that future season (Luke 17:22-37), anticipating many remarks to be made again a week or so later in His Olivet discourse. Still on an eschatological theme, He spoke a parable about faith, the vindication of His believing people at His coming (Luke 18:1-8), and final justification. He employed a parable about a ridiculously pompous Pharisee who thought a recital of his own supposed virtues a sufficient ticket to heaven and of a truly contrite publican who knew he must trust the redemptive grace of God alone (Luke 18:9-14). The former is made to appear truly ridiculous and despicable while the latter is seen to be truly justified, fully in possession of evangelical righteousness.

As they hiked together down the east bank of Jordan, Jesus delivered Himself on the subject of divorce (Mark 10:1-12; Matt. 19:1-12), a matter on which the rabbis were divided. He showed how far short the prevalent Jewish standards, allowing a sort of temporary companionate marriage even for respected rabbis, fell from the original divine standard and the now-forming Christian idea of marriage.

During a pause He even found time to teach a new Christian standard for the love and care of little children (Mark 10:13-16; Matt. 19:13-15; Luke 18:15-17). Children never found their rightful place in the care and affection of men until Jesus taught it. The short discourse on children marks the point where all three Synoptics become generally closely parallel and remain that until the end of the story of Christ's earthly career.

Let us treat somewhat more at length one incident with accompanying discourse. One morning, as their journey resumed, a rich ruler of the Jews, a young man to whom Jesus was immediately drawn in affection (Mark 10:17-31; Matt. 19:16-30; Luke 18:18-30), very respectfully addressed the Lord: 'What shall I do that I may inherit eternal life?' It turned out that the young man, while sincere, was still putting treasure on earth ahead of riches in glory. Attention to details of the conversation of Jesus with the young man and, shortly after, with the disciples, helps us to understand what Jesus and others of the time – quite aside from visible establishment of Messiah's reign on earth – thought the kingdom of God to be. The young ruler first asked about *eternal life* (Matt. 19:16). Jesus then referred to the same as entering into *life* (Matt. 19:17). Later Jesus spoke to the man of the same, or some aspect of it, as having treasure in *heaven* (Matt. 19:21); and then to the disciples, as entering into the *kingdom of heaven* (Matt. 19:23); and again to the disciples, as entering into the *kingdom of God* (Matt. 19:24). The disciples understood this as being *saved* (Matt. 19:25), and Jesus finally referred to the same as *inheriting* (Matt. 19:29) eternal life, but in the same connection Jesus connected all of these with a time when earth would have a *regeneration* (Matt. 19:28), when the *Son of man* would sit on the *throne* of His *glory* (Matt. 19:28, 29) and His disciples would likewise *judge* (or reign). These ideas have a common core, and he who throws some out to favor only one or two does not understand Jesus' message of the kingdom. We regret that the young man left sorrowful (Matt. 20:1-16), but we may hope he later believed. Jesus closed the episode with a striking parable about how God rewards His servants faithfully, yet sovereignly, not affected by human ideas which sometimes confuse the *just* with the *equal*. God is a great King, not an egalitarian democrat!

The movement quickens. He now a third time (after a first at Caesarea Philippi [Mark 8:31-33] and a second as the four descended the mount of transfiguration [Mark 10:30-32]) informed the disciples clearly about His passion, death, and resurrection (Matt. 20:17-19) now immediately to come at Jerusalem; but they were dull, 'and they understood none of these things: and this saying was hid from them...' (Luke 18:31-34). Man's soul is sluggish about the genuinely spiritual. God must enlighten him and, of course, in this case not only did the disciples need to grow some more but prediction had to become history. How little they understood is disclosed by the request which James and John then made through Salome, their mother (Mark 10:34, 35; Matt. 20:20-25), for a special place in the kingdom[1] they expected to

---

1 'Let us suppose,' said John Chrysostom, 'that there is an umpire, and a good many athletes enter the lists. Two of the athletes, who are very intimate with the umpire, approach him and say: "Cause

unfold upon the mountain tops of Judah in a few days. They moved through Herod's Jericho, though not so fast that two blind men could not be healed and that the benighted publican Zacchaeus could not be saved and blessed by Jesus as his overnight guest (Mark 10:46-52; Matt. 20:29-34; Luke 18: 35-19:10). (See excursus 12, pp. 187, 188, on the apparent discrepancies in the Gospels' accounts of the events at Jericho.)

Sometime during that last overnight (a Thursday night), still a few miles and a hard climb from Jerusalem, Jesus proceeded to speak a parable about stewardship of God's gifts and patient waiting (Luke 19:11-28). The disciples needed correction of one of their ideas about the kingdom of God on earth. They were not necessarily wrong to expect it but certainly wrong to have 'supposed that the kingdom of God was immediately to appear' (Luke 19:11 ASV). Again He spoke of a second advent after a long time in the far country of heaven.

This was essentially the end of the pilgrimage of Jesus and His friends. On the morrow, a Friday, the malice of Jerusalem reached out and drew Him up the ancient Ascent of Blood[2] and set Him down to await at Bethany, over the Sabbath, the baptism of fire and blood to follow.

---

us to be crowned and proclaimed victors," on the strength of the good-will and friendship between them. But he says to them: "This is not mine to give, but it is for them for whom it has been prepared by their efforts and sweat."' Quoted in SDHF, p. 380.

Jesus' rebuke sank in. Decades later John wrote, as from the mouth of the ascended Christ: 'He that overcometh - I will give him to sit with me on my throne, as I overcame and sat down with my Father in his throne' (Rev. 3:12, my translation; cf. II Tim. 2:12).

2 This is the ancient and modern name of the route of the road up to Jerusalem from Jericho. 'The valley... coming up from Jericho is the valley of Adummim, or [in English] the Ascent of Blood (Josh. 15:7; 18:17), the name by which it is still known today. It is so called because of the patches of red ocher exposed along its course, which can be clearly seen near the present Inn of the Good Samaritan.' BGB, p. 165.

The road followed by Jesus did not even approximately follow the route of the present asphalt highway, except for five miles or so in the central portion. The ancient and modern routes converge on the steep slopes about midway at the inn – in recent times a police check-point. (The red patches can clearly be seen here.) The ancient road began at New Testament Jericho – completely avoided by the present highway and for its entire length followed a generally direct line toward the north wall of Jerusalem. It passed to the north of the summit of the mount of Olives, not approaching Bethany. So when Jesus and His party got to a point a mile or so north of Bethany, they left the road to follow a path to the home in Bethany of His friends Lazarus, Martha, and Mary. The route taken from Bethany to Jerusalem on Palm Sunday was not the road from Jericho, even though that is often assumed by visitors to the Holy Land today. John Wilkinson, 'The Way from Jerusalem to Jericho,' BA 38 (1975): 10-24.

In Old Testament times one would have taken a day to pass from the oasis of Jericho (Elisha's Spring) at about 1,000 feet below sea level, through barren desert where rainfall is less than six inches per annum, to the caravanserai at midpoint where rainfall is about ten inches per annum and a few shrubs grow. The second day (we assume here that Jesus and the Twelve took only one day) one would have

A QUIET WEEKEND AT BETHANY

Late in the afternoon Jesus and the caravan topped the first summit of the Mount of Olives at Bethany.[3] The crowds passed on to whatever lodgings they had, but Jesus and the Twelve stopped in the village, their hostess being Martha with her brother Lazarus and sister Mary, dear friends of some months at least. Their view of Jerusalem was hid by the south shoulder of the mount, and likewise were they veiled from the malign view of that city now committed to kill Him (John 11:53) and thereby to seal its own doom. But Jerusalem, for days in a state of excitement of fear and hope that He would come, knew where He was.

Luke 19:28
John 12:1
12:9-11

John takes note of two responses, one positive and one negative. Jesus was now a common man's celebrity (John 11:48, 56). The people knew, however, of the Sanhedrin's purpose to arrest Him (John 11:57). Perhaps notices had been posted even in Bethany. With the general feeling of near riotous excitement about what He might do, the Galileans, present in large numbers, some of them still fair-weather disciples of a year before in that province, were recovering their admiration for Him and hopefully expecting to join a march in strength to inaugurate Messiah's kingdom, with Jesus of Nazareth as Messiah. There was another popular drawing card in Bethany – Lazarus, Jesus' host. Lazarus had been restored to life by Jesus after four days in the grave, not many weeks before.

---

ascended to a height of about 2,500 feet at the mount of Olives where rainfall begins to approach twenty-five inches per annum-about the same as at Berlin and London. Forests grew there in ancient times, remnants of which remained until the beginning of the modern era. See BGB, pp. 165-67. 3 There are four summits to the ridge that lies east and northeast of Jerusalem. Writers sometimes refer to them all as part of the mount of Olives. Each of these, however, has its own name, and the native people of the district do not think of them as one. 'Today the name et Tur, "the Mount [of Olives]," applies exclusively to... the height which is opposite the Temple and to the slope stretching down from it to the Kidron Valley... There is every reason to believe that this continues ancient Hebrew usage.' KBA, p. 396.

This mount, especially the summit and parts facing Jerusalem, was crowded with churches and other buildings in Byzantine times (fourth to seventh centuries). Even now the small tetrahedrons (cubes) of stone used in mosaic walls and floors can be found everywhere. After centuries of abandonment (except for a small village at the summit, three or four memorial churches, and the Jewish cemetery), it is coming to be heavily built again. On Palm Sunday Jesus would have walked to the left of the summit, perhaps following the now-ancient but still-used route pointed out to pilgrims and tourists. A Franciscan chapel known as Dominus Flevit ('the Lord wept;' Luke 19:41) indicates the traditional place where Jesus wept over Jerusalem. A cemetery of the first, second, and fourth centuries AD has been found there. Many ossuaries (clay chests for interring the bones of the dead) found there are inscribed with names found in the Gospels: e.g., Jairus, Martha, Mary-and even Simon Barjona See FLAP, p. 333. Many competent researchers feel that our Lord's route on Good Friday, however, was to the left, farther down the south slope of Olivet. See SDB, p. 2246 (col. 2). Somewhere from the mount our Lord ascended to heaven (Luke 24:50; Acts 1:11, 12).

Hence there was a double reason for resorting there in numbers.

The visitors to Jerusalem on Friday and Saturday were chiefly pious people who took their religious duties seriously, being on hand several days before Passover to care for certain necessary ceremonial purifications after incurring some sacral defilement (John 11:55). So they would not have had entirely unworthy motives in seeking out the house of Lazarus in Bethany. So much for positive response to Jesus' weekend presence at Bethany.

Meanwhile the Sanhedrin trembled, and all of resident Jerusalem with them. What they had been fearing for weeks had happened. The disciples of John the Baptist now augmented the Galilean partisans of Jesus. Jesus had attracted still more disciples – however fickle they would turn out to be – in the preceding six months of an exceedingly impressive campaign, in Jerusalem itself for a while, then in Judaea and the Trans-Jordan. So an immense, friendly crowd had accompanied Jesus (many already speaking of Him among themselves as the Christ) up the Ascent of Blood as far as the side path to Bethany on the left. The object of Jerusalem's fear and hate rested in Bethany over the Sabbath. But Jerusalem, however outwardly quiet on that fateful Sabbath, was not at rest. Plans for the terrible deed of next Friday, which would result in desolation of their house and judicial divine abandonment (Luke 13:35; Matt. 23:35) of their people, were even now being formulated in their hearts, and careful schemes were being put together.

Assuming that the Christian consensus[4] which places the arrival at Bethany on a Friday evening is correct, it seems clear that the supper reported by John (12:2-8) was served next day, on the Sabbath (Saturday) evening, and is the same as that described a bit later in their narratives by Mark (14:3-9) and Matthew (26:6-13). This is acknowledged by many competent writers. They regard the Synoptics' reports of the supper as parenthetical flashbacks to explain Judas's treachery on Tuesday evening.[5]

John's account seems to say that the obviously friendly villagers of Bethany planned and provided the supper (John 12:2-8; Mark 14:3-9; Matt. 26:6-13), and that may have been the case. If so, it was held in the house of one Simon, called 'the leper' because he had formerly been a leper. Perhaps he was one of the many lepers cleansed by Jesus, and, having the largest house available, offered it gladly for the occasion.

A truly remarkable anecdote is reported in all three accounts of this

---

4 ELTJM, 2:357ff.; ALOL, p. 422; SGG, p. 501; John 12:1.

5 ALOL, pp. 425-28; ELTJM, 2:358, contra RHG, p. 187.

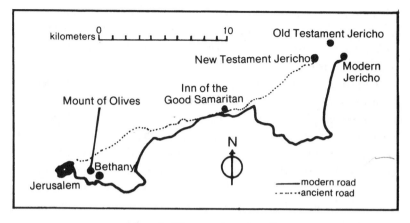

Map 4. The road to Jericho

supper. (It should be noted that none of the Synoptics ever elsewhere mentions Lazarus, and only Luke [10:38-41] mentions Lazarus's sisters, Martha and Mary. Hence it is not surprising that John, the supplementor, provides the information about this loving family.) Lazarus was an honored guest. Martha - mistress of her own house - was apparently in charge of serving in Simon's house. Mary, ever thoughtful and reflective, appeared on the scene, bearing an alabaster box of very costly, perfumed, anointing oil, worth a sum competently calculated as sufficient to buy food to serve a meal to fifteen thousand adults and their children or to pay a daily wage to three hundred laborers.[6] As Jesus reclined at the board, Mary sorrowfully anointed both His head (Matthew and Mark) and His feet (John), then, as that woman of Magdala had done months before, wiped His feet with her hair. It seemed like a daring act, and it was. But apparently Mary alone, of all those present, pondering the many times Jesus had spoken of His coming passion, truly understood His purpose in His present mission to Jerusalem. Preferring to lavish her wealth on the living to the employment of it for sad memorials, she did what her heart desired. Jesus both defended and praised her, predicting the world would never tire of hearing the report of the loving deed whereby she anointed His body, yet living, for burial only a few days later. This act achieves great poignancy if those interpreters are correct who insist that the sinful woman of Magdala (Magadan, Dalmanutha)

---

6 ELTJM, 2:358.

whom Jesus reclaimed for life and chastity and who, in the house of that other Simon, anointed His feet, is no other than Mary the beloved sister of Martha, now restored to her home and family – both Mary of Bethany and the Magdalene.[7]

Perhaps the most presently applicable feature of the story derives from Judas's professed shock at the alleged waste of resources. Here is the professed philanthropic social-activist seen in the worst possible light. A recent writer laconically observed: 'Often, concern for the poor comes to the forefront when other people's money is involved.'[8] The critics of Mary should have considered that the precious box was Mary's own to dispose of as she wished. Jesus, also a poor man, saw nothing to criticize and everything to praise. Judas really was not interested in the poor at all, for he was already embezzling company funds. John says, 'he was a thief.' Jesus and Mary alone seem to have understood one another that evening.

It was the end of any sympathy Judas ever had for the cause of Jesus and His kingdom. That night he hatched his plan (Mark 14:10, 11; Matt. 26:14-16; Luke 22:3-6), for the next two days he pondered it, on the third he proposed it to Jesus' enemies, and on the fifth he executed it.

THE TRIUMPHAL ENTRY

Mark 11:1-11
Matt. 21:1-11
21:14-17
Luke 19:27-44

The Jerusalem multitudes who participated in the events of that first fateful Palm Sunday understood somehow that a King was presenting Himself (John 12:12, 13). Two crowds participated in His triumphal march. The one, composed of Passover visitors already in the city, 'when they heard that Jesus was coming to Jerusalem, took the branches of the palm trees, and went forth to meet him, and cried out, Hosanna: Blessed is he that cometh in the name of the Lord, even the King of Israel' (John 12:12, 13 ASV). Another crowd came with Him. Some 'went before' and some 'followed,' crying out, 'Blessed is the kingdom that cometh, the kingdom of our father David: Hosanna in the highest' (Mark 11:10 ASV). But the great redemptive and (if we dare to use the word) 'dispensational' meaning was missed by all, for 'these things understood not his disciples at the first: but when Jesus was glorified, then remembered they that these

---

7 This view, ardently and impressively set forth in SDHF, pp. 202-11, citing views and evidences ancient and modern, ought to be examined before scornfully rejecting it as most modern writers do.
8 GJM, p. 266.

things were written of him, and that they had done these things unto him' (John 12:16 ASV).

Concerning the relations of Jesus, the Messiah, with the House of Israel to whom He came, this was the critical day. Let no one doubt it. On this and the two following days came His final break with the nation of Israel.

Somewhere the student of the significance of Jesus must come to understand certain crucial truths about His mission. Let us summarize these as put by Samuel J. Andrews, whose *The Life of our Lord upon the Earth Considered in Its Historical, Chronological, and Geographical Relations* has stood for a long time as a landmark in such matters.[9]

First, Jesus came to a nation in covenant relation with God. They were an elect people living in a land apart, set aside for them, under laws prescribed by God and blessed with promises. They were a kingdom of priests, a holy nation. Their own Messiah and the world's Redeemer was to come through one of their tribes and families. This people interpreted their covenant documents, the Scriptures, in such a way as to expect the Messiah to be primarily a political personage and after that a spiritual restorer, instead of the other way around. They had no inkling of how unprepared they were for either the spiritual or distinctly national ministry of the Messiah. 'Hence it was that Jesus could not openly assume the name of Messiah, because it had become the exponent of so many false hopes, and would have gathered around Him a body of followers moved more by political than spiritual impulses.'

'*Second*, it was the will of God, but not His sovereign purpose, that the Jews should receive His Son. We cannot here avoid the problem that assails us everywhere in history, whether biblical or otherwise – the sovereign purpose and foreknowledge of God on one hand and man's un-coerced freedom and responsibility on the other. According to the former Jesus Christ was "the Lamb slain from the foundation of the world" – thus announced in countless Old Testament types and prophecies and according to the latter slain by the wicked acts and counsels of evil men. Peter put the two sides together: '... him being delivered by the determinate counsel and foreknowledge of God, ye [i.e., the Jewish people] by the hands of lawless men did crucify and slay.'

'Third, as the covenant of God with the Jews was a national one,' so must 'their acceptance or rejection of Christ be. God had dealt with the

9 New York: Charles Scribner's Sons, 1891.

people as a corporate body. Their blessings were national blessings, their punishments national punishments. What was done by the heads of the nation was regarded as the act of all, and involving common responsibility. Only in this way could the purpose of God, in their election to be His peculiar people, be carried out. Hence, in this greatest and highest act, the acceptance or rejection of His Son, must be a national one. It must be done in the name of the whole people by those who acted as their rightful representatives... if... He was rejected by the nation acting through its lawfully constituted heads, this national crime must be followed by national punishment. Individuals might be saved amid the general overthrow, but the people, as such, failing to fulfill God's purpose in their election, must be scattered abroad.' Though the gifts and calling of God, being without repentance, guarantee an ultimate restoration, as Paul says (Rom. 11:25-29), in the meantime a different people (not a new Israel as is sometimes asserted) must be gathered out of all the nations.[10]

All the details of Jesus' ministry and, just now, especially the details of the great final presentation to Israel, the so-called triumphal entry, must be interpreted in light of these facts.

When we arrive at this difficult point, all reverent minds must bow before the mystery of the divine ordering of history whereby sometimes the eternal plan of God is carried out by the evil deeds of wicked men. A justly famed author wrote: 'Jesus had formally made an offer of Himself to the capital and authorities of the nation, but met with no response. The provincial recognition of His claims was insufficient to carry national assent. He accepted the decision as final.'[11] The same writer also said: 'There is no point in the life of Jesus at which we are more urged to ask, What would have happened if His claim had been conceded – if the citizens of Jerusalem had been carried away with the enthusiasm of the provincials, and the prejudices of priests and scribes had been borne down before the torrent of public approval? Would Jesus have put Himself at the head of the nation and inaugurated an era of the world's history totally different from that which followed? These questions very soon carry us beyond our depth, yet no intelligent reader of the Gospels can help asking them.'[12] We add in Jesus' own words: 'How then should the scriptures be fulfilled, that thus it must be?' (Matt. 26:54 ASV). And how

---

10 Quoted and condensed from ALOL, pp. 125-28.
11 SLC, p. 112.
12 ibid.

would the world have been redeemed, considering that 'the Son of man came... to give his life a ransom for many (Matt. 20:28)?

As at many points in the Gospels, the whole background of the Old and New Testament doctrines yet to appear must be brought to bear. Thus, when some of the Pharisees from the crowd lately sprung from the eastern gate of the city, offended deeply by the messianic proclamations in the crowds' Hosannas,[13] cried, 'Master, rebuke thy disciples,' He responded, 'I tell you that, if these shall hold their peace, the stones will cry out' (Luke 19:40 ASV). A hundred Old Testament prophecies pointed to the hour of the Messiah's presentation to Israel. A lesser number pointed to Israel's misunderstanding of Him and their consequent rejection of Him. A marvelous array of New Testament texts relating to Jesus' royal dignity and atoning work point back to it. Now was the time. Jesus had been delaying it for months, but now was the hour that the Son of man should be glorified. That hour could no longer be delayed. Someone had to announce the arrival of the King. The crowds were conducting a messianic demonstration.[14] He therefore no longer concealed the character in which He now came to Jerusalem. The prophet had said: '... thy King cometh unto thee: he is just, and having salvation: lowly, and riding upon an ass, and upon a colt the foal of an ass'[15] (Zech. 9:9; cf. Matt. 21:4, 5). So accepting the accolades of the multitudes and thereby their demand that He assume the style of a King, He secured an ass colt, and after some of His disciples spread their coats on it, He rode in the midst of the people and their festive palm branches in lowly triumph. There will be another day when He shall come in power and glory with the armies of heaven. But this was not the day. He came, as Zechariah said, having salvation, riding upon the common man's beast, the lowly ass.

As the city broke into view, perhaps near the spot on the western

---

13 Hosanna is a rendering into Greek of the third and fourth words of Psalm 118:25 and means simply 'save, please' (not 'save, now,' as is commonly held, for the 'now' corresponds to the first word of the verse). One must resist finding more in the passage than is strictly justifiable.

14 Just how fully the crowd understood the messianic meaning of the Psalms they were citing, much relating to the second advent, is a matter of dispute among scholars. See ELTJM, 2:368; SBCNT, 1:845-55. That Jesus so understood it then and that the Apostles did so later seems clear from John 12:16, for after citing the crowd's recitation of the Hallel Psalm, John writes: 'These things understood not his disciples at the first: but when Jesus was glorified, then remembered they that these things were written of him, and that they had done these things unto him.' The cries of the people quoting Psalm 118:25, 26 were part of the customary Hallel Psalms sung at all three pilgrim festivals - Passover, Pentecost, and Tabernacles.

15 'In the Pseudepigrapha there is nothing to be found with reference to Zech. 9:9; on the contrary, in the rabbinical literature the significance of the text for Messiah is the usual thing.' SBCNT (on Matt. 21:5), 1:842 (my translation).

slope of Olivet now marked by the buildings of *Dominus Flevit*, a spot where the entire city lies in impressive panorama, especially in the light of the morning sunlight, our Lord broke into tears. Perhaps He stopped for a while. He spoke of that day as Jerusalem's day, a day in which, had her people known it, she might have secured her peace (Luke 19:41-44). There is again a strong prophetic undertow drawing the student to the prophecies of Daniel (Dan. 9:24-27), a portion which predicted that at the end of a certain sixty-nine weeks of years, the Messiah would be presented (Dan. 9:26). But, says the prophecy, after presentation the Messiah would be killed and then the city would be destroyed by the people of the prince that should come a cryptic reference to Antichrist, as almost all interpreters agree. Jesus did not quote the prophecy, but through His tears, and knowing well that He would soon 'be cut off' (Dan 9:26) – that is, die – as the prophet had said, He spoke sadly of how the enemies of Jerusalem would soon lay siege to the city, dash both her and her 'children' to death, and make the city an utter ruin, all because on that Palm Sunday 'thou knewest not the time of thy visitation.' All came to pass in less than forty years. No one else wept. Neither the disciples nor the crowd were in a weeping mood. But none of them knew what He knew nor saw Jerusalem the way He saw Jerusalem!

As the joyful procession moved on, slowing as it narrowed at the gate, the residents of Jerusalem would call from their doors and balconies and the arches over the street, 'Who is it?' The answer would come from the passing procession, 'This is the prophet, Jesus, from Nazareth of Galilee' (Matt. 21:10, 11). But there is no evidence that the natives of the capital city joined in the glad acclamation. This was not their doing and, led by the scholarly Pharisees and the worldly Sadducean hierarchy, held themselves aloof. They would wait and see. Their leaders planned to postpone dealing with Jesus till the crowds went home in a week or so – and would have done so had not Judas Iscariot, the traitor Apostle, provided what they thought to be a better way.

ARRIVAL AT THE TEMPLE

Matt. 21:14-17

Mark 11:11

As Jesus continued through the streets and into the temple, the blind and lame appeared before Him 'and he healed them.' As He entered the temple children were present who picked up the procession's chant: 'Hosanna to the son of David' (Matt. 21:15). Hermann L. Strack and Paul Billerbeck, commenting on Matthew 21:15, asserted that children were

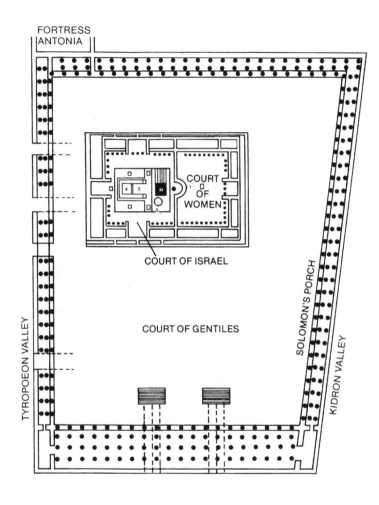

Diagram 2. The temple precincts. Marked by numerals are (1) the "great gate", (2) the great altar, (3) the holy place, (4) the most holy place, and (5) the court of the priests. Scientific archaeological excavations on the south and west sides since 1967, still incomplete and only partially reported, render previous efforts at precise representation of those areas out of date and any present attempt still premature. A covered walk, or cloister, surrounded the temple area on the west, north, and east sides. Solomon's porch was simply the east section of this cloister.

trained at as early an age as possible to wave the festive branches at the singing of the Hallel when it was sung at the temple during the feast of Tabernacles. This they did when they heard the word *hosanna.* These learned authors add that the *tosephta* (glosses in certain commentaries) report that children were at an early age accustomed at school to read or recite the Hallel so that the cry 'Hosanna' could not have been unknown to them.[16] The children may have been there with their parents for the temple services, or they may have been boys and girls dedicated to the temple and regularly there as part of the choirs. In any case, though their youthful repetition may have been with little comprehension of the meaningful occasion, they greatly angered the chief priests. Matthew used a word unique to the New Testament[17] in referring to Jesus' miracles of healing in the temple that day. These 'wonderful things' angered the chief priests (Sadducees) too. They say, to Jesus, as if He had told the children to start their sing-song and ought to put a stop to it: 'Don't you hear what these mindless brats are saying?' Jesus' answer was not haughty, but He did turn them off with words which told them He both approved and accepted the children's words of praise and acclamation: 'Yea; have ye never read, Out of the mouth of babes and sucklings thou hast perfected praise?' (Matt. 21:16; cf. Ps. 8:2).

A tremendous day's work, full of several emotional climaxes, was now over for Him. The leaders of the Sanhedrin feared the crowds of pilgrims with whom He seemed recently to have gained increased popularity. What had happened looked like a clever bid for power and a *coup d'etat.* They surely wondered why He had not already carried through with it. But He did not do so on that Sunday. Monday and Tuesday passed without any effort on His part to use the enthusiastic crowds for a bid to power. The Jewish leaders did not fail to take advantage of His deliberate refusal to use popular support for political advantage while it was still strong.

In any case the decision lay with the properly constituted heads of the Jewish nation, not the crowds. Jesus had handed over the initiative to them, and He was waiting for their decision. It had really already been made, and it would be executed with fearful, malign cruelty on Thursday night and Friday.

Meanwhile the Lord simply walked back to Bethany. He had completed

---

16 SBCNT, 1:854.
17 *Ta thaumasia.*

six-and-a-half-months of journeyings on to Jerusalem. He would now await Jerusalem's answer to His presentation of Himself.

Excursus 12 – Some Apparent Discrepancies

As a sample of the apparent discrepancies which not infrequently assail the careful reader of the Gospels, let us examine more closely the incident of the healing of the blind men at Jericho (Matt. 20:29ff.; Mark 10:46ff.; Luke 18:35ff.). There are two primary difficulties in the three accounts, centering around these two questions: (1) Did Jesus heal one blind man (Mark and Luke), named Bartimaeus (Mark), or two (Matthew)? (2) Did the healing occur when Jesus was leaving Jericho (Mark and Matthew), or when He was approaching Jericho (Luke)?

At least a dozen solutions have been proposed to the double discrepancy. Some of the more plausible follow.

1. Luke's 'drew nigh' means simply He was in the neighborhood, not specifying whether He was entering or departing. Thus there is no variance from Mark and Matthew.

2. Jesus spent some time at Jericho. He left on a short excursion out of town on one day, as Mark and Matthew say, and upon His return He healed the blind man, as Luke says.

3. Three blind men were healed – one as mentioned by Luke as Jesus entered Jericho; two, as Matthew says, as He left, of whom Mark mentions the outstanding one, by name.

4. Matthew condensed the story, the exact time and place being unimportant. The other two accounts supplement the story, showing one was healed as Jesus entered Jericho, the other as He left it.

5. As in no. 1, 'drew nigh' means 'in the neighborhood.' But two were healed, both as Jesus entered; Mark mentioned only Bartimaeus because Bartimaeus was well known.

6. One blind man besought Jesus for healing as He entered, but was not healed. As Jesus left the city next day, the blind man brought another with him and both were healed by Jesus as He departed. Luke's story is condensed, leaving out any reference to the overnight at this point, choosing to keep the story separate from that of Zacchaeus.

7. There are two Jerichos, Old Testament Jericho at the great spring called Elisha's fountain, and, a mile or so south and west of this, the New Testament, or Herod's, Jericho. This town got water through an aqueduct coming down out of the mountains to the west. The healings

took place as Jesus left the former and was entering the latter.

These and other explanations, each with some degree of plausibility, serve to show only that there is no need to accept the stories as discrepant if all the relevant facts should become known. This and many similar apparent discrepancies are no serious obstacle to believing the facticity of the Gospels.

Excursus 13 – On the Idea of a 'Life of Christ'

A popular classification of the twenty-seven books of the New Testament divides them into four books of biography (the Gospels), one of history (Acts), fourteen of doctrines (Epistles), and one of 'prophecy' or prediction (Revelation). The classification is correct in a rude sort of way, but everyone who has read the New Testament carefully knows that while the four Gospels are concerned with the words of Jesus and events in his life (Gr. *bios*, hence our word *biography*), they are not biographies in the sense that James Boswell's *Life of Samuel Johnson* is a full-scale biography or Dr Samuel *Johnson's The Lives of the English Poets* is a series of brief biographies.

The Gospels are called 'Memoirs of the Apostles' in some very early writings of the Church Fathers, exactly what Christians have always thought they are – recollections of apostles regarding the time they were with Jesus as disciples and authorized 'messengers.' Two writers (Matthew and John) were personal eye witnesses, Luke, companion of Paul, was a researcher of eye-witness testimony (Luke 1:1-3), and Mark reported what he was told by the eye witness Peter.

Yet these four accounts, however accurate, do not approach their subject biographically. They are *Gospels*, reporting the redemptive career of Jesus of Nazareth, the Messiah of Israel, the Savior of the World. Each author has certain different major emphases. It is not quite correct to speak of these as different theologies. The most important study of these four Gospels has therefore always been of the distinct message of each one.

If, however, the accounts are factual, if the conversations, sermons, and apostolic interpretations thereof are truthfully reported, as Christians have always asserted they are, then there is validity to putting it all together in something like a consecutive narrative account. Jesus does not come through to us as a disembodied spirit out of 'no-space' and 'no-time.' The more we know of the space and time (call it *Sitz im Leben*) the more we understand of the words, events, and deeds. John the Baptist may have characterized himself simply as a 'Voice' in a nameless 'Wilderness,' but Jesus did not do so.

The earliest known attempt at something like a 'Life of Christ' was put together in the Aramaic (Syriac) language about AD 170. A Syrian Christian named Tatian tried to weave the four accounts together, including all but avoiding repetition, so that there was a continuous narrative of all that Matthew, Mark, Luke and John say. Though it was very popular at the time, only bits and pieces have come down to us.

Most efforts to tell a continuous story with the actual words of the Gospels take the form of a 'harmony' which places the four accounts in parallel columns. Only rarely do all four contribute something to the same event. For example, only Matthew and Luke give birth accounts and genealogies of Jesus, and they are markedly different. Mark starts at a point about thirty years later with the opening of Jesus' public ministry. Only a few incidents (e.g., the miracle of the feeding of the five thousand) are reported by all four.

Once the efforts of scholars have produced 'harmonies' other scholars can produce exposition on the composite result. A famous example is *Calvin's Commentary on a Harmony of the Gospels Matthew, Mark and Luke.* Other scholars can put the narrative together in an interpretive summary of the redemptive career of the Lord Jesus Christ. This is what almost every author of a 'Life of Christ' tries to do.

This book is one of many such efforts. It is a modest project. The goal is simply to pass on in interpreted, coherent, and organized form the whole of the Gospel story designed for a particular kind of readers.

Certain scholars claim to believe the project of a life of Christ, even when so narrowly defined, is wrongheaded and misleading. They object to any attempt at any unified, coherent story derived from the four canonical Gospels. Their objections have no basis in religion, devotion, or piety, but in their theories as to how the Gospels came to be written. See *Excursus 14* and the appendix.

CHAPTER 10

His Last Ministries in Jerusalem

The importance of the climax of the Lord's earthly career in His passion, death, resurrection, and the forty days is clearly indicated by the disproportionate amount of space the four Gospel writers devote to it. John, for example, devotes the last ten of his twenty-one chapters to events after the last arrival at Bethany. A very large proportion of these materials reports His controversies with the Pharisees, scribes, Sadducees, lawyers, and Herodians. Another large part contains His last discourses to the disciples. Each Synoptic reports a long discourse about the future destruction of Jerusalem and the second advent – two of Matthew's longest chapters (24 and 25) are devoted to it. John captured forever the intimate final instructions and prayer of our Lord in the portion, unique in the entire Bible, found in chapters 13-17.

A book treating mainly the *teachings* of Jesus might therefore extend to hundreds of pages in interpreting these matters and relating them to the life of the church. The present study, however, emphasizes the life of Christ. Hence, we may rightfully highlight the action – things done to, for, and by Jesus – and drape about that structure only as much of what He said as serves to flesh out the story.

The Lord and His party had arrived at Bethany on Friday afternoon to lodge at the home of Martha, Mary, and Lazarus. After the Sabbath rest

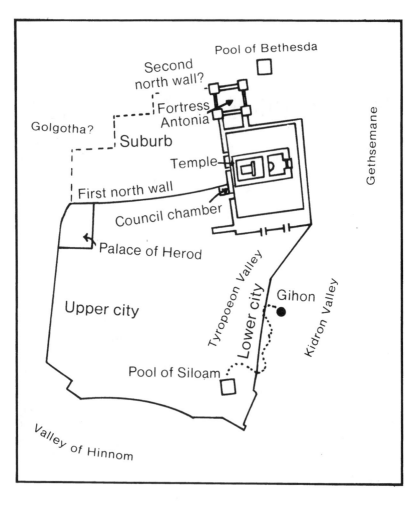

Map 5. Jerusalem

(sundown Friday to sundown Saturday), there had been a feast in His honor, apparently supplied by the friendly villagers, at the house of one Simon. It is likely that at this feast Judas, being greatly annoyed by Mary's lavishing on Jesus a large amount of expensive ointment, and by Jesus' praising her for this, had resolved to betray Jesus into the hands of the Sanhedrin.

On the next day, Sunday, the Lord had officially presented Himself as the Messiah of Israel, the provincial crowds joining in acclaiming Him the long-expected Son of David.

On Monday He again entered the city and the temple. Likewise Tuesday – an enormously long and busy day for Him – was spent in the city. Wednesday was apparently spent quietly in Bethany. There is no report in the Gospels of this day. Not until Thursday afternoon, having left the friendly house at Bethany, did He cross the shoulder of Olivet, pass on across the Kidron for the last time, and walk to the house of the Last Supper in the southwest part of the city. Before night was over He was bound and in the hands of His enemies. Let us follow Him closely through Monday, Tuesday, Thursday, and perhaps even the very early hours of Friday morning.[1]

MONDAY

It was common for the Jews to begin the day without food. Jesus therefore next day was hungry as He walked with His disciples toward the city.[2] Sunday had been a strenuous day. Thus we understand the occasion of the cursing of the fig tree (Mark 11:12, 20-25; Matt. 21:18-22) which had no fruit.[3] The fulfillment of the curse in twenty-four hours greatly impressed the disciples. But even the lesson in prayer which Jesus made of it and the manifest evidence of the joining of our humanity (His great physical hunger) with deity (power of judgment) in Jesus seem insufficient to justify including the story. Devout minds have always sought a deeper meaning. Rather, our Lord was acting out a parable (Luke 13:6-9) spoken many months before and one spoken six hundred years before by Isaiah (Isa. 5:1-7). 'Israel was that barren fig-tree; and the leaves only covered their nakedness as erst they had that of our first parents after their Fall.

Mark 11:12-18 Matt. 21:18, 19 21:12, 13 Luke 19:45-48 John 12:20-50

---

1 As usual herein, we adopt the modern custom of dividing the days at midnight rather than the ancient Jewish custom of dividing them at sunset.
2 It was very early, as prôi, sometimes used of the last watch of the night, suggests. See Mark 1:35.
3 ELTJM, 2:374, 375, gives an excellent discussion of the horticulture of figs, important to understanding the incident.

And the judgment, symbolically spoken in the parable, must be symbolically executed in this leafy fig-tree, barren when searched for fruit by the Master.'[4] Peter was impressed only by the miraculous blasting of the tree – sudden, complete. The Lord then, as always, emphasized the spiritual meaning. Our own age, preoccupied with data analysis, empirical verification, and the like must almost be struck down before men will think of spiritual meaning in natural events. Even typological interpretation of Scripture has recently become almost extinct.

The symbolical judgment of the fig tree (Mark 11:12-14, cf. 11:15-20; Matt. 21:12, 13, cf. 21:19-22) on the way was shortly extended literally and symbolically to the ritual efflorescence of the temple, that most showy, but empty, aspect of the nation of Israel. When our Lord had entered the national sanctuary on Sunday, the previous afternoon, the main rituals had been completed. The priests as well as the vendors of sacrificial victims and other supplies had dismantled their tables, removed their merchandise, and gone home. So He had merely looked about, spoken a few words, and, 'it being now eventide,' gone back to His lodgings (Mark 11:11). Today, the garrulous chatter of hawkers in 'the shops' – an area reserved in the court of the Gentiles – and the shuffle of worshipers' feet mingled with the chants, songs, and ritual acts in the court of the priests about the sacred building. Jesus had always thought of the temple as His Father's house; He had often used its precincts in quiet hours for meditation and discourse. Three years earlier He had driven out the merchandisers and now, as the time drew near when neither 'in this mountain nor yet in Jerusalem' (John 4:21) but in all the world, men of every kindred, tribe, tongue, and nation would worship God in Spirit, our Lord determined to use messianic authority to purify the venerable old place once again for at least a few hours of proper worship. In language reminiscent of Isaiah 56:6, 7 and Jeremiah 7:11, Jesus spoke out against the invasion by gross secularity. After that He took charge of the premises in the capacity of God's great High Priest and *Messiah Nagid* (Dan. 9:25) ('Christ-Ruler'). What kind of force He used is not specifically mentioned, but physical force was necessarily employed. Hard looks did not overturn the tables and chairs, 'and he would not suffer that any man should carry a vessel through the [outer courts of the] temple' (Mark 11:16 ASV).

The significance of the fig tree incident and the forcible cleansing of the temple must not be slighted. Israel (the fig tree) is God's. So is the

---

4 ibid., 2:375.

temple. The Messiah is the prince of Israel and Lord of the temple. Both Israel and the temple are now coming under divine judgment.

The immediate result among the Jerusalem leadership was the same as that upon every display of Jesus' holy power: 'But the chief priests and the scribes and the principal men of the people sought to destroy him...' (Luke 19:47 ASV; Cf. Mark 11:18).

Perhaps while Jesus still lingered at the temple, perhaps in the court of Israel, certain Greeks came as far as an entrance to that court and, beckoning Philip – likely the most Greek of the Apostles[5] – asked him to intercede with Jesus for an interview (John 12:20-36). Philip consulted Andrew, the man of counsel, and together they brought the request to their momentarily withdrawn Master. His seemingly distracted answer has the ring of something true but far away. We do not know if Jesus then spoke in the hearing of the Greeks or not. He did make it clear that He was soon going to die. Then, like the kernel of wheat planted and decomposing, yet producing blade, stalk, and ear of precious grain, His death would produce much fruit. It was another promise of the favor of God being extended to all men. Moments later, while the Son trembled briefly before the awful prospect of His passion, as at the baptism and transfiguration, the Father spoke audibly in support and praise of His Son.

At this point, as is his wont (1:38; 1:41; 2:21, 22; 4:9, 25; 7:35, 50; 9:7), the author of the Fourth Gospel interrupts his narrative with an interpretation (12:37-43). This one is of supreme importance. It places responsibility for Jesus' rejection on the Jewish people who saw His miracles, and it traces that rejection to providential hardening of their hearts. A day like ours, in which many believers misunderstand the ideas of human responsibility and divine sovereignty in their own religion and in which almost no one countenances the idea either of national crimes or virtues and all seem to reject the idea of group responsibility of any sort, John's words seem unreal. But there they stand. There were a few believing exceptions, but the bulk of the Jewish nation followed their leaders either actively or respresentatively in rejecting the Savior. John's Gospel several times makes a point of the national Jewish rejection of Christ.[6] They rejected their Messiah in spite of

---

5 Conjecture supposes both Philip and the Greeks to have hailed from the same part of the Decapolis (a mainly heathen-Greek area), and hence to be already acquainted.

6 'The Jews' is a phrase appearing only sixteen times in the Synoptic Gospels but at least sixty-eight times in John, usually as a designation of the Jewish people in some act of suspecting, reviling, or rejecting the Lord Jesus. In the ninth or tenth decade of the first century, when John likely wrote, though there were still many Jewish Christians, it was clear that the bulk of the nation had rejected their Messiah.

the most overwhelming evidence of His authenticity. The root was their hardness of heart. For reasons God never fully explains, God hardened their hearts – a way of saying that their hearts, initially hard by virtue of innate human depravity, were never effectually softened by God's Holy Spirit. Hence it is also correct to say they hardened their own hearts. 'For this cause they could not believe, for Isaiah said again, He hath blinded their eyes, and he hardened their heart; lest they should see with their eyes, and perceive with their heart, and should turn, and I should heal them' (John 12:39, 40 asv). These verses should be considered in connection with Jesus' remarks on the necessity of a divine effectual calling in John 6 and the effects of hardening of the heart in Matthew 13:14-15.

These sentences, so grim in their meaning for Israel, seem to be a verdict on the results of Jesus' amazing and now-completed ministry of word and work to the nation. We may think of them as following His fierce controversies with the leaders on the morrow – His last words to them – and His utterly unrestrained fierce condemnation of them and all they stood for. These controversies now come before our attention.

TUESDAY MORNING AND AFTERNOON

Mark 11:19-B37
Matt. 21:19-25:46
Luke 21:37, 38
20:1-21, 36

Very early the next morning He was again in the outer court of the temple (Mark 11:20; Luke 21:38), as if by appointment, speaking to the people. This day was to be His last to enter those hallowed precincts, and it was to be the greatest day of debate and controversy there. Every element of partisan leadership in the nation asserted itself against Him sometime that day, without pause or let.

1. First came the chief priests and scribes (Mark 11:27–12:12; Matt. 21:23–22:14; Luke 20:1-19). They were within their formal rights. Yesterday He had assumed jurisdiction of the temple precincts – not entering upon priestly service Himself (not being of the house of Aaron) but regulating and judging the practice there as was the duty and right of the Davidic king. They wanted to know by what authority He had acted and from whom He had obtained it. He had, of course, been presenting messianic credentials by repeated and overwhelming signs over a period of more than three years. But as seen already in this chapter, their, hardened hearts did not permit them to see or hear the truth about Him. Hence, Jesus declined to offer further evidence or to answer, choosing rather to close their mouths by a truly clever question of His

own: 'The baptism of John, was it from heaven, or from men?' He promised to answer their question if they answered His. If they said 'From heaven,' then they stood condemned, for they had almost unanimously rejected John; if they said 'From men,' they would alienate the crowds standing about, most of whom acknowledged John as a prophet. So they chose not to answer at all and thereby lost 'round number one' of that amazing day of contest. Jesus made full use of His forensic advantage and convicted His questioners of their own sins of unbelief, immorality, and obdurate hardness of heart by a series of three parables (Mark 12:1-12; Matt. 21:28-22:14; Luke 20:9-19). In these parables, especially the second, about a householder and his vineyard, He predicted their coming act of murdering Him as their fathers had the Old Testament prophets. He also announced that the divine favor was now to pass over to the world of Gentiles, that God would pass by the chosen nation. He added that a severe divine judgment would soon come on them, His present questioners. Those standing by did not wholly miss His point, for 'when the chief priests and the Pharisees heard his parable, they perceived that he spake of them' (Matt. 21:45, 46); they would have seized Him on the spot except that He had not quite yet lost the support of the Passover crowds, who still expected Him to pull off some effective bid for civil power. Thus the end of the first round.

2. Next to assail Him was a combination of Pharisees and Herodians (Mark 12:13-17; Matt. 22:15-22; Luke 20: 20-26). Between them they skillfully devised what looked like a question fatal for Him to answer: Is it lawful to give tribute to Caesar or not? But Jesus handily disposed of it – The coin in use is Caesar's; it bears his embossed image; therefore pay Caesar what is his. Then observing, perhaps silently, that His questioners bore the image of God, He cleverly added: Render to God the things that are His, your own selves. Jesus had won again, and His questioners' silence bore witness to it.

3. Then came a bold assortment of Sadducees (Mark 12:18-27; Matt. 22:23-33; Luke 22:27-40) – the religiously skeptical party of the priests, men who denied the existence of angels, spirit, immortality, and resurrection. Their question about the woman who survived seven husbands simply voiced their theological denial of immortality and resurrection. His totally unprecedented response drew from the fact that hundreds of years after the death of the three great patriarchs, God said, 'I am' their God. Since God is God of the living, their spirits live with God! This was the last round. The Pharisees no doubt congratulated

themselves on Jesus' effective new answer to Sadducean negative theology (Mark 12:28; Matt. 22:34).

All of this controversy moved on the plane of rabbinic theological method. Jesus was never more fully the most excellent Jewish Rabbi than on this last day in the temple. This was the end of all efforts to ensnare Him with hard questions. He had won a clear victory over all comers (Luke 20:40).

4. The Pharisees now held counsel, and one of them, called both a *scribe* and a *lawyer* (Mark 12:28-34; Matt. 22:34-40), asked what seems to be a sincere, searching question. It called forth our Lord's greatest pronouncement on the central teaching of the Law, echoed later by Paul (Rom. 13:7-10): Love God with all your being, and your neighbor as yourself.

5. Then, almost as if mocking the Pharisees, while they were still gathered in counsel nearby, He asked them a question (Mark 12:35-37; Matt. 22:41-46; Luke 20:41-44): 'Whose son is the Christ?' They answered, 'The Son of David.' Then calling attention to how in Psalm 110 David calls Messiah, Lord (as the rabbis acknowledged), He asked, 'If David called him Lord, how is he David's son?' If the Pharisees had been in the slightest degree open to conviction of truth, they would have recalled His many claims to divine prerogatives and powers, how He forgave sin and raised the dead. The holy light of the truth as it is in Jesus Christ would have dawned on them, and they would have acknowledged Him as Lord. But their hearts were hardened.

6. Having now carried the contest to His enemies' ground, there followed something unique in the life of our Lord. He stood still on His two feet (it is almost impossible to think of Him as seated for this fearful tirade) and, eyes flashing, countenance flushed with holy anger, scathingly denounced the leaders of Jewry until He was apparently out of breath. All this, while addressed to Jesus' disciples, was in the hearing of all the people and of as many of His enemies as had the fortitude to hear Him out. This storm of deliberate, controlled, detailed criticism expressed the pent-up anger of a lifetime, reaching back to His twelfth year. 'Ye that love God, hate evil,' the Psalmist commanded, and so He did, though not without compassion (as His yearning for Jerusalem, near the end of the outburst, expresses vividly). While His relentless but defeated foes were still cowering before Him, He unstopped the vials of wrath upon them. It is almost like the Apocalypse of John. 'He called attention to the high position of these teachers and how they had

degraded their office. They hid the truth, they made proselytes worse than they were before, they were mere hair-splitters, they put wrong emphasis on truths, they were professional religionists, boasters of heredity; in a word, hypocrites, serpents, offspring of vipers, with the judgment of hell upon them. It was terrific. Before this hailstorm and lightning His enemies shrank away and the crowd dispersed. The heart of Jesus bursts out in lament over Jerusalem, soon to be desolate, while the disciples gather in silence apart.'[7]

Jesus has been criticized for lack of restraint. Admittedly His repeated 'woe unto you' (seven times), with characterizations such as 'hypocrites' ('play actors'), 'son of hell,' 'blind guides,' 'fools and blind,' 'full of hypocrisy and iniquity,' 'ye serpents, ye offspring of vipers' are the strongest possible terms of acrimony. But they deserved every word of it. Jesus placed guilt for every prophet martyred from the beginning of the Old Testament (Abel)[8] to its end (Zacharias)[9] at their door as a people and foretold that shortly – until their fateful judgment by the Roman armies in AD 70 – they would be persecuting and murdering His own accredited prophets and Apostles.

Very significant for interpretation of the final rejection of Jesus is the Lord's final word of explanation for His fierce denunciation: 'Verily I say unto you, all these things shall come upon this generation.' This is unwelcome news to people of our century who generally think of God only as merciful and if He is a philosopher, certainly an individualist democrat, one who would never bring a whole nation to time for the accumulated evils of past generations. But the Scripture doctrine starts in Genesis. God delayed the judgment of the Amorites of Canaan until their last generation brought their iniquity to the 'full' (Gen. 15:16), 'and

---

7 RELJ, pp. 142, 143.

8 The Hebrew Bible of Jesus' time, like the Christian Old Testament, began with Genesis, in which Abel's martyrdom is reported (chap. 4), and it ended with Chronicles, in which a certain prophet named Zechariah (not the author of the Old Testament book by that name) is reported to be murdered at King Joash's command (II Chron. 24:20-22). The Hebrew Bible is commonly, by modern Jews, called *Tenach*. This is a manufactured word, the consonants of which are derived from the initial letters of *Torah* (the Pentateuch), *Nebhi'im* (the Prophets-the former, Joshua through Kings; and the latter, Isaiah through Malachi), and *Kethubhim* (the Writings, a section containing all the rest of our thirty-nine books, so arranged that Psalms is first and Chronicles last).

9 Zacharias (or Zechariah), the last martyr of the Jewish Bible, was Jewish, but Abel, the first martyr, was pre-Jewish. Hence, Jesus may, it has been suggested, be referring very obliquely to universal human guilt of some sort for His death. The famous prophecy of Isaiah 53:6, 'The Lord hath laid on him the iniquity of us all,' is apparently intentionally ambiguous. The speakers of this part of Isaiah 53 might be a converted nation of Israel in the future, or perhaps confessing believers of all ages, or some other group. One's view of the fulfillment of Old Testament prophecy in general and one's view of the atonement, whether universal or limited, will affect his interpretation.

then the abominations of [the] ages were at once completely and awfully avenged, so the iniquity of Israel was allowed to accumulate from age to age till in that generation it came to the full, and the whole collected vengeance of heaven broke at once over its devoted head [i.e., head devoted to judgment]."[10]

The 'great indictment'[11] closed with an anguished reversal of tone – anguish over the stubborn rejection of love extended by the pre-incarnate Logos over the groaning centuries of Israel's past and now rendering judgment certain by rejection of the incarnate Son with His prophets and apostles. The horror of Tuesday is exceeded only by that of the Friday of the crucifixion.

At this point the Lord, exhausted from the controversies, left the scene for a vista point somewhat higher but still in the sacred enclosure. As He sat there – with the dazed disciples, some scattered here, others huddling there – He viewed a scene which gives us one of the rarest vignettes of beauty in the life of the Savior (Mark 12:41-44; Luke 21:1-4). On the pavement a few yards below the stair where He sat were the slotted boxes in which the last straggling worshipers of the day were placing their voluntary cash gifts to the temple ministry. He called the disciples to Himself, directing their attention to the scene below. In His remarks the nameless rich are the backdrop for the similarly anonymous poor widow. She gave more than they all, 'for all these did of their superfluity cast in... but she of her want did cast in all the living that she had' (Luke 21:4 ASV).

6. Sometime in the afternoon Jesus and the Twelve departed the temple. As they did so, one of them (like the untravelled provincials they all were) commented on the grandeur of their national shrine. They continued to talk about the temple until they had left the city. They mounted part of the eastern hill called the Mount of Olives. With the temple and the city lying clear before them, laced with the lengthening shadows of the declining sun, Jesus sat down. The disciples Peter, James, John, and Andrew, now full of curiosity about Jesus' two predictions earlier in the day of the doom of Jerusalem and its people, came close for what turned out to be our Lord's most extensive discourse (all privately given) regarding the future – Jerusalem, His second advent, the end of the age (Mark 13:1-37; Matt. 24, 25; Luke 21:15-36).

---

10 JFBC, 2:56.

11 The visit of the Greeks would have been appropriate to the story here, and that is where SDHF places it.

There are several reasons why, informative as the Lord's words are, they remain wrapped in considerable obscurity. All Biblical prediction, of course, is limited by the readers' range of understanding. We are all 'first graders' as regards the future. Even great prophets were sometimes mystified by the marvelous oracles they received (Dan. 4:19; 7:5, 28; 8:27; 10:12; 12:8-10). History makes prediction clear to everyone. There was also the fact that the disciples still had no conception of the great age of the church lying between the advents and to be inaugurated fifty days after the near approaching Passover. Even deep in the forty days of Jesus' post-resurrection ministry they did not understand (Acts 1:6). Though the second advent looms large in the sermon, it merges with other critical incidents of the future, especially the destruction of Jerusalem, which was indeed a coming of Christ the King in destruction of 'their city,' as He had earlier set forth in an important parable (Matt. 22:1-14, esp. v. 7).

Every generation of Christians has found warning and instruction in the sermon. Without doubt its salient lesson is watchfulness, watchfulness for the Lord's return after Jerusalem's destruction and after His protracted absence in heaven.

Jesus expressly disclaimed personal knowledge of the time of His return, but He was sure of several things. The kingdom of God would soon be taken away from Israel and given to the Gentiles. The disciples would be persecuted by both Jews and Gentiles in the process of this transfer. Terrible afflictions lay ahead for the elect before the consummation. Only those who endure to the end will be saved. They must be ready. When the Son of man comes, those not ready will be taken away (as the wicked people were by Noah's flood) for judgment (Matt. 24:39-40 cf Matt. 13:43), whereas the spiritually prepared will shine forth in the kingdom of God, then to be visible on earth as now only in heaven. The uncertainties of the future, as well as the certainties, call for Christian fortitude and watchfulness: 'Watch therefore: for ye know not on what day your Lord cometh' (Matt. 24:42 ASV).

TUESDAY EVENING AND NIGHT

It was now Tuesday evening at Bethany. Thursday afternoon the Passover lambs would be slain and in the evening eaten by groups of ten to twenty, in and about the city. By the following sunset Jesus would be slain and buried in Joseph's tomb.

Mark
14:1,2;
14:10,11
Matt.
26:1-5;
26:14-16
Luke
22:1-6

Already this Tuesday evening the climax would be taking shape.

Judas, son of Simon Iscariot, the only non-Galilean of the Twelve, had been disaffected in heart for a long time. Over a year before, without identifying him, Jesus had said of Judas, 'One of you is a devil.' On that day in the Capernaum synagogue the crowds of Galileans, with revolution on their minds, intending to carry Jesus at their head to national power, had been brusquely turned aside by the Lord. So the multitudes abandoned Jesus. Judas should have left Him too. Jesus challenged him to do so. But he did not. Throughout the year to follow, he had no heart for Jesus' message or program. The feast of the past Saturday in Simon's house, when his venal thief's interest in the ointment with which Mary anointed Jesus had been severely rebuked, was the last straw. Now three nights later he stole away from Bethany back to Jerusalem (Mark 14:10, 11; Matt. 26:14-16; Luke 22:3-6), where he skulked and slithered through the stony lanes until, with discreet inquiry, he found the Sanhedrin in session and offered to solve their problem for them. He had a plan for taking Jesus quietly into custody in such a manner as not to inflame the numerous supporters who still remained from His earlier campaigns in Galilee and more recently in Peraea, Judaea, and Jerusalem.

The Sanhedrin, on the other hand, had been in tense situation for months as regards Jesus. His early collisions with them, while serious, were not such as to create any concerted effort to destroy Him. They had been embarrassed by His first cleansing of the temple three years before. After that they had sent expert rabbis to follow His movements in Galilee, where they charged Him not only with Sabbath breaking (healing on the seventh day) but with blasphemy for claiming power to forgive sins. He had utterly overwhelmed them on the Sabbath question and had effectively rebutted their charges of blasphemy. They also had charged Him with being in league with Satan. More recently He had performed a remarkable healing of blindness which greatly discomfited them. Twice in recent months their partisans had failed in efforts to stone Him. To top off their discomfiture, He had attracted excited support and astounded the nation by raising from the dead one of their own class, Lazarus, a prosperous citizen of nearby Bethany. So favorably affected toward Jesus had the Jerusalem crowds become that when Jesus had stopped with Lazarus at Bethany on the previous Friday, 'the Pharisees... said among themselves, ... lo, the world is gone after him' (John 12:19 ASV). The crowds of Palm Sunday frightened them even more. Then on Monday He had assumed messianic power and again driven the moneychangers and the sellers of animals and their merchandise out of the temple. Now just today (Tuesday) He had in high dudgeon denounced the entire national leadership: priests, lawyers, Pharisees and their scribes, and Sadducees and their Herodian cohorts. Jesus simply had to be stopped.

So that august body of learned fools met that night in their hall in the temple complex (Mark 14:1, 2; Matt. 26:15; Luke 22:1., 2) to devise a way to apprehend Jesus by stealth and then to kill Him. A knock on the door; admission to the lighted room where the frustrated men of the Sanhedrin sat, a brief haggling, a messenger sent to obtain money from the temple vaults, delivery of the money to the strange caller (Judas), and the meeting disbanded. Their problem had been solved.

Meanwhile out in Bethany Jesus explained to the disciples assembled in the host's house that the Sanhedrin would be successful; He would soon be 'delivered up to be crucified.'

Sometime that night the weary Savior and His exhausted Eleven lay down to sleep the sleep of the just. Judas slunk away to think about his pondered crime, the seventy members of the Sanhedrin went to bed with a sense of accomplishment (Nicodemus and Joseph excepted), and Jesus' puzzled hosts lay down to fitful rest.

THURSDAY AFTERNOON AND EVENING

Wednesday seems to have been a day of rest for Jesus and His Apostles at their retreat in Bethany. Not until Thursday was well advanced did Jesus dispatch two (Peter and John) to a certain room in the city, there to make ready the Paschal meal.[12] *Mark 14:12-25 Matt. 26:17-29 Luke 22:7-29 John 13. 14*

Whether or not the choice of house involved a miracle of direction seems best decided in favor of the idea that Jesus had arranged for the room with some citizen of means. The sign of a *man* (rather than, as usual, a *woman)* bearing a water pitcher may have been prearranged as a device to avoid letting Judas the traitor know, and thereby have opportunity to deliver Jesus over to the officers of Caiaphas before the evening began. In such a case several important events – His conversation with the Apostles, the institution of the Lord's Supper, instruction in the doctrine of the Holy Spirit, the 'high priestly prayer,' and the agony of the garden – would never have taken place. The host would doubtless have been a disciple.

---

12 On the distinction between the Passover and Paschal meals, see note 16 in chapter 12.

After the room[13] had been located, they fetched a sacrificial lamb, procured on the 10th of Nisan, three days earlier. Early in the afternoon one of their number, with countless others, according to an orderly temple scheduling carried their lamb to the temple and, according to Mosaic ritual, slaughtered it, a priest catching the blood to be poured out at the great altar and also removing certain portions for burning on the altar. The other elements of the supper were bought, including at least sufficient wine, unleavened bread, bitter herbs, and vinegar. The lamb had to be roasted whole. The proper festival lamp was put in place with supplies of oil. There would be thirteen of them at the table – more than the required ten, less than the upper limit of twenty.

Several questions occur to readers at this point of the Gospel story. Was the Last Supper the Jewish Paschal meal? On what day of the week did the crucifixion take place? With a measure of confidence, we can affirm that the day was Thursday, the crucifixion taking place on Friday. That Jesus ate the genuine regular Jewish Passover with the Twelve can hardly be denied on any grounds.[14] These have been the opinions held by most Christians interested in the questions from earliest Christian antiquity.

---

13 It has been assumed on the basis of ancient tradition and inherent likelihood that this room is the one in which the disciples (120 in all) met throughout the forty days.

14 In recent times certain scholars have proposed that Jesus and the Twelve ate the Passover, in keeping with alleged Essene rules, a day earlier than the followers of rabbinic Judaism. Another variation is that they ate it in keeping with an alleged Galilean custom, a day earlier than the followers of rabbinic Judaism. A dependable discussion that will introduce the reader to the basic data of the problem and to the literature is Harold W. Hoehner, 'Chronological Aspects of the Life of Christ: The Day of Christ's Crucifixion;' *Bibliotheca Sacra* 131 (1974): 241f. Though I do not support Hoehner's conclusion, I do recommend his discussion as an introduction to the subject.

CHAPTER II

His Last Night:
With the Twelve and
at the Jewish Trials

Tourists to Israel nowadays are invariably led by Israeli guides to the national shrine known as the Tomb of David, outside the south wall of the old city near the southwest corner but within the city of Jesus' time.[1] What the Israeli guides seem not to know or care is that a large room in the second floor of that building has been reverenced for at least a millennium and a half as the Cenacle – i.e., dining room the scene of the Last Supper and of the first Christian Pentecost[2]. The great Dormition (sleep of Mary) Church of the Benedictines hard by on the north is the highest thing in old Jerusalem and the most visible from almost anywhere in the neighborhood. It signalizes the fact that Roman Catholic dogma asserts Mary slept here – body and soul after her death – before being bodily 'assumed' to heaven. Throughout the ages Christian tradition – and lately considerable scholarship also – has located the 'upper room' in this southwest corner of the Jerusalem of the time of Pilate and Herod Antipas, Annas and Caiaphas, Jesus and the Twelve. Hence there appears to have been plenty of time for the discourses of Jesus in John 15 and 16 to have been spoken on the way as the party moved slowly on the diagonal, across the entire old city toward

---

1 FANT, pp. 147-52.
2 VIG, pp. 110-16.

Gethsemane. The garden seems to have been at a considerable distance eastward from the north part of the eastern wall. Hence if, as seems likely, they left the upper room about 11 pm, it might have been near midnight when they arrived at the garden (better, the field or farm) of Gethsemane and near 12:30 or 1 am when the betrayal took place.

IN THE UPPER ROOM

The evening did not begin auspiciously. With what must surely have been a poignant sigh, almost too deep for utterance, Jesus spoke of how He had cherished the desire 'to eat this passover' with the Apostles 'before I suffer' (Luke 22:14, 15), for, said Jesus, He would not eat another Passover on earth until the coming of God's kingdom. The Apostles, still unable to understand their Master's gentle care for them and still too 'dull of hearing' to discern the reality of what would happen on the morrow and still expecting 'the kingdom of God immediately to appear,' fell to quarreling about their order of precedence in the coming kingdom. One writer suggests the quarrel may have been induced by the grandeur of the fine room which their brave host, in the face of official reprisals, had furnished them.[3] Or was it sparked by the seating order at the table? Jews paid considerable attention to such matters. It was the custom in dining to recline[4] on the left side at a low table, the left arm and a pillow providing the elevation necessary for conversation and eating (see diagram 3). We may assume that the chief place was for Jesus and that John was at the end just beyond Him, reclining 'on Jesus' breast.' Evidently next, and back of Jesus, was Judas Iscariot. The rest were in no special order, but we may assume that Peter was not near the head, perhaps taking the thirteenth and last place. Though their quarrel seems trivial (and it was), it only serves to highlight the form of the Lord's words that night, especially when He said 'I have yet many things to say unto you, but ye cannot bear them now' (John 16:12). He did nevertheless promise them future glorious office in which they would rule from twelve thrones over the twelve tribes of Israel (Luke 22:30).

Old Testament sources, present Jewish observance, and the Talmud inform us just about how the supper proceeded. Since three to five cups of wine were required, the Passover supper began with mixing (i.e.,

---

3 SDHF, p. 438.

4 The KJV and even the NEB render Mark 14:18 'they sat.' But the word here and at Matthew 26:20 is *anakeimai*, which means 'to lie down or lean back.' So there can be no doubt about it, the Twelve and Jesus reclined on the floor or on divans at the Last Supper.

diluting with water, but not so as to lose the taste and color) the first cup of wine. Then the food was brought to table – bitter herbs to symbolize the bitterness of Egyptian bondage; the 'sop' – a paste of crushed fruits moistened with vinegar, symbolizing the clay of Egypt wherewith their forefathers had made bricks; a supply of unleavened bread; and, of course, the roast lamb carved in small pieces for eating with the hand.

Their feast was opened by a prayer of blessing and by the drinking of that first chalice of wine – passed from hand to hand. After a second blessing the bitter herbs were dipped in the 'sop' and eaten. Then a second chalice of wine was mixed. At this juncture the father, or head of the company, as enjoined by Moses, explained the meaning of the meal. Choosing therefore a most unusual method of giving this explanation 'before the feast of the passover' (John 13:1) (i.e., at the beginning of the entire week of the Passover festival but 'during supper,' or the Paschal meal [John 13:2]), Jesus arose, girded a towel about Him, and, taking water and basin, began to wash those twelve pairs of feet. True, among ancient Romans and Greeks, as well as Jews, a servant washed the feet of guests *as they arrived*. More to the point, in ancient understanding,

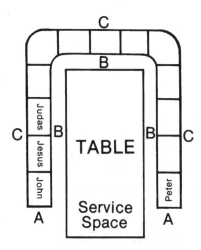

Diagram 3. Table positions at the Last Supper. (A) represents the two rows of single divans on which the Apostles reclined on their left sides, with their heads (B) nearest the table and their feet (C) stretching back towards the floor. The least certain feature in the diagram is the position of Peter.

unwashed feet symbolized lack of preparation for high responsibility. Jesus was not observing any ordinary usage at all. As His words show clearly, He was teaching the need which regenerate, 'blood-washed' believers have for the daily intercession of Christ and His cleansing by the Word, if they are to give effective service.[5] Interpreters of the highest order, from Aurelius Augustine onward, have seen this and commented on it.

The supper being resumed, the Lord sadly asserted that one of them was about to betray His presence to the officers of the Sanhedrin. Peter beckoned to John from his place at the foot of the table, signaling him to ask who the betrayer might be. John leaned back and asked Jesus. Jesus 'therefore answereth, He it is, for whom I shall dip the sop, and give it him. So when he had dipped the sop, he taketh and giveth it to Judas, the son of Simon Iscariot' (John 13:24-26 ASV). From this it is inferred that Judas, the treasurer, reclined immediately behind Jesus.

This was a climax of the evening. It was important to keep Judas there long enough that he not exit and draw the police back before Jesus could finish those treasured, memorable words of John 14:17. Satan now took over Judas, who became an incorrigibly damned soul. 'What thou doest, do quickly' (ASV), Jesus quietly said to him. When Judas now left with the company purse, the Eleven supposed He left to buy food for the festive meals of the next day and of the rest of the Passover week (i.e., the week of the feast of Unleavened Bread). From then on the traitor to Jesus (and to them) was gone. Our Lord was alone with His own and only His own.

After Judas's departure an atmosphere of deep calm prevailed, obvious in John's lengthy reports. Jesus quietly spoke (Mark 14:27-31; Matt. 26:31-35; Luke 22:31-38; John 13:31-38) of how they would all 'be offended' at Him that night as He, the Shepherd, would be smitten and all the sheep scattered. He told them to depart for Galilee where in a few days He would 'go before' and meet them. (This they delayed to do until many days after His resurrection.) Over Peter's protestations of undying fealty to Jesus, the Master calmly prophesied: '... this night, before the cock crow [twice], thou shalt deny me thrice' (Matt. 26:34). Later the Lord instituted the ordinance of the broken bread and of the wine, the twin memorials of His redemptive work. He did so in connection with one of the later cups of the Paschal wine, as Luke makes plain (22:17 *contra v.*

---

5 SDHF, p. 441.

30). (Three to five cups were drunk.) The church's memorial ordinance was instituted near the close of the main part of the Paschal supper or shortly after its close.[6]

After the supper was over, the party of Jesus and the Eleven lingered on for a while. Jesus employed the precious moments to do what He could to prepare the Apostles for the shocks of the morrow. He spoke of His going away (His ascension) to prepare in the Father's house a home for them (John 14) and of His coming again. Of great importance are His remarks on the advent of the Holy Spirit in a new and special way, to be not only *with* them as heretofore but *in* them (John 14:17; cf. Matt. 3:11). Thus Jesus would fulfill the Baptist's prophecy of how Jesus was going to baptize "in the Holy Ghost" and His own earlier prophecy (John 7:37-39) at the latest feast of Tabernacles. Jesus told how the Holy Spirit would enable the Apostles, who had been with Jesus through His ministry, to recall the many things He had said to them (John 14:25-27). Then as if a chill had entered, and first pronouncing a peace upon them and exhorting them not to fear but to love, He announced that His words must soon end. He declared that Satan was coming and that He would now willingly face the prince of this world's assault in order to let 'the world... know that I love the Father.' Abruptly He announced, 'Arise, let us go hence.'

IN GETHSEMANE

As they passed through the moonlit streets of the ancient walled city, perhaps pausing in the shaded privacy of a wayside fig or olive tree outside the east or south wall, Jesus continued to bare His heart in concern for them. The allegory of the vine and the branches (John 15)

---

6 The events of the Last Supper should be related to the usual order of events at a normal Jewish Paschal supper of the time of Jesus. Authorities agree on the following (see ALOL, p. 484): (1) Supper opens with a glass of wine mingled with water, preceded by a blessing and followed by washing of the hands. (2) Thanks are given and the bitter herbs eaten. (3) Unleavened bread, the sauce, the lamb, and the flesh of the chagigah are brought in, and thank offerings are made. (4) The benediction is offered and the bitter herbs, dipped in the sauce, are eaten. (5) The second cup is mixed, and the father explains to his children the origin of the feast. (6) The first part of the Hallel (Ps. 113, 114) is sung, prayer offered, and the second cup drunk. (7) The father washes his hands, takes two loaves of bread, breaks one and blesses it, takes a piece, wraps it in bitter herbs, dips it in the sauce, and eats it with thanksgiving. After giving thanks he eats of the chagigah, and after giving thanks again, he eats of the lamb. (8) The meal continues, each eating what he pleases but eating last of the lamb. (9) He washes his hands and, after giving thanks, takes the third cup. (10) The second part of the Hallel (Ps. 115-18) is sung. (11) The fourth cup is taken, and sometimes a fifth. (12) The supper concludes with the singing of the great Hallel (Ps. 120-27). For this summary I am indebted particularly to ALOL, p. 484. Andrews noted that 'upon several of these points there is dispute among the Jewish writers.'

with its lesson that 'apart from me ye can do nothing' was spoken at this time. He also foresaw a time when through their written word (the New Testament), as well as their spoken word, the Holy Ghost would perpetuate among men the same infallible witness which He Himself had begun.

He said that although they would be put out of the Jewish synagogues, the Holy Spirit would be their comforter. The Holy Spirit would convince men of their sin, of true righteousness and just judgment. He spoke of a new stage of prayer experience, directing that all prayer now be addressed to the Father in the Son's name and expecting sure response (John 16). Then, the chill of a cold night augmented by utter sadness (they all must have shuddered as He spoke), He announced that in moments they would all be scattered and He left alone.

As they approached an enclosed field, called Gethsemane, on the nearer slope of Olivet, perhaps after they had entered this familiar haunt, our Lord lifted His eyes to heaven and prayed. There followed the most intimate intercourse of earth with heaven in human annals (John 17). In calm cadences Jesus 'reported in' from His earthly mission - anticipating by a few hours the agonies of the morrow: 'I have finished the work which thou gavest me to do' (John 17:4). Then He prayed for His immediate disciples, announcing to God their final loyalty, proclaiming their eternal salvation. He prayed for their service for God and deliverance from an evil world. Then His intercession turned toward all those who through the ages would be won to God by the written and spoken word of those Apostles. No Christian believer was omitted from that marvelous prayer.

After that He took Peter, James, and John, companions of several other holy hours, and moved deeper into the shadows. There He experienced the final agony of temptation (Mark 14:26, 32-42; Matt. 26:30, 36-46; Luke 22:39-46; John 18:1). He was contemplating the fatal moment of the next afternoon when as the Lamb of God He would suffer the turning away of His Father's face. The Lord God would then lay on Him the iniquity of us all. For the moment Jesus could hardly bear even to think of it. At three intervals Jesus prayed: 'O my Father, if it be possible, let this cup pass from me: nevertheless not as I will, but as thou wilt.' Except for the appearance of an angel who strengthened Him, the agony might have killed Him, for 'his sweat became as it were great drops of blood falling down upon the ground' (Luke 22:43, 44 ASV).

But it ended quickly. He announced His betrayal to be at hand. Shortly after that, likely seeing the party of Pilate's soldiers accompanying the Sanhedrin police now moving out of the shadows from one of the eastern

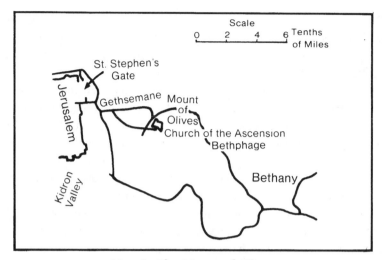

Map 6. The Mount of Olives

gates, or perhaps rounding the northeast corner of the wall, Jesus calmly and regally walked out of the garden to meet His destiny in the hands of wicked men. The traitor kissed Him; Peter bravely swung his sword to defend Him; Jesus spoke to Judas in stinging rebuke, to Peter with command and instruction, and to the arresting party in righteous protest. His amazing majesty flashed momentarily, but in a few minutes He was bound and on His way to the house of Annas.

THE INTERROGATION BY ANNAS

The plot of the Sanhedrin involved having Jesus condemned by their court at the earliest possible moment and then by Pilate too, before the crowds, possibly still friendly to Jesus, could be aroused. That would be very early in the morning, for the Near East, then and now, does most of its work in the morning, beginning with the first streak of dawn and on until shortly before noon. (I once accidentally surprised a woman stealing olives from a tree near the village of et Tur, at the very summit of Olivet, half an hour before daybreak, and already people were on the street about their business.)

The leading ecclesiastic of the time was an old man named Annas. He was a sort of high priest emeritus. Caiaphas, his son-in-law, was the sixth younger member of Annas's family who, after him, and without interruption, had held the high priest's office. Though not a sinecure, the financial rewards greatly exceeded the national service rendered.

Annas's family controlled a large part of the market, located on the Mount of Olives, for ritual and sacrificial goods. They also got their 'rake-offs' from other sources connected with the religion business to which the central national worship had given occasion.[7]

So while messengers went out to awaken the members of the Sanhedrin, calling them to an early extra-legal session, Jesus was required to cool His heels in the presence of Annas. Whether this was an apartment in the house of Caiaphas or some other residence cannot now be determined.

It is hard to identify all the trials and hearings Jesus went through that day. There were at least six of them three Jewish and three Roman. Of the latter, two were before Pilate and one before Herod.

The first was a brief interrogation by Annas. This aged man, though put out of office by the Romans, was a man to be reckoned with. With the verdict of guilty and the sentence of death already agreed upon by the Sanhedrin, this interrogation was only the first act of a play. Jesus had well called these men 'play actors' (hypocrites). Annas inquired in the manner of a disinterested diplomatist concerning Jesus' disciples and His teachings. There were no charges and no witnesses for the prosecution. The questions were therefore irrelevant, incompetent, and unnecessary. If, responded Jesus, Caiaphas, in capacity of judge, wanted to know these things, let him ask those who heard Him. All His ministry had been public - spoken 'in synagogues, and in the temple, where all the Jews come together.' This answer got Him a blow with the hand from an officer. Jesus' answer was a chin-up challenge either to bear witness to the falsehood of what He had said or to apologize. Let all observe that at this stage Jesus is not silent before His accusers and persecutors and that He does not 'turn the other cheek.' Annas's questions were irrational; the action of his stooge was both irrational and unjust, and Jesus let them know that it was so.

THE SANHEDRIN HEARING

From Annas's presence the Lord was soon led away, His hands bound with rope, to the house of Caiaphas the incumbent high priest. Christian tradition has always placed this house somewhere on the southwest hill known as Zion. The tradition has been confirmed in a measure by recent archaeological and historical research.[8] Evidence has convinced many

7 SDHF, p. 441.
8 FANT, pp. 152-54.

scholars that remains of the high priest's palace are located in a small area about 260 yards east of the Cenacle (Tomb of David, Church of the Dormition) on the eastern slope of the southwest hill. Recent researches and excavation confirm that the very early Christians so believed. A broad stairway-street from Roman times, uncovered in recent times, ran from near the Cenacle eastward down the hill to the pool of Siloam. Though outside the present walls, all of this lay within the walls of Jesus' time. Jesus might have walked this street from the upper room to Gethsemane. It goes beside the modern Church of St. Peter in Gallicantu (i.e., 'of the cock crowing'). It is, as noted above, about 260 yards down the slope and eastward from the Cenacle or upper room. Inside this great church (St. Peter in Gallicantu) lie the reputed scene of Jesus' two trials by the Sanhedrin, the courtyard of Peter's three denials, a dungeon with holes in the rock to which the Savior was bound while being detained between the predawn trial and the one after dawn some hours later. The reverent visitor cannot help but be impressed that these stones may indeed enclose some of the scenes of our Lord's trials before the Sanhedrin.

The first Sanhedrin trial could have been as early as 2 am. A legal trial could not be held before sunrise, according to their own rules. But their interest had drawn a quorum, and they were eager to get on with the business. So an informal but deadly session ensued. In it the charges, evidences, and even decision could be enacted, or at least put in shape, so that after sunrise the formal, legal trial could be done within minutes. They planned that after sunrise they would quickly formalize what had just been put in shape but what had been decided months before. They would then hustle Him off to Pilate. Pilate, the procurator, meanwhile would be put on notice and be present at the Praetorium, the Roman fort and headquarters, just off the northwest corner of the temple enclosure.

The hearing turned up no clear, verifiable charges. They were in great disagreement among themselves, for Pharisee crime might be Sadducee virtue and vice versa. The Pharisees, for example, would not have grieved over Jesus' interruption of the Sadducees' (the family of high priests were Sadducees) graft in the sales at the temple. Then someone remembered His saying of three years earlier about destroying the temple and restoring it in three days. But this loose talk, if such it was, was no crime. To this Jesus made no response or defense at all, even when goaded by the high priest himself. They were left, at this point, with a prisoner in the dock and a house full of judges, but no charge, no prosecution witnesses, and no evidence.

But the Sanhedrin had already decided on His execution. They were desperate for some publishable grounds. So the presiding officer, Caiaphas, took steps to compel Jesus to talk, hoping thereby to involve Him in self-incrimination. First, in the Jewish manner, he put Jesus under oath (rather than the witness placing himself under oath as in the British and American courts). Then the high priest demanded, '...tell us whether thou be the Christ [the Messiah] the Son of God' (Matt. 26:63). Of course various superpatriots and cracked pots had been making claims to be Messiah for years – but more to the annoyance of Roman governors than the scandalizing of the Jews. Being now under oath, He had to answer truthfully. Jesus, surprisingly, answered in a way that gave Caiaphas all he wished. He not only acknowledged Himself, indeed, to be the Messiah and Son of God[9] but added: 'Henceforth ye shall see the Son of man sitting at the right hand of Power, and coming on the clouds of heaven' (Matt. 26:64 ASV; cf. Ps. 110:1 and Dan. 7:13). These were assertions of divinity in the cryptic fashion of Old Testament prophecy but with which these self-acclaimed experts were fully familiar. Now that he had what he wanted, the high priest rent his clothes in the approved manner when capital crime is observed or confessed, and the assembled leadership of Israel pronounced Him 'worthy of death.' They then covered the face of the condemned man. After that, contrary to either justice or civilized behavior and, in a manner which Jewish apologists have never satisfactorily justified, insulted and abused Him.

THE OFFICIAL SANHEDRIN TRIAL

We do not know how many hours passed until sunrise. They were probably spent by the Lord in an uncomfortable posture, tied to the pillars and walls in the dungeon below, if indeed St. Peter in Gallicantu is the true

---

9 We have observed that throughout His public ministry Jesus was repeatedly challenged to tell people plainly if He was indeed the promised Christ. He never denied it but never overtly asserted it either. The reason was almost certainly Jesus' concern not to precipitate the crisis of persecution by the Jewish authorities and execution by Caesar's procurator prematurely. But now Jesus knows that His hour has come; He had come from God and is about to return (John 13:1ff.). He is about to be lifted up (crucified, John 3:14), so there is no reason to make His claim obliquely. When Caiaphas asked Him, 'Tell us if you are the Christ, the Son of God' (Matt. 26:63 RSV), therefore, He replies, 'Thou hast said' (KJV) or 'You have said it *yourself*' (NASB). This is almost certainly a literal translation of an Aramaic *vorlage* (i.e., source document or saying) meaning 'Yes, I am.' This was the idiomatic way of answering a yes or no question in the affirmative; Aramaic, like Biblical Hebrew, had no word equivalent to *yes*. This apparently is the sole straight-out affirmation of Christ on this subject.

location. In any case He remained bound while the Sanhedrists dispersed for rest and refreshment. Then at sunrise they all assembled again (Mark 15:1; Matt. 27:1; Luke 22:66-71) – at least a quorum of them did. This likely took place in the 'hall of hewn stones,' hard by the sanctuary, their usual meeting place. We would like to know where two of the members of the Sanhedrin, both disciples of Jesus, Nicodemus and Joseph of Arimathaea, were and what they were doing. Did they speak up at all? At the end of the day, they did not fail to step forward to show themselves His friends. Now in legal session (at least the Sanhedrin held it so) their previous work on the case paid off in quick results. The high priest repeated his question and, apparently still under oath, Jesus repeated His answer. They pronounced Him guilty of blasphemy and worthy of death. Then, after again binding His hands, they led Him off to Pilate.

Meanwhile two of the Lord's erstwhile Apostles were each going through his own private agony: Judas, the remorse of the damned; Peter, the repentance of the contrite, one of the things which accompany salvation. Peter's defection (Mark 14:54, 66-72; Matt. 26:58, 69-75; Luke 22:54-60; John 18: 15-18, 25-27) is not difficult to explain. All the Apostles had fled Gethsemane like scared rabbits. Peter's rash, unlawful resistance to lawful (if unjust) civil power had been rebuked by Jesus, and no miracle of self-defense – such as they doubtless expected – followed. Peter's defection was no more blameworthy than that of all the others (save John); it was only more public and noteworthy. His impetuous, incautious speech, characteristic of the outdoorsman that Peter was, put him out on a limb as regards his fellow Apostles. In a way his very leadership ability smote him. Then the same tendencies, coupled with an unfamiliarity with grand surroundings and his own social inadequacy, pressed him to vulgar, loud speech in response to female mockery before other men. The set of strengths that caused him to follow Jesus to Caiaphas's house were not sufficient as yet to carry him through. Satan was sifting him as wheat (Luke 22:31), but ultimately, though it faltered, faith did not fail. Peter has been strengthening the brethren ever since.

Judas, on the other hand, is inexplicable (Matt. 27:3-10; cf. Acts. 1:18, 19). Never did Jesus say why He chose him to start with. No one knows just why Jesus let Judas's peculiar weakness for covetousness be tempted by custody of company funds. Scripture prophecy is involved. The sovereignty of God in delivering Jesus into the hands of wicked men, as Jesus had several times announced, was overruling Satan's designs in poor Judas. Certain it is that Judas not only made his own responsible choice, but when as son of perdition he died and went to the place of eternal loss, he went 'to his own place.' Again, as several times before in the narrative of our Lord's career, the believer is asked not to explain mysteries, but to do what it is the part of a believer to do – believe.

Excursus 14 – On Critical Theories of Gospel Origins

As long as writers of Christian books about Christianity regarded the four Gospels as essentially factual reports (the four authors were reporting what they had seen and heard or knew from first-hand testimony), there were no serious scholarly objections to Gospel harmonies and books on 'the life of Christ.' The real objections today are rooted in doubt or rejection of the facticity of the Gospel reports. A century ago learned Christians of 'liberal' theological persuasion still wrote and read on the subject (E. W. Farrar's *Life of Christ* was published in 1884), but not so today.

The story is complicated but traceable in brief space.

Serious destructive criticism of the Gospels began with the deistic writers of the late 1700s who rejected the supernatural element of the Bible. They sought to replace Christianity with 'natural religion.' Reimarus and Voltaire are remembered for this effort. The first serious attempt to rewrite the story according to wholly naturalistic theory was *Leben Jesu* (Life of Christ), 1835, by David Strauss. He thought the Gospels were written a century or two after Jesus' death and that through the years the church had gradually accepted the supernaturalistic hopes of the Jews about their Messiah. The stories about Jesus were unconsciously exaggerated. The Jesus of the Gospels is not the Jesus of history who really lived. The remarkable stories of birth and infancy, all the miracles, events of His passion and resurrection are myths. The authors of the Gospels really lived after the myths were formed. Strauss' theory is not widely accepted today, for even destructive critics acknowledge the Gospels were written within the lifetime of men who knew Jesus and were familiar with the history of the period.

Criticism took a more 'learned' turn in the writings of F. C. Baur (1792-1860) of Tübingen University. He attacked the authenticity (i.e., denied the claimed authorship) of most of the New Testament. Only Romans, Galatians, and I and II Corinthians were written by Paul. The Gospels were composed in the late second and third centuries and were spurious books composed to validate the beliefs which the church endorsed at the time. Baur invented a history of Christianity in conformity with a theory of conflict between a Pauline type of Christianity and another promoted by the other apostles. This is now a theory discredited in detail, but Baur's basic theory remains: we determine when, how, and by whom the Gospels were composed 'by a careful investigation of the motives which apparently actuated their authors.'

This and similar assumptions gave the world the optimistic liberalism of late nineteenth century: Albrecht Ritschl (1822-1889) and Adolf Harnack (1851-1930). This system of belief, which prevails to a degree in many pulpits and in much literature today, makes Christ simply the first Christian. He is not the Savior of the world, second person of the Trinity; His miracles never occurred. The supernatural element of the story of Jesus is not factual. It is important that He modeled the finest kind of ethical living men are capable of. If one follows that model, it is unimportant whether he believes the miracles, the resurrection, the doctrine of the atonement, and all the rest. The historical element of the Gospels may be largely true, less the supernatural elements. But Christian faith is not necessarily faith in Christ. It is faith – period: the kind of faith Jesus had. When we have that faith God makes His own impact on our individual souls. Revelation is essentially *our* private experience. Those familiar with the idea of revelation in Karl Barth and 'orthodox neo-orthodoxy' will observe the similarity.

During the 'liberal period' what is called *Source Criticism* came to occupy the attention of New Testament critical scholars. They tended to think that the Synoptic Gospels originated during the apostolic age. Their independence as eye-witness accounts, however, came to be silently rejected by critical scholars, even many conservative ones, and the 'Two-Document Theory' appeared. Mark was written first. At about the same time a now non-extant source was written (called Q for *Quelle,* a German word). The authors of Matthew and Luke used Mark and Q as main sources for their Gospels. Many of these critics regard John as a second-century document, though some think it is authentic, written by John, the Apostle, late in his life.

Form Criticism of the Gospels, beginning with publications by K. L. Schmidt and M. Dibelius in 1919, shifted the interest in a new direction. They theorized that by AD 60 the churches were employing in their liturgy and instruction many small pieces, or units, now found in the Gospels. These units were in the form (hence form criticism) of legends, sayings, parables, miracle stories, narrative tales, and the like; many of which now appear in Mark, Matthew, and Luke. These units were not parts of a connected narrative. They were simply amplified or invented remembrances, like individual beads in a box, to be used as necessary in liturgy, sermon and instruction. The Gospel writers furnished the narrative (the string) on which first Mark, then Matthew, and Luke connected the items they chose. The German name for this sort of 'criticism' is *Formegeschichte (form criticism)*. Rudolf Bultmann came to be the most influential and radical noted advocate of this theory of Gospel origins.

Form Criticism has been modified by emphasizing the personal theological aims of the individual authors in what is called *Redaction Criticism*. Redaction is editing. This theory accepts the more or less standard results of source criticism and of form criticism. The redaction critics ascribe the variations between Matthew, Mark, and Luke – word choice, order of presentation, materials included and excluded, interpretive comments and the like – to the theological purposes of the authors. No effort should be made to 'harmonize' the accounts since there can be no harmony. There was no particular order to the 'beads' of Gospel materials 'created' by the church in three decades after AD 30. So when in the 60s or thereabouts the three 'authors' [= editors] put some of the beads each on his own string [narrative, transitions, etc.] each let his own theological purpose determine what and how and in what order. Each molded the materials to suit his own purpose without much concern for historical fact.

In a 'scholarly' atmosphere such as this it is no wonder that the whole idea of a history of the career of Jesus or 'life of Christ' is commonly rejected in certain quarters.

CHAPTER 12

His Last Day:
At the Civil Trials
and on the Cross

It is only a short walk from the hall of the Sanhedrin in the temple area to the Fortress Antonia. This combination palace-fortress-garrison headquarters is almost certainly the place where Pilate lodged when in Jerusalem. This large structure, erected by Herod the Great and named in honor of Mark Antony, lay adjacent to the temple. Here likely was located Pilate's 'pavement' outside an official house of judgment.[1] The buildings of today crowd closely to the street, but the level of the street before the leveling of Jerusalem by Titus in AD 70 and again sixty years later by Hadrian is at least ten feet below the present street. There in the excavated basements of three adjacent church structures,[2] the contemporary visitor to Jerusalem stands on ground where Jesus walked if one does so anywhere in Jerusalem. Somewhere on these stones He in all likelihood stood for all the trials before Pilate, and there He was beaten and crowned with thorns.

---

1 Recent scholarship does not usually favor Herod's palace as Pilate's residence in Jerusalem and as the scene of the final Roman trials, though some writers still favor it. Likewise the high priest's residence has been advocated as the scene of the formal Sanhedrin trial, but it is now generally disclaimed.
2 FANT, pp. 159-62.

BEFORE PILATE

At this season the Jews were fastidious about avoiding any heathen edifice lest they contract ceremonial defilement and thereby be excluded from the Passover. Though engaged in a nefarious enterprise, they did not wish to be excluded from participation in further parts of the eight-day festival. So Pilate, to accommodate their scruples, stepped out of his chambers and court to set up his *béma* on the pavement before the door. There Jesus stood before Pilate.

We have had occasion before to remark about this man. Though he has gained evil fame for his part in the evil proceedings, when his situation is fully assessed, he appears in great measure to have been a victim of circumstances. Several early Christian writers refer to him with pity. One tradition even makes a repentant believer and saint out of him.[3] He was an ordinary Roman, not unprincipled, yet opportunistic; above all he was practical, contemptuous of all popular religions as mere superstition. As an upper-class Roman he had great respect for civil order as well as love for orderly society. In spite of some of his well-known mistakes of civil administration, his apparent wanton destruction of life, and his disrespect for local custom, they were, as is so often true, miscarriage of good principles rather than opposition to them. It does not take an expert in Roman history to see that Pilate knew why the Jews wanted Jesus put out of the way. He knew in his heart they were wrong. Pilate really wanted to save Jesus from execution but yielded out of weakness and fear for himself rather than out of avarice, greed, or disregard of justice.

The Sanhedrin had a large amount of legal jurisdiction over the rest of Jewry. To allow native magistrates such authority helped Rome keep a lower profile among a subject people. In fact the Gospels clearly show that in the countryside outside of garrison centers like Caesarea and Jerusalem there was scarcely any Roman presence – even the collectors of Roman taxes were mainly Jews. Thus Rome sought to avoid unnecessary local conflict. As the Sanhedrists bitterly acknowledged to Pilate, they brought Jesus to his court only because they could not legally inflict death penalties (John 18:31) – though this did not prevent an occasional, officially inspired lynching (Acts 7:54-60).

First they thought to stampede the governor into condemning Jesus

---

3 SDHF, p. 477.

without a specific charge, simply on their say-so that He was an 'evil-doer' (John 18:30). The Sanhedrin condemnation for blasphemy was not mentioned, for they knew Pilate would not regard that, if true, as anything worse than self-delusion and error, of no concern to intellectually liberated Romans. Someone in the crowd shouted something about Christ's claiming to be a king.

So Pilate interrupted the public trial and took the accused with him into the 'judge's chambers' within the palace (Mark 15:2; Matt. 27:11; Luke 23:3, 4; John 18:33-38), leaving the wretched religionists outside where their ceremonial purity could remain intact. There he privately interrogated the prisoner. During the brief questioning session Jesus courteously answered Pilate's questions as directly as his darkened mind could allow. Pilate learned that Jesus' kingdom was to be established by no human force and that it was a kingdom of truth. At this point the governor came forth to the crowd and pronounced the accused innocent of their implied charge of sedition, i.e., political rebellion.

Then the accusers took a new tack (Mark 15:3-5; Matt. 27:12-14; Luke 23:5). They charged Him with disturbing the peace, of using the respect in which He was generally held to disturb the populace 'throughout all Judaea, beginning from Galilee.' The word *Galilee* was eagerly seized by Pilate (Luke 23:6-12) as a way out. Hoping to have Herod decide Jesus' fate, Pilate ignored the charges and fired Jesus off to Herod, whose chief civil jurisdiction was the Jewish province of Galilee. Herod was in the city for the Passover festival and gladly received Jesus. This was the man against whom the Pharisees had warned Jesus when a few months earlier He was sojourning in Herod's Trans-Jordanian dominions. At that time Jesus fearlessly called him 'that fox' and now showed no more esteem for Herod than then. That dissolute monarch feared Jesus as he had John. Now assured that Jesus was not John's ghost and - having witnessed no miracles such as Jesus was reported to perform – thinking he had nought to fear from Him, Herod had Him mockingly arrayed with a kingly robe and then fired Him back to Pilate. For some reason both Herod and Pilate liked one another better after this shameful incident.

It was now painfully evident that Jesus was more of a problem to Pilate than the other way around. Jesus knew full well how matters stood and simply did what was true and right. Pilate, on the contrary, was grasping for straws, caught between essentially just Roman law, his conscience, and basically superstitious fears on the one hand, and the strident, threatening demands of the Jews on the other. He therefore proposed scourging, a flogging with leather whips weighted with bone or metal laid on so hard that weaker men sometimes died from it. This would, he supposed, satisfy the Jews' taste for some of Jesus' blood, but Jesus' life would be spared. This did not appeal to Jesus' accusers in the least (Luke 23:13-16).

Another bright idea came to Pilate's mind. Someone had just reminded him out loud of his own recently established custom of releasing some noted insurrectionist or robber at the annual Passover festival. So Pilate suggested release of their accused insurrectionist – Jesus the selfacclaimed king of the Jews. At this point both Mark and Matthew inform their readers that Pilate believed the real Jewish objection to Jesus to be jealousy of Him by the leaders (Mark 15:10; Matt. 27:18). But this sort of reason must never be given. Hence other excuses must be advanced for what passion wants. At this point Matthew reports (Matt. 27:19) that Pilate received a message (a note?) from his wife (Claudia Procula, in Christian tradition) telling of a dream she had that day, warning about Jesus. Claudia's message proclaimed Him righteous and warned her husband not to do Jesus any harm. This was a very unusual thing for a Roman wife to do, and it no doubt affected her husband greatly. That Matthew knew about it (and about Pilate's awareness of the Jewish jealousy) tends to support Christian traditions that both Pilate and Claudia became Christians in later years and would naturally have shared the information. While the governor reflected on his wife's message, the chief priests improved on the time by stirring up the people (Mark 15:11; Matt. 27:20) to call for the release of one Barabbas, a notorious, but evidently popular, brigand and insurrectionist.

At this point the crowds increased clamor for release of Barabbas. In response to Pilate's question, 'What shall I do to him whom you call the king of the Jews?' (Pilate liked that way of speaking of Jesus, thereby annoying the Jews by the spectacle of a Jewish king bound in the presence of a Roman procurator), they cried, 'Crucify Him!'

At this juncture – the narrative of John suggests it may have been a bit earlier – Pilate had Jesus scourged in the Roman manner referred to above. Then Jesus was mockingly crowned with a circlet of sharp thorns, arrayed in royal purple, and abused by the soldiers. This must have taken place inside the palace, for afterward Pilate went out to the Jews again, stood Jesus before them, and proclaimed, 'Behold the man' – no doubt hoping that seeing Jesus in such hideously bruised and bleeding condition would mollify the Jews. If so, he would then release Jesus without further harm.

It was not so to be, because there went up a new demand that Jesus be crucified – and now they mention the Sanhedrin charge, blasphemy: He claimed to be the Son of God. This frightened Pilate. Jesus' magnificent composure and Claudia's dream now must have mingled in his mind together with the new information. So he took Jesus 'into chambers' again. Where are you really from? he wanted to know. Jesus remained silent until the exasperated governor said, 'Don't you know I have power to crucify you?' This brought forth from Jesus an important pronouncement bearing on civil power, even civil power unjustly used: 'Thou wouldest have no power against me except it were given thee from above' and added that the Jews who were pressing Pilate to use that power were more blameworthy than he. This should be connected with His refusal to let Peter use a sword to resist a lawful (if unjust) arrest.

Pilate then, leaving Jesus within, went out to the Jews alone to persuade them to give up their demand. But the wily leaders then delivered what was to be the winning stroke. They claimed that to release Jesus would be against the emperor's interest. Now, Pilate knew the moods of the capricious, gloomy Tiberius, that this caesar might not bother carefully to investigate plausible charges of *lese majesty*. Pilate knew his own record was not good. So he brought Jesus out of the palace while he as judge sat down in the temporary *bçma* set on 'the pavement' (in Latin, *lithostratos*). He called for a basin of water wherein he symbolically washed his hands of complicity in (though scarcely of responsibility for) Jesus' execution. 'And all the people answered and said, 'His blood be on us and on our children.' Then after decreeing the release of Barabbas he delivered Jesus to his officers to be led off for crucifixion.

A noted author commented on the frightening words of the people and Pilate's surrender to them: 'Pilate, of course, could not escape full legal and moral responsibility for his cowardly surrender to the Sanhedrin to keep his office. The guilt of the Sanhedrin (both Pharisees and Sadducees unite in the demand for the blood of Jesus) is beyond dispute. It is impossible to make a mere political issue out of it, and to lay all the blame on the Sadducees [chief priests] who feared a revolution. The Pharisees began the attack on Jesus on theological and ecclesiastical grounds. The Sadducees later joined the conspiracy against Christ. Judas was a mere tool of the Sanhedrin, who had his resentments and grievances to avenge. There is guilt enough for all the plotters in the greatest wrong of the ages.'[4]

Of the hour of the day and the day of the week when Pilate emerged

4 RHG, p.225.

from the Praetorium for the final episodes of the trial, John writes, 'And it was the preparation of the passover, and about the sixth hour' (John 19:14). What does that mean in modern terms? Every Friday was preparation. That was how Jews designated the day when they readied themselves and their homes for Saturday Sabbath. 'The Passover' refers to the whole Paschal week which this year began on Friday evening (it could be any day of the week). It does not refer to the Paschal meal as such, with which the week-long festival had begun the night before. 'The sixth hour' is 6 am, by the Roman reckoning employed by John, writing in pro-consular Asia some sixty years later and about twenty years after the Jewish commonwealth had passed away. Mark, writing while the Jewish commonwealth still existed, or at least shortly thereafter; says Jesus was crucified at the third hour (Mark 15:25). This is by Jewish reckoning, which started counting hours at sunrise, hence 9 am. So we know that about three hours were consumed in gathering the two other condemned men, preparing the means and site of execution, and traveling to the site. All the Gospel data fall into harmony on this basis.

THE WAY OF THE CROSS

We may safely presume that the gathering of the whole garrison of the Praetorium was to witness the stripping of Jesus and the attendant mockery, for 'the soldiers of the governor took Jesus into the Praetorium and gathered the whole Roman cohort around Him.'[5] There is no way of knowing how long the soldiers' cruel sport with the Lord lasted. After it was ended He was compelled to pick up His cross and carry it toward the scene of execution.

A number of points of interest on the walk westward (the way of sorrows, *via dolorosa*) to the mount of crucifixion are mentioned in Scripture – all embellished by Christian tradition and each assigned some geographical spot on the route. Tradition has added several points, too.[6] The distance is

---

5 This is conclusive that the pavement on which the trial took place and the Praetorium were at the Fortress Antonia, for a cohort *(speira* in Greek) is the tenth part of a Roman legion, a legion consisting of 4,500 to 6,000 men. The Antonia fort, near the temple, had been built to accommodate such assemblages of persons, as the old Herodian palace was not.

6 Every Friday, during most of the year, at Jerusalem, processions of pilgrims, sponsored mainly by Roman Catholics, form near the Church of the Flagellation (near the site of the Antonia fort at the northwest corner of the temple enclosure [*al Haram*] in the open space between an old school and the Haram wall). Then they, sometimes one or two bearing a cross of wood and following a printed order of service, proceed through all the fourteen 'stations of the cross,' terminating at the Church of the Holy Sepulchre, at which are the last several stations. But the procession may be held

not far.[7] Under ordinary conditions it requires less than ten or fifteen minutes. Yet, with the crowds present in the city for the Passover festival, the grim procession would have moved slowly. A man named Simon of Cyrene (Mark 15:21; Matt. 27:32; Luke 23:26, cf. Ps. 16:13) (mentioned in such a way as to indicate that his sons and perhaps he himself became Christians), perhaps just coming home from his farm in the country, was compelled to bear Jesus' cross for him - evidently the scourging and other abuse had rendered Him unable. Luke notes that a large company of wailing women followed, lamenting Him (Luke 23:27-31; cf. Hos. 10:18). Whether they were friends or the voluntary professional mourners yet today prevalent in the Orient, we do not know, but probably they were the former. Some of them remained with Him through the day. Jesus was allowed to pause in order to address them as friends. He told these 'daughters of Jerusalem' to weep not for Him but for their city, which, now that its inhabitants were murdering Him and bringing judgment to harvest for themselves and their children, was shortly to experience the ultimate of human vengeance. The national life was then still green; soon it would be dry, and then, Oh, what a fire (Luke 23:31)! Luke is the only one to report that two genuine malefactors were 'led with him to be put to death' (23:2). Shortly they passed through one of the city gates and on to a small mount – for some unknown reason called Golgotha,

---

elsewhere. Sometimes these stations 'are set up in regular order round the nave of a church... with meditation and prayer, at each station; the devotion being a substitute for an actual pilgrimage to Palestine and a visit to the holy places themselves. The fourteen stations of the cross represent-1. Jesus is condemned to death; 2. Jesus is made to bear His cross; 3. Jesus falls the first time under His cross; 4. Jesus meets his afflicted mother; 5. the Cyrenian helps Jesus to carry his cross; 6. Veronica wipes the face of Jesus; 7. Jesus falls the second time; 8. Jesus speaks to the women of Jerusalem; 9. Jesus falls the third time; 10. Jesus is stripped of his garments; 11. Jesus is nailed to the cross; 12. Jesus dies on the cross; 13. Jesus is taken down from the cross; 14. Jesus is placed in the sepulchre.' 'Stations of the Holy Cross,' in John McClintock and James Strong, eds., *Cyclopaedia of Biblical, Theological, and Ecclesiastical Literature*, 12 vols. (New York: Harper and Brothers, 1867-1887; reprinted – Grand Rapids: Baker, 1970), 9:997.

7 Countless generations of pilgrims, churchmen, and scholars pretty much accepted the traditional location of the mount of crucifixion (Golgotha, Calvary) and likewise the site of the tomb. Both are within the walls of the present 'old city.' These walls, however, are mainly of Turkish construction. For many decades previous to World War II, there was a lively debate on the basis of archaeological evidences and, it must be admitted, a good bit of anti-Catholic feeling from the Protestant side, seeking to locate these so-called holy places outside the present wall. In spite, however, of several generations of search for evidence, scholarly consensus now seems to be that the investigations of Helena, Emperor Constantine's mother, which were based mainly on locally supplied information (and a helpful miracle or two?), are at least as trustworthy as the latest contrary opinions. Gordon's Calvary and 'the garden tomb' are wonderful places to stand and remember what the Savior of the world went through nearby, but they are hardly authenticated sites of the crucifixion and inhumation of the Lord Jesus Christ.

'the place of a skull' (in anglicized Latin, *Calvary*). Immediately a drugged potion[8] (Mark 15:23; Matt. 27:34; cf. Ps. 69:21) to dull the pain was offered Jesus, but choosing to act consciously and responsibly, after tasting it, He rejected the drink.

THE CRUCIFIXION

The cross has been described as a ghastly instrument. Sometimes this form of execution employed a single pointed stake on which the victim was impaled through the chest or in the belly and out the mouth. A blunt post or tree was sometimes employed, the victim being tied by the arms and allowed to hang until dead. More frequently it was compounded of two pieces, which might be joined like the letter *X* (St. Andrew's cross), like the letter *T* (St. Anthony's cross) or with the upright extending above the transom in the manner familiar among Western Christians (†). The last was commonest and probably used on that dark Friday. 'The victim... was first... stripped naked [9]... then he was laid across the transom with outstretched arms, and his hands were made fast to either end, usually by nails hammered through the palms or wrists but sometimes, to prolong the suffering, merely by cords. Thereafter the transom with its quivering load was hoisted on the upright; and, to support its weight which else must have torn the hands, the body rested, as on a saddle, on a projecting peg... Sometimes the feet, like the hands, were merely tied, but usually they were nailed to the upright either through the instep by two nails or through the Achilles tendon by a single nail... the victim hung in agony, lingering on... as long as two days.'[10] These details are amply supported by ancient sources.

God's Word, the Bible, delicately draws a veil over most physical details of the crucifixion of Jesus. We should be grateful. It is, in fact, much more explicit concerning the agony in Gethsemane. It is well to be so. We are not edified by either the merely touching or the sensational. The only details are that the soldiers took possession of His clothing, casting lots for the seamless tunic (Mark 15:24; cf. Ps. 22:18) – as Scripture predicted – and that the time of day was the third hour (Matt. 15:25) (Jewish time), that is, 9 am.

---

8 See Proverbs 31:6 – 'Give strong drink unto him that is ready to perish...' According to Talmud tractate Sanhedrin 43:1, there was a charitable society of Jerusalem ladies who supplied this potion to condemned men. Several drugs were available.
9 The Gospel of Nicodemus says Jesus was furnished a loincloth. SDHF, p. 495.
10 Ibid.

Afterward a title or superscription written by Pilate (Mark 15:26, 27; Matt. 27:39; Luke 23:33; John 19:19-22) on a board or panel was affixed over His head. All four Evangelists report it. In full it read – in Hebrew, Latin, and Greek – 'This Is Jesus of Nazareth, the King of the Jews.' Pilate, now having recovered a little of his independence and self-respect and still cherishing his spiteful joke on the Jewish leaders (identifying a bound and now-crucified man with their king), refused to take it down, though the Jews protested. (Was Pilate at the scene, or were messengers sent to the Praetorium?)

The two malefactors who were led out with Him were crucified to His right and left. Some of the crowd reviled and mocked Him, as at first did both the malefactors.

During the first three hours after being crucified the Lord spoke only three times – each time with gracious words to meet the needs of those around Him, needs which, though they knew it not, were truly greater than His. First, as they elevated Him, He prayed: 'Father, forgive them; for they know not what they do' (Luke 23:34; cf. Isa. 53:12). This saying is missing in some ancient Greek manuscripts and versions, and though perhaps not a genuine portion of Luke's Gospel, one can hardly doubt that Jesus said it. It is utterly like Him. Stephen seems to have paraphrased it in his own dying moments (Acts 7:60). For whom was He interceding? All mankind? Jews and Romans? The Jews? The Romans who were indeed proceeding ignorantly? Henry Alford's explanation that He referred primarily to His executioners seems best. Certain it is, as Alford also remarked, that between the first member of the prayer and the last 'lies the work of the Spirit leading to repentance.'[11]

The second saying was His own forgiving response to the repentance of one of the malefactors. This thief, clearly speaking as a Jew expecting the Lord some day to come back 'in thy kingdom,' timidly confessed his faith: 'Jesus, Lord, remember me' (Luke 23:42). Our Lord's words – important to a sound doctrine of the state of the believing soul after death – have comforted every dying Christian ever since: 'Verily I say unto thee, Today [not merely in some far-future, coming kingdom] shalt thou be with me in paradise.'

The third was to His mother and to John. A number of faithful women who throughout His ministry had cared for His physical sustenance did not forsake Him in His last extremity. Seeing among them His anguished mother, the sword of which He had spoken now truly piercing her heart,

II ANT, p. 440.

He committed her, in her mature years, to the care of the sole (and youngest) Apostle standing by, John[12] the beloved: 'Woman, behold thy son! ... [John,] Behold, thy mother.'

All three Synoptics report that beginning at noon, the sixth hour of the day by Jewish reckoning, a strange darkness prevailed over the land until the ninth hour – 3 pm. Whether a natural phenomenon or a supernatural event, the Scripture does not say. A miracle is not suggested. It was not an eclipse, for the sun cannot be eclipsed at the time of full moon – as the fifteenth day after new moon would certainly have been. Residents of Syria (i.e., the eastern Mediterranean littoral) are well acquainted with hot winds which move in from the desert bearing high temperatures, low humidity, and sometimes darkened skies – called hamsin by Arabs and Israelis. 'A bad storm will approach the observer like a wall of gigantic height.[13] W. M. Thomson called attention to similar phenomena as preludes to earthquakes in the area, as old residents of California speak knowingly of 'earthquake weather.' Thus, said Thomson of the prelude to a Beirut earthquake on January 1, 1837: The time was a 'quiet Sabbath evening. A pale smoky haze obscured the sun, and threw an air of sadness over the closing day, and a lifeless and oppressive calm had settled down over the face of nature.'[14] Eclipses have a similar effect. I well remember a period of recess at the village grade school, one warm spring day. The hundred or so children, grades one through eight, were frolicking and playing – I with other seventh and eighth graders playing baseball. For reasons none of us realized at first, schoolyard activity slowed down and finally all became very quiet. We did not know why we had become quiet until it dawned on me, at least, that the world had become almost dark. In a day when people lived their own thrills instead of being bombarded with concocted ones (TV drama) or titillated with doctored stories of others' experience (the news shows), we all responded naturally. If a voice had sounded from the sky announcing the judgment day, none of us would have been surprised however frightened. We were already scared. Such must have been the state of men and minds at Calvary that Friday afternoon. Most of the people there, except the soldiers in charge, the three sufferers nailed to the premises, and their most loyal friends, quietly stole away home. There were ritual and festive matters to attend to anyway.

---

12 John as usual in his Gospel, conceals his own identity by a cryptic reference (19:26, 27).
13 BGB, p. 64.
14 Quoted in ibid., pp. 69, 70.

For nearly three hours all was silent save for the sufferers' moans. Then at the ninth hour the Son of God cried out with a loud voice in Hebrew (the fourth saying): *'Eli, Eli, lama sabachthani?'* ('My God, my God, why hast thou forsaken me?'). It was appropriate that He who all His life did indeed 'in God's law meditate day and night' should phrase the first of His dying shouts and cries in the language of Psalm 22. In a way the Psalmist never fathomed, He could say: 'The cords of death compassed me, and the pains of Sheol [the grave] gat hold upon me' (Ps. 116:3 ASV). It was not mere human extremity that pressed this shout from the Savior. Jesus was suffering a divine visitation of judgment. It was the desolation to which sin, He being 'the Lamb of God which taketh away the sin of the world,' had now brought Him. It is probably not correct to say He endured the sinners' hell in that hour, but that He was shortly to die in the room of sinful men is not unrelated. He was made a curse for us (Gal. 3:13). Surely contemplation of this desolation was part cause of the intense suffering of Gethsemane the night before. Jesus died as no good man before or since has ever died – loved by God but abandoned by Him *(contra Ps.* 23). For the first and last time in His own eternal existence, He was alone. He is thoroughly able to succor those who are tempted because He, in His own temptation (Heb. 2:18), suffered all that man can suffer.

The Hebrew 'Eloi' was mistaken by some non-Hebrew-speaking persons as a call for Elijah. The intense thirst caused by pain, loss of blood, and exertion, exacerbated by the abnormally oppressive heat of the day, were bringing the end swiftly. He, knowing His work was now nearly over, quietly said, 'I thirst' (John 19:28; cf. Ps. 69:21), His fifth saying. It was an implied request for a small deed of mercy. Someone nearby, persevering over the mild objections of others present, dipped a sponge in the diluted wine supplied for the soldiers and held it up to His lips. It is not necessary to suppose use of a pole to reach up, for the victim was not elevated far above the ground. Knowing the end had now arrived, our Lord triumphantly hailed its arrival. Matthew, Mark, and Luke simply say He shouted again, but John articulates this marvelous, one-word cry (the sixth word from the cross): 'It has been [now] finished' (in Greek, one word, *tetelestai).* The one truly wise and prosperous man had brought His fruit to completion.[15] The Old Testament dispensation – its types and prophecies of the Suffering Servant, Messiah, Son of man – was all

15 In Psalm 1:3 'shall prosper' means 'shall bring to completion.' See Isaiah 52:13.

finished. To seal that fact and to show it to the very priests of the temple, God rent the veil of the temple from top to bottom. That which had for ages separated the innermost recess (where God dwelt) from the access of men was now as open as God alone can make it. This was God's way of showing some of the meaning of what the death of Christ had accomplished. God had put Him to grief (Isa. 53:10). It pleased the Lord to bruise Him so that all believing 'brethren' might have boldness to enter into the holy place by the blood of Jesus (Heb. 9:12; cf. 10:19-22).

Immediately, in the language of another Psalm, but adding what no Old Testament writer would have dared to say, that is, 'Father,' the most blessed of Adam's children quietly whispered, 'Father, into thy hands I commend my spirit' (Ps. 33:5). Then He bowed that noble head – held erect throughout a victorious life – and gave His spirit back to God.

The rending of the veil was accompanied, perhaps caused, by an earthquake. Stones broke apart. Remarkably and inexplicably 'many bodies of the saints that had fallen asleep were raised; and coming forth out of the tombs after his resurrection they entered into the holy city and appeared unto many' (Matt. 27:52, 53 ASV). Though the opening of tombs occurred at the time of the earthquake, the resurrection of a number of dead saints took place 'after his resurrection.' These were probably recently deceased persons, for they were known to people still living in Jerusalem. 'Thus, in the opening of the graves at the moment of the Redeemer's expiring, there was a glorious symbolical proclamation that the death which had just taken place had 'swallowed up death in victory'; and whereas the saints that slept in them were awakened only by their risen Lord, to accompany Him out of the tomb, it was fitting that "the Prince of Life" should be *the First* that should rise from the dead"' (Acts 26:33; I Cor. 15:20-23; Col. 1:18; Rev. 1:5). Whether these people lived on in natural bodies and died again, or were in glorified bodies and later translated, is a matter of conjecture. Most interpreters seem to prefer the former explanation.

The people, for there were some who stayed through to the end, were impressed greatly. More importantly, the Roman officer (Mark 15:39-41; Matt. 27:54-56; Luke 23:47-49) in charge, seeing Jesus' behavior, especially hearing those last several sayings, said, 'Truly this man was a son of God.'

BURIAL (BY A SANHEDRIN MINORITY)

After that, disposal of the Lord's body was necessary to end the story of that Sabbath preparation day. The Mosaic Law required the bodies of executed men to be buried out of sight before sundown. 'And if a man has committed a sin worthy of death, and he be put to death, and thou hang him on a tree; his body shall not remain all night upon the tree, but thou shalt surely bury him the same day; for he that is hanged is accursed of God; that thou defile not thy land which Jehovah thy God giveth thee for an inheritance' (Dent. 21:22, 23 ASV). How utterly pathetic! How unthinkable that these words should be prophetic of the end of the career of the Savior of the world!

So Pilate had the suffering thieves dispatched, and then no doubt their mangled corpses were carted off to the town dump or some such place. Jesus' body would have been likewise disposed of except that now, as the Father had decreed (Isa. 53:9), the humiliation was over and the hands of wicked men were never to touch Him again. Also, Scripture type, the Passover ritual, predicted that no bone should be broken (Exod. 12:46; Num. 9:12; Ps. 34:20; John 19:36, 37). So His legs were not broken as the thieves' were. John says he is eyewitness to these facts (John 19:35). So a rich disciple and Sanhedrist named Joseph, with Nicodemus, another Sanhedrist, took the corpse down after gaining Pilate's permission. The time was short-no time for full burial preparation. So they wrapped the body with one hundred pounds of myrrh and aloes in a clean linen sheet and laid it in the new garden tomb near at hand, which the wealthy Joseph had caused to be prepared for his own burial. Before leaving, they rolled the heavy stone door across the opening. Further preparation and dressing of the body in the Jewish manner would have to wait till after the Sabbath.

Though Joseph and Nicodemus acted alone, they were not unobserved. Some of the ladies who had followed Jesus throughout His journeys and travails were watching from a spot nearby; they noted carefully where the body was placed and before the closing of shops at sundown, the beginning of the Sabbath, returned to the markets, purchased, mixed, and cooked the spices for final washing, anointing, and dressing of His body for what they thought would be permanent interment. The Pharisees[16]

---

16 It is important in harmonizing the Synoptic accounts and John, all of which place the death of Jesus on 'the preparation,' that this expression be understood as a designation for Friday, the recurring preparation-for-Sabbath day. All the Synoptics place the crucifixion on the day called the

had their sentinels out observing too. And, evidently understanding the Lord's predictions of His resurrection better than the disciples did, they requested from Pilate an armed guard to keep His disciples, so they asserted, from stealing the body. They thought the disciples might steal it in order to claim some sort of miraculous resurrection of Jesus' body. Pilate, in a mood of disgusted concession, granted the guard. So the Pharisees sealed the stone door and left the heathen guard behind at the grave.

As far as anyone that day did see, or could see, Christianity was now dead – annihilated with the utter destruction of its founder and sole leader.

---

preparation (Matt. 27:62; Mark 15:42; Luke 23:54). John twice (19:31, 42) says the same. Hence his expression (19:14) about Jesus' trial before Pilate beginning at the sixth hour (sunrise) of the 'Preparation of the Passover' is most certainly to be understood not as the day Jews prepared the Paschal meal but as the preparation, i.e., the recurring weekly preparation for-Sabbath day (Friday) of the week-long festival of Passover and Unleavened Bread. They had eaten the Paschal meal the night before and prepared it on the 14th of Nisan. 'Today,' the 15th, was Friday of the Passover week, and that is what 'preparation of the Passover' means. 'The Passover' is a name for the entire week of festivity. So after sundown on that Friday (preparation), the beginning of Jewish Saturday, according to Matthew 27:62, the Pharisees asked for and got their Roman watchmen for Jesus' tomb.

Part 4

'I am... going to the Father'

CHAPTER 13

The Denouement:
His Resurrection and Ascension

It is common in expositions of this part of the story of the Savior's personal intercourse with His disciples to devote much attention to the psychological state of the disciples, tracing it from utter despair, by stages, to strong faith. We likewise shall consider that aspect of the subject. Yet, since the subject of this series of studies is the career of the Lord, we shall devote most attention to details of the narrative – What happened? Who was involved and how and when and where?

Let us begin with the summary statement of one who, among learned believing students, has been held in greatest respect and whose work, though now no longer recent, has not been superceded: 'The number of our Lord's appearances after the resurrection during the forty days following, or to His ascension, as given by the Evangelists, is generally said to be nine. Of these, five were on the day of resurrection, one on the Sunday following, two at some later period, and one when he ascended. As regards place, five were in Jerusalem, one in Emmaus, two in Galilee, and one on the Mount of Olives. If to these we add that to James, mentioned only by St. Paul (I Cor. 15:7), which was probably at Jerusalem, we have ten recorded appearances. We may well believe that these were not all, the language in Acts 1:3, RV: 'appearing unto them by the space of forty days, and speaking the things concerning the kingdom of God,' clearly implying that the Lord met the apostles often for instruction.'[1]

This paragraph furnishes a natural outline for what now follows. It does not seem strange to devout Bible readers that such a sensible plan might in all truth be followed. We are rightly both annoyed and surprised that the several independent contemporary accounts, all either by eyewitnesses or their reporters, should be said to be confused and full of discrepancies. One modern theologian, denying both the physical removal of our Lord's body in resurrection and any physical corporeality of the Lord's resurrection body, speaks of the 'manifold discrepancy'[2] of the reports and reduces their experiences to subjective visions. A widely used recent Bible atlas makes out all our Lord's resurrection appearances to have been 'visions.'

APPEARANCES ON SUNDAY MORNING

Matt. 28:1-15
Mark 16:1-11
Luke 23:56b 24:1-12
John 20:1-18

The Scriptures noted in the margin should by all means be read first. They describe a condition of amazed excitement over events unprecedented in the annals of human events. The obvious purpose of the four writers is not to present an orderly scientific account, such as a lawyer might prepare, to prove something to a reluctant judge or jury. It is rather simply to report initial happenings to certain of the Lord's circle of friends which led them to gather again, there to recall His several predictions of resurrection after three days in the grave and to consider favorably the testimony of certain of their small group that divine messengers from heaven had announced His resurrection. They also heard testimony of some of their number that they had actually seen Jesus alive.

Many data which would be essential to form an airtight reconstruction of that eventful morning are missing. But this is not by any means to acknowledge that the four narratives are inharmonious. Each Evangelist provides the particulars which suit the particular slant of purpose he is following. They are not in every case the same particulars. The writers are not to be faulted for this, for not even Luke intended to give a complete account, including all details.

For those who prefer to think the Gospel writers did not have firsthand information, there may seem to be discrepancies and even contradictions, 'but a thorough investigation shows that the points of real difference are

---

1 ALOL, p. 596.
2 H. Emil Brunner, Eternal Hope (Philadelphia: Westminster, 1954), p. 144.

very few, and that in several ways even these differences may be removed. While thus we cannot say of any order which we can frame, that it is certain, we can say of several that they are probable; and if they cannot be proved, neither can they be disproved. This is sufficient for him who finds in the moral character of the Gospels the highest vouchers for their historic truth.'[3]

Sometime after sunset on Saturday, our Lord's spirit returned from the Father. That spirit trustingly committed to the Father at 3pm. Friday afternoon, reentered and reanimated His dead body sometime after sundown on Saturday night (Jewish Sunday). At the same time His body was transformed into an eschatological, that is to say, glorified, body. What the nature of that body is may be known, so far as can be known, from Jesus' previous teaching, from statements in the Gospels about it, and from remarks about the body of the resurrection in the rest of the New Testament. We shall note some of these matters at appropriate junctures of the narrative of the forty days.

At the crack of dawn on the morning after the Sabbath (Sunday morning) (Matt. 28:2-4), a severe earthquake occurred, not involving the whole area as had the one at 3 pm. Friday, nor even affecting the city – for the Gospel narratives would hardly have failed to report the effects on the feelings and opinions of the populace which such an event would have made. It affected only the immediate area of the tomb of Jesus and its startled Roman guards. The tomb, being of the usual type that contained a room inside, would have had a small opening which one would stoop very low to enter, and it was shut by a round solid stone wheel set in a gutter that sloped down to the door sill. The door would have weighed five or six hundred pounds. Swiftly after the earthquake, and in full view of the guards, 'an angel of the Lord descended from heaven, and came and rolled away the stone, and sat upon it. His appearance was as lightning, and his raiment white as snow' (Matt. 28:3 ASV). The guards were understandably terrified, rendered immobile.

Apparently immediately afterward Mary Magdalene and another Mary,[4] mother of a James and Salome, came with the spices they had prepared to anoint the body of Jesus and (now that the Sabbath was past) to finish the Jewish burial (Matt. 28:1; cf. 27:56, 61). There may have been other

---

3 ALOL, pp. 607, 608.
4 Interesting details are furnished of names and relationships and children of the women of Jesus' intimate following. The data were sufficient to clarify these matters for the early Christians, but now connections are tenuous. The commentaries are usually helpful, as are Bible dictionaries

women also. They had obviously agreed to come for this service – evidently normally 'women's work' – but, coming from different homes or lodgings, they did not arrive at precisely the same moment. Apparently the angel was no longer sitting on the stone, and now the women suddenly were troubled about how to roll back the heavy stone so they might enter the tomb (Mark 16:1-3). They apparently knew nothing about the seal and guard. As they drew near they saw that the stone had been rolled back, the opening exposed. Mary Magdalene walked no further, but, seeing nothing inside in the dim light of early morning, supposed the tomb to be empty, robbed of Jesus' body (Why else would anyone open it?). She ran back into the city where she found the lodgings of Peter and John (whether at the same place we cannot know) and in helpless anguish exclaimed, 'They have [i.e., somebody has] taken away the Lord out of the tomb, and we [the women] know not where they have laid him' (John 20:1, 2).

Meanwhile the other women whom Mary Magdalene had left behind had cautiously proceeded on into the sepulchre and there were met by two angels – said to be 'a young man' (Mark 16:5) and 'two men' (Luke 24:4) – who informed them of Jesus' resurrection and directed them to bear a message to 'the disciples and Peter' that the Lord will be preceding them to Galilee and expecting to meet them there. But instead of heeding the instruction, the women, dazed and fearful, fled in terror and said nothing about it to anyone for some hours.

Shortly thereafter Peter and John came on the run, electrified by the Magdalene's report of the empty tomb. John, the fleeter, arrived at the sepulchre first. He stooped, looked in, and saw by the gathering light of morning a linen coverlet lying, but no corpse. Shortly Peter arrived and stepped past his younger and more cautious companion into the empty tomb, soon to be followed by John. The latter, as he wrote of himself some sixty years later, 'saw and believed' (John 20:8), while Peter marveled. That is, at first they believed in His resurrection because of what they saw, not because Scripture had prepared their minds for it. Something about the emptiness of the tomb and the arrangement of the linens impressed John and caused him to believe Jesus had been supernaturally resurrected.[5] Perhaps it was that the linens showed no

---

5 As John 'beholdeth' (in Greek, *theorai*), he sees three signs that Jesus had tranquilly divested Himself of the grave clothes and walked away rather than being carried away as a corpse: (1) the grave clothes are there, not carried off, as would be the case if the body had been snatched; (2) the various wrappings are disposed in an orderly manner; (3) even the separate head wrapping lies folded separate.

sign of discard by robbers but were in some orderly array, for there is no proof that Jesus simply 'evaporated' through them, though this is today commonly supposed. In what manner and by what means the resurrection body of Jesus was clothed, the Gospels give not one shred of information. Perhaps no one noticed! We may safely assume our Lord did not appear naked to the Christians during the forty days. The appearance of angels had not yet been reported by the temporarily silenced female witnesses.

An earthquake has struck, mighty shining angels have been seen, the stone has been rolled back and seen to be so by several women, Mary Magdalene has run to report the removal of the stone and apparent theft of the corpse, Peter and John have entered and viewed the tomb, but still no one has seen Jesus – all this before the first resurrection appearance. But the Magdalene, out of breath from having run to tell Peter and John, was being drawn irresistibly – if in brief exhaustion – back to the garden with its empty tomb. After all others had gone their astonished ways, and with no knowledge of the apparition of angels which occurred in her absence from the tomb, that tearful lady approached it a second time – apparently alone (John 20:11-18). As she then stood weeping at the opening, she for the first time stooped to look inside. Now she sees the two white angels, one at the place where the head and the other where the feet of Jesus had lain. She apparently thought them to be men. When they asked why she wept, she repeated her opinion about the theft of His body and simply drew back out of the tomb – to behold Jesus Himself standing before her. *This is the first post-resurrection appearance of the Lord Jesus Christ.* She did not at once recognize Him and, supposing Him to be the gardener, come early for his work, addressed Him: 'Sir, if thou hast borne him hence, tell me where.' Then in clear, gentle tones Jesus called her by name: 'Mary!' There was instant recognition. At this point recent Greek language studies help us know what happened. Mary cried out, 'Rabboni!' and evidently grasped some part of His body, for a proper rendering of Jesus' following words is'"Do not cling to me' (NEB), or better, 'Stop clinging to me' (NASB) (John 20:7). Research into usage clearly indicates that the tense and mood of the verb mean to cease doing what is now being done. Our present project does not allow an interpretation. What must be noted is that as she released Him, Jesus gave her a message for the Apostles of His impending ascension to the Father, as He had told them in the upper room. He thus provided her a sort of voucher of authenticity, for only the Eleven had heard that message of ascension on the previous Thursday night. So now Mary had still another swift trip to make into the city.

Shortly came Jesus' second resurrection appearance – to the party of women frightened dumb by the angels' appearance and words awhile before. Having recovered their senses, they were now hastening to tell the Apostles of the empty tomb, the angels, and the angels' message, but in the way the Lord met them, saying 'All hail. And they came and took hold of his feet, and worshipped him' (Matt. 28:9, 10). Then after hearing Him repeat the message of the angels – Go to Galilee – they went away to report to the Apostles. But the Eleven 'and all the rest' did not believe, for 'these words appeared in their sight as idle talk' (Luke 24:11 ASV; cf. Mark 16:11).

Sometime during these happenings the unfortunate soldiers of the guard stumbled back into the city, told their tale to the chief priests who had got them into their predicament, and found a typical military-political way around an unpleasant but unchallengeable fact (Matt. 28:11-15).

So we have clear Scriptural witness to at least two appearances of angels and two of the risen Christ on the morning of Easter. They were not 'to all the people' (Acts 10:41), but only to chosen witnesses. Think what a sensation would have been made if the first two appearances had been to Annas or Pilate or Caiaphas! Another appearance – whether in morning or afternoon we do not know – in private, to Peter, took place that day (1 Cor. 15:5). The Lord had graciously sent a special message to Peter by the women, perhaps as leader of the apostolic band and certainly to let him know that in spite of Peter's defections, he was still an accepted and loved disciple.

This summary cannot treat all the data given by the four Evangelists, but the framework of two or three appearances of an angel or angels (also called young man or men) and two appearances of the risen Christ on Sunday morning is not likely to be overturned. There is a possibility of a third appearance of angels to the two Marys, but the above reconstruction of only two seems to satisfy the requirements.

AN APPEARANCE SUNDAY AFTERNOON

Mark 16:12,13
Luke 24:13-32
Neither Matthew nor John speaks of this appearance, perhaps the longest continuous presence of the risen Christ with any disciples and certainly the most fully reported.

Early Sunday afternoon two men disciples set out from Jerusalem to walk to Emmaus, one of them named Cleopas. Though some identify him with Clopas or Alphaeus, husband of a certain Mary, thought to be Jesus' mother's sister, it seems very unlikely that there would have been two living sisters with the same name. This is part of an effort to identify James and Joses, the sons of Alphaeus (or Clopas, or Cleopas) with the 'brethren' of the Lord. It is likely that they were two men with similar names.

The location of Emmaus has always interested Christian people. The name 'is a Greek reproduction of a Semitic place name, *Hamma*, which means "warm well.""[6] So like such names as Trout Lake, Round Lake, Rockford, etc., there could be and were several cities of that name. Emmaus is one of the few towns (less than fifteen) which Jesus is specifically reported to have visited in His entire ministry and hence of considerable interest to everyone. On the advice of some modern scholars and several ancient ones, the village is said to be Imwas in the *Shephelah*[7] nearly twenty miles west of Jerusalem. In spite of the preservation of the ancient name in the modern Arabic, another village called *Qubeibeh*, less than ten miles from Jerusalem as the crow flies west-north-west of Jerusalem, fits the requirements of Luke's report (sixty stadia equals seven-plus miles; two trips between Jerusalem and Emmaus, and a leisurely meal by the same people in one afternoon). Since the fourteenth century it has been seriously proposed.[8] A modest Franciscan church, set on Crusader foundations, stands on the supposed site of Cleopas's house. Its modest but beautiful stained glass windows illustrate Luke's story. Nearby are lovely gardens and woods. The location fits the narrative exactly.

These men had left Jerusalem after the amazing reports of the early morning angelic appearances had been shared by word of mouth but before reports had gone out of Jesus' being actually seen. Their mental condition speaks volumes on the state of the believers yet Sunday afternoon. Jesus had, entirely unrecognized, joined them on their walk. When he asked what their conversation was about, this revealing sequence followed (Luke's beautiful prose can hardly be reported except by quoting it): 'And they stood still, looking sad. And one of them, named Cleopas,

---

6 KBA, p. 409.

7 *Shephelah*, a name supplied by the Bible itself, is still used by geographers for an area of low hills and intervening, rather smooth valleys between the highlands of Palestine and the coastal plains. It is the word rendered 'vale, valley, low country, plain(s)' in numerous Old Testament passages (examples: Dent. 1:7; Josh. 9:1; I Chron. 27:28; and II Chron. 28:18).

8 *A Guide to Jordan* (Amman Jordan: Jordan Tourist Department, n.d.), p. 34. See also FANT, pp. 177-80.

answering said unto him, Dost thou alone sojourn in Jerusalem and not know the things which are come to pass there in these days? And he said unto them, What things? And they said unto him, The things concerning Jesus the Nazarene, who was a prophet mighty in deed and word before God and all the people: and how the chief priests and our rulers delivered him up to be condemned to death, and crucified him.[9] But we hoped that it was he who should redeem Israel. Yea and besides all this, it is now the third day since these things came to pass. Moreover certain women of our company amazed us, having been early at the tomb; and when they found not his body, they came, saying, that they had also seen a vision of angels, who said that he was alive. And certain of them that were with us went to the tomb, and found it even so as the women had said: but him they saw not' (Luke 24:17-24 ASV).

The Christians were already a fellowship, sharing the matters of deepest concern on their hearts. Their entire hope was already centered in Him. Means were being employed to operate as a vital organic body. Now, even before the effusion of the Spirit, Jesus began to effect that spiritual enlightenment which constituted the Jewish Scriptures forever a Christian book (Luke 24:25-27; cf. vv. 40-48). He showed them that the subject matter of every part of it is part and parcel, root and branch, through and through a message about Christ. The name of Christ now no longer designates an office with limited Jewish reference but a world-wide office, and His church a body of people with a worldwide evangelistic mission. Not long afterward Christians began to employ 'Christ' as a personal name for their Lord, referring to Him as Jesus of Nazareth only in conversation with unbelievers. As they reclined at the supper table with Jesus as their guest and as He blessed and broke the bread, they suddenly recognized Him. But He vanished immediately. Filled with wonder, joy, new discernment, and new information, the two men forthwith left for a quick return trek to Jerusalem. There they informed the apostolic Eleven, their acknowledged leaders in the absence of Jesus, of the marvelous things which they had seen and learned.

AN APPEARANCE SUNDAY EVENING

Luke
24:36-
49
Mark
16:14-
18
John
20:19-
25

It is just possible that Mark does not intend to distinguish this appearance from a second Sunday evening appearance a week later (John 20:26-29).

9 That generation held the Jewish religious-civil rulers directly responsible for the crucifixion.

His summary style of language may intend to merge the two deliberately.

A problem will occur to the reader who compares the three accounts. Luke states that when the two Emmaus messengers reported the Lord's long conversation with them of that afternoon, they found the Eleven already joyfully affirming that 'the Lord is risen indeed, and hath appeared to Simon' (Luke 24:33-35). Mark, however, who seems to refer to this visit of the Eleven by the two from Emmaus, says they did not believe them (Mark 16:12, 13). If, as we think, the occasions are the same, there is apparent discrepancy. A mixture of not believing with joyful believing is the near certain answer. Luke himself says of their response to the appearance of Jesus Himself in the room a few minutes later: 'And while they yet believed not for joy, and wondered, he said unto them...' (Luke 24:41). Some were more believing (or disbelieving) than others, an entirely natural state of affairs.

It has been assumed by many that because He is said to have stood in the midst of them and that the doors (probably of the same room as the room of the Last Supper) were shut for fear of the Jews, Jesus simply 'materialized' in the room without opening the door and entering by it. It is the same sort of gratuitous assumption which has Jesus 'evaporate' through the grave clothes. Just what the properties and powers of a glorified body are, we do not know fully, but this does not justify gratuitous assumption. He submitted to spatial limitations in becoming man. He can, as man, never escape them. This is part of the meaning of the ascension. 'He is not here,' said the angel to the women, for He was now somewhere else. So the fact of the *empty* tomb is also connected.

As He lingered with the disciples in the closed room in Jerusalem that Sunday evening, He did several things. He assured them indeed of His resurrection. He was no longer dead, though truly He had been so. To demonstrate, He showed them His hands and side, presumably bearing the scars of crucifixion. We probably should not generalize from these pieces of information concerning the resurrection body of believers, for there was a memorial and apologetic purpose in the scars remaining on Jesus' body. He also announced their mission to go forth as the Father had sent forth Him and, in apparent anticipation, proclaimed their reception of the Holy Spirit. The effusion of the Spirit was still promise (see John 7:39), for He later commanded them to wait awhile for it. He made some cryptic remarks to the effect that they would have power to remit or retain the sins of others – something the present limitations cannot allow us to interpret save to say that He was giving hints of the foundation of the church and of its powers.

Nothing which happened that evening exceeds in importance His act of opening 'their mind, that they might understand the scriptures' (Luke 24:45). Henceforth they would understand the Bible as Christians, not as Jews. Their eyes would see that Scripture required that Christ should suffer, die, and rise; a world redemption had always been God's plan; that thereby repentance and remission of sin should be preached to all nations. It is no exaggeration to say that henceforth 'Scripture saith' is a stronger expression, implying additional meanings and insights, than 'Moses saith' or 'the prophet saith.' Christian writers[10] have been entirely within the bounds of necessary and important truth in asserting that 'What saith the Scripture?' is now, in the light of the Messiah's coming and career, a larger matter than 'What did Isaiah or David mean?' Jesus had now begun to open His disciples' eyes to these things. Ever after they would see the Hebrew Scriptures as an 'Old Testament' preparatory to the events of which they were witness. These events, interpreted, as they came to be, by New Testament Apostles and prophets and written down by them, constituted a New Testament.

AN APPEARANCE THE NEXT SUNDAY

The Apostles still delayed departure for Galilee. Why? The answer is not far to seek. They were aware that as an Eleven they were a college of specially designated and empowered men. They must be together in faith and action (no disunity in the body of Christ). But Thomas had been an absent member of the Eleven when Jesus had first met with them and was still unbelieving as, indeed, they also had been (John 20:24, 25). As long as one of their number remained unconvinced, they must await further direction from the Lord. They would not disperse again, as they had last Friday, until directed by Him to do so. Why Jesus waited a week to reveal Himself to them again we do not know. Likely it was to allow the meaning of recent events and His most recent words to be discussed and absorbed. At any rate, exactly one week later, in the same room, with similar conditions prevailing, He appeared, Thomas being present (John 20:28, 29). He again pronounced a peace upon them and challenged Thomas to examine His scars as the others had done a week before. John, the only one of them present to witness the thrust of the spear into the dead Christ's side as He still hung on the cross, reporting the present

---

10 Alfred Edersheim, Franz Delitzsch, Adolph Saphir, Albert Barnes, et al.

occasion, notes the challenge to inspect the wounded hands and side; in speaking of Jesus' resurrection body in His appearance of the previous week, Luke speaks of the hands and feet (Luke 24:39).

Thomas's answer was immediate, comprehending, and truly magnificent; he was the first clearly to confess the deity of Christ in utterly unambiguous terms: 'My Lord and my God.' Peter's confession at Caesarea Philippi (Matt. 16:16), as also that of Martha of Bethany (John 11:27), implied it, but Thomas's confession is explicit. A few weeks later Peter would teach the doctrine (Acts 2:33-36) to assembled thousands of Jews, with great success.

Jesus' words of reproof really applied no more to Thomas than to them all, in view of the way matters had stood a week before. His declaration 'Blessed are they that have not seen, and yet have believed' (John 20:29 ASV) points ahead to the manner in which Christian faith must ever after begin and grow. For, as Peter (who heard Jesus say this) wrote long afterward: '… Jesus Christ: whom not having seen ye love; in whom, though now ye see him not, yet believing, ye rejoice greatly with joy unspeakable and full of glory' (I Peter 1:7, 8 ASV).

APPEARANCES IN GALILEE

This part of the resurrection story is found in John 21: 1-23, Matthew 28:16-20, and possibly Mark 16:15-18, though this part of Mark – all, in fact, of 16:9-20 – is regarded by textual authorities as not a genuine part of the New Testament: 'Mark 16:9-20 is neither part nor parcel of that Gospel.'[II]

John's lengthy chapter tells how the disciples returned to the old haunts near Capernaum. Peter got out his old fishing gear and checked his boat. Never one to wait for the future to come to him, that restless disciple said, 'I am going fishing,' and so he did, with Thomas, Nathanael, James, John, and two unnamed disciples-seven of them in all. With proverbial fisherman's luck, a night of toil got them nothing. Then, at dawn of day, just as they headed toward shore in the morning calm, an unrecognized man on the still-distant strand asked about their catch. When He heard of their empty nets and boats, He said, 'Cast the net on the right side of the boat, and ye shall find. They cast therefore, and now they were not able to draw it for the multitude of fishes' (John 21:6 ASV). Nothing is more calculated to demonstrate the natural characteristics of

---

II GCTNT, p. 5II.

the seven men – at least of some of them – than what next happened. John – reflective, perceptive, and cautious – quietly said to Peter, 'It is the Lord.' Peter – abrupt, impulsive, ardent, a man of action – paused only long enough decently to cover his body (not wishing to appear before Jesus in underwear only), jumped overboard, and swam for shore, heedless of the catch. The others, mindful of practical things, anchored the boat (*ploion*) and, dragging the net, rowed ashore in a skiff (*ploiarion*) kept in tow behind the larger vessel and used in setting nets. Jesus had already laid a cooking fire and called for more fish (He had some already cooking to fill the hungry men with its odor). By now Peter, having recovered his calm, helped draw to shore the oversize catch of 153 (as John, the youngest and hence probably the one who counted them, notes carefully). More fish were laid out to roast, and when ready, Jesus served them the fish with bread which He had provided – no one knows how (Had an early-rising baker been unwitting witness of the risen Christ?) Though not quite all the Eleven were present (unless they were meanwhile called, which seems not at all unlikely), John remarks that this was Jesus' third post-resurrection appearance to the apostolic group (John 21:14).

After the breakfast Jesus took great care to explain to Peter that he was still to shepherd the Lord's flock – surely indicating some leadership for Peter among the Twelve (they would shortly be twelve again). He also gently reproved Peter for his too-quick confidence that his love for Christ was steady and true. Jesus also intimated the manner of Peter's martyrdom in the time of old age and delivered a gentle rebuke for insufficient attention to his own rather than others' service for the Lord.

We are sure only of one further appearance in Galilee. Paul refers to it as an occasion when Jesus 'appeared to above five hundred brethren at once' (I Cor. 15:6 ASV). Matthew says simply that 'the eleven disciples went into Galilee, unto the mountain where Jesus had appointed them' (Matt. 28:16 ASV). Like the lake shore, it was another old haunt – very likely the mount of the famous sermon, for the place of the transfiguration was most likely not in Galilee. This had been their instructions right along, given both before the crucifixion during the last week and by the angels to the women after the resurrection. The Galilean pilgrims at the feast had gone home many days before. Now word was sent to known, trusted followers throughout the northern province to gather at a certain place on a certain mountain at a certain time, the Lord promising to meet them there. These instructions must have been repeated and made specific at one of the two Sunday-evening appearances in Jerusalem.

We have meager report of this meeting (Matt. 28:16-20). We know that now for the first time they all worshiped Him when they saw Him, even though some, for whom this was the first meeting with the risen Christ, doubted for a while if it were really He in the flesh and not some temporary phantasm of Christ.

The record of the appearances, including the showing of pierced hands and feet and of wounded side, breaking bread and eating before them, walking beside them, conversing with them, even expressly denying that He was ghost or phantasm, shows how important it was to Him and to the future church that the permanent corporeality of the second Person of the Godhead be fully demonstrated, understood as true, and believed. His physical ascension before the Apostles' eyes a few days later was only the final touch to this emphasis.

At the meeting on a mountain of Galilee, He made the boldest possible assertion of authority – all there is in heaven and on earth. They must understand that what He is commanding is of utmost urgency and certain truth. Then He made a single command (the Greek text is very clear on this): 'Make disciples of all nations.' They were to do this as they would now soon be going into all the nations of the earth. Most would go on business and economic errands – spreading believers everywhere. Some would be going for education or recreation. These causes still send Christians to 'every nation under heaven.' A few would be called, commissioned, and supported as special church-sponsored missionaries, of whom Paul, Barnabas, Silas, and their helpers – Mark, Timothy, Titus, Demas, Luke, Trophimus, and many others – are examples. But the commission was for all, whether *sent* away from home or not. Everyone has gone somewhere in the world. The emphasis is as much *anywhere* as *everywhere*. All believers are under the commission. They are to carry it out in connection with and in the context of and with the authority of local churches, planting local churches everywhere, confessing disciples and receiving them by means of water baptism in the name of the Father and of the Son and of the Holy Ghost. The baptism must be preceded, accompanied, and followed by teaching men all things that Jesus said, in connection, of course, with what He did.

Thus Jesus laid the foundation of the Christian mission several days before the actual spiritual formation of the church at Pentecost. Thereby He made provision for effective custody of the saving news, the gospel. He entrusted it to that human, yet divinely constituted and sustained, organ which the Bible calls the *ekklesiā*, (church, assembly).

There was then an appearance to a certain James. Paul alone mentions it and does so in such a way as to require that it took place after the appearance to the five hundred but before the final appearance at the ascension (I Cor. 15:7). This James is generally conceded to be James the Lord's brother in the flesh – the son of Joseph and Mary. If James and the other brothers and sisters were, indeed, as is close to certain, the offspring of Joseph and Mary, we may be sure of the solicitude of Jesus, their older brother, for their spiritual redemption. Christian history reports several incidents about them. We know that James the Lord's brother quickly came to a place of leadership in the Jerusalem congregation and remained so, long after most of the Apostles (save that other martyr James) had scattered on their journeys of worldwide ministry.

FINAL APPEARANCE NEAR JERUSALEM

Jesus remained to the end of the Gospels a Jewish Messiah. The Jewish capital, Jerusalem, had attracted Him from earliest days. He moved His ministry there as early as possible and stayed as long as He could. He made dangerous excursions into Jerusalem and its environs many times, long after the city's leaders had clearly shown their intention to destroy Him by any means necessary. He had yearned over the city and finally chose, in keeping with Scripture prediction, that His passion and crucifixion should be there. Finally, at Jerusalem He arose from the dead and made His first appearance to believers. Now His last resurrection appearance and ascension would be in the same neighborhood.

On the fortieth day after His resurrection, Jesus gathered the Eleven somewhere on the mount of Olives. On the first Sunday after Easter, He had renewed 'the promise of the Father' to send the Spirit and had instructed them to tarry in Jerusalem until fulfillment of the promise. But the command to go to Galilee for a meeting there with the great body of His disciples intervened, hence a return trek from Galilee was necessary for the Eleven (Luke 24:49). How much walking these men did in pursuit of their Lord's errands! Now they were back, and the final meeting (or meetings) took place (Acts 1:3-5). Luke is fully capable of being interpreted to mean that several meetings took place, most of them probably in Galilee. 'Here the Apostles were at home and among friends.' 'Amidst the scenes of His former teachings His present words would be among His enemies, and in a state of disquietude, if not of positive fear.'[12]

---

12 ALOL, p. 630.

We may conjecture that it was near the fortieth day when they finally and forever broke free from the friendly neighbors, beautiful countryside, and cheerful skies – land where their crafts and skills had been learned and practiced – for the stark, stony, infertile hills of Judaea and the grim old walls of Jerusalem. It was not just to be present for the feast of Pentecost, ten days after Jesus' ascension, but by Jesus' appointment. There is no hint that they expected Him to leave them forever, short of the last, great day, for they were still unable to conceive of the coming age of the Holy Spirit. Their hopes of an earthly kingdom, many Christians will say, were not utterly false, rather very inadequate. The change in their thinking came after Pentecost, when the present spiritual kingdom and the future visible manifestation of it, according to the Old Testament hope of Israel, were put in clearer perspective. Only a few days after Pentecost, Peter preached to an assembled group of interested Jews in that part of the temple called Solomon's porch, the exact place where Jesus at the time of the feast of Dedication in the previous December had preached His sermon on eternal life (cf. John 10:22ff.). After noting that 'all the prophets' had said something of Christ's suffering (first advent) and delivering a challenge to repentance, Peter added that God would 'send the Christ who hath been appointed for you, even Jesus: whom the heaven must receive until the times of restoration of all things, whereof God spake by the mouth of his holy prophets that have been from of old' (Acts 3:20, 21 ASV).

After assembling them for the last time, Jesus commanded the group (we learn there were 120 of them) to wait in Jerusalem for the promised baptism of the Holy Spirit (Acts 1:4; cf. Luke 24:49). He was interrupted briefly by a question, the last lingering articulation of hope for a Jewish kingdom on earth at that time: 'Lord, dost thou at this time restore the kingdom to Israel?' (Acts 1:6 ASV). All His words about the kingdom of God being given to the Gentiles on account of Israel's rejection of it were still below their level of apprehension.

Jesus did not affirm that their hope was entirely wrong; it was certainly out of time, as the words of Peter (cited above) later clarified (Acts 3:18-21). God had a new and different program in mind for the long age ahead. Judicially blinded in obdurate unbelief, Israel would be set aside, Jerusalem would be trodden down of Gentiles, God would gather children from every kindred and tribe, tongue and nation, until the fullness of the Gentiles should come in. The Apostles' immediate future was to be witnessing in the world, not judging the twelve tribes at Jerusalem.

ASCENSION

Then Jesus led them out toward Bethany. If, as the account implies, they were already on the mount of Olives, then they moved on to some eminence on the east slope southeast, to be exact – several hundred yards from the several claimed sites to the north and south of the present Arab village of *et Tur* at the peak of Olivet's highest summit.

When they arrived, He repeated and enlarged their commission by commanding them to witness of Him, not beginning at Jerusalem this time, but as the Greek (*te... kai... kai... kai*) requires, 'not only in Jerusalem but also at the same time in Judaea, Samaria,' and everywhere Christians are (cf. Luke 24:47). The commission again emphasizes not so much that believers are to go somewhere, but that they are to witness wherever they are.

Then Jesus raised His hands in blessing and while doing so He visibly ascended until a cloud took Him out of view (Luke 24:50, 51). As they continued to look in amazement, 'two men stood by them in white apparel [the same two angels who appeared to the women in the garden of entombment?]; who also said, Ye men of Galilee, why stand ye looking into heaven? this Jesus, who was received up from you into heaven, shall so come in like manner as ye beheld him going into heaven' (Acts 1:10, 11 ASV).

Although the event itself is described only by Luke (Luke 24:50, 51; Acts 1:11), the ascension is referred to in the New Testament at least seven times in prospect. One reference comes shortly after the transfiguration (Luke 9:51). Several more appear in the story of the Last Supper (John 13:3; 14:2, 28). Others fall later in the same evening as Jesus and the Apostles walked toward the garden of Gethsemane (John 16:7, 10). The text which has furnished the outline for this book (John 16:28) is among the Lord's words to His own as they made that same last trek together through the city; the last words of that text are 'I... go to the Father.' The ascension is mentioned also in the Received Text's ending to Mark (16:19) and in the liturgy-like Christological summary in I Timothy 3:16, which concludes with 'received up into glory.'

It is an important part of our Lord's great work of redemption and is freighted with great theological and practical meaning, according to the New Testament. It was a 'finishing touch' to our Lord's redemptive career, as He Himself said (John 16:28). Jesus also regarded His return to the Father as necessary for the special descent of the Spirit and for the inauguration of the church and the special work of the Holy Spirit in it during the period leading up to Jesus' second advent. This seems clearly to be taught in the Gospels as interpreted by Paul (cf. John 7:37-39 with John 16:6, Matt. 3:11, and I Cor. 12:13). Christ's giving of the gifts (apostles, prophets, evangelists, and pastors and teachers) are likewise connected with this striking event (Eph. 4:7-16).

Practically considered, the public quality of the ascension should protect believers from a serious error. Jesus did not simply quit appearing from time to time; He enacted a distinct farewell. As regards His physical presence, therefore, He was visibly taken up into heaven. Until the second advent He would never be literally and physically seen on earth – as some claim Him to be in the broken bread or poured wine of the ordinance of the Lord's Supper. We are clearly to believe in His spiritual presence (Matt. 18:20; 28:20) with us at every private or public occasion of worship or need. He is completely present to faith (II Tim. 4:17) in all His glorified humanity, but not as to time and space. The ascension settled that: Peter said of Jesus that 'the heaven must receive [Him] until the times...' (Acts 3:21). The disciples will not see Him again, as He was seen during the forty days, until He comes 'in like manner as Ye have seen him go into heaven' (Acts 1:11). Christians are taught to view this spectacular consummation of the Son of God's career as strong assurance of a similar destiny for themselves. This calm trust becomes for them an anchor of the soul (Heb. 6:18-20), lodged firmly in heaven which their Forerunner has entered before them.

An earthly life which began with a miracle ended with another. Men have been blessed by that life ever since, and shall continue to worship and serve Him till He comes again, in His kingdom, with power and great glory.

A Preamble to Modern Criticism of the Parables of Jesus

One hears frequently today that great advances in the study of the parables of Jesus have been made in recent times. Indeed many books and articles have been written on the parables in the last century. The Society of Biblical Literature has held seminars on the parables as part of its meetings recently. Let us take notice of this surge of interest and explain how it does or does not affect our understanding of Jesus' sermons and evangelism.

Until the time of the Enlightenment (eighteenth century), Christian understanding always accepted the Gospels' own testimony and the testimony of the early church about the time of their writing and the identity of the authors. The Gospels' were considered apostolic and authentic, which is to that they were viewed as accounts written by members of the circle of Twelve (Matthew and John) or by one under immediate sponsorship of an apostle (Mark by Peter) or by one associated with an apostle and whose Gospel was received by an age of the church supervised apostles (Luke). One of the earliest post-New Testament Christian testimonies called them 'Memoirs of the Apostles' (Justin Martyr, Apology I, 66-67).

No dependence of one Gospel author upon another Gospel author or mutual dependence on a third source was felt necessary or appropriate.

Luke's assertion that he researched sources who were eyewitnesses from the beginning was taken at face value, and the other Gospels were held to be eyewitness accounts.

Such a view of the Gospels was in keeping with Christ's explicit promise to the apostles during their last evening together (John 13:7; 16:12-13) of a divine enablement to recall, to understand, and to explain the events of his career (words and deeds). Throughout most of the history of Christendom those assurances from the Lord's most tender moments with the Twelve had been regarded as true, as have been the penultimate words of the Gospel of John. John was the youngest of the apostles and thus prepared his account some fifty to sixty years after the death of Christ. Just before the close of his Gospel he made the strongest possible assertion of the truth of what he had written: 'This is the disciple who bears witness of these things, and wrote these things; and we know that his witness is true' (John 21:24).

Since the Enlightenment, writers of every degree of scholarship and devotion (or lack of either) have sought to penetrate the approximately three decades before the three synoptic Gospels (Matthew, Mark, Luke) were written. They have sought information about sources (written or oral), occasion, and motives for writing. Since there is scarcely any information except the Gospels themselves and several early epistles of Paul, those materials have been examined, combed, sorted, distilled, and redistilled. Certain theoretical conclusions (hardly scientific results) among several prominent theoreticians have emerged. These have achieved sufficient attention that certain tentative results are widely – if not firmly – recognized by a circle of writers who write largely for one another and their students and the libraries that deposit their books for later writers of scholastic theses.

In this school of opinion generally it has been held that Mark's was the first Gospel to be written (and indeed it may be true, though the same data has been turned upside down to 'prove' that Matthew or Luke was first). There is said to have been another 'source,' German *Quelle*, hence Q, which existed as contemporary with mark but earlier than Matthew or Luke. It is asserted that when Matthew and then Luke composed their gospels they employed Mark and Q as sources. This is said to account for the materials common to Matthew and Luke but not in mark. Finally, since Matthew reports things not in Luke or Mark, and Luke things not in Matthew or Mark, two other sources have been proposed: a source for Matthew called M, and a source for Luke called L.

Those who are interested in such theories can and do confidently refer to 'the four sources' of the synoptic Gospels – Mark, Q, M and L. This is the *Four Document Theory.* If one wishes, he may assume divine guidance in the use of these sources, hence divine inspiration, and many do so. Or one may suppose that three authors or groups of unknown authors simply did their fallible best with what they had. It is then up to the enlightened reader to judge their words rather than be judged by them. Those not enamored of such theories wonder why, in that age when hundreds of eyewitnesses were still living, and when, as is well known, the actual words of Jesus from the mouths of people who heard Jesus speak them were treasured far more than the written word, writers should have turned to something called Q, M or L as sources for their permanent records. They suspect that such documents as Q, M or L may never have existed outside the minds and writings of the literary critics. Certainly no *bona fide* copies have ever turned up, though considerable documentary remains have been preserved from that epoch.

More recently it has been proposed that during the decades AD30-60 the churches circulated various small units, oral and written, about Jesus. These pieces regarding His career were in various forms: miracle stories, parables, legends, sayings, prayers and short stories, all used in liturgy, devotion and instruction. As the years passed, the material was embellished and worked over to meet the changing constituency (Jewish dominance to Gentile dominance) and outlook (soon return of Christ to later) of the church. These pieces were possessed in the churches like beads in a coffer until Mark furnished a narrative framework for the units, putting 'the beads' on the string of his narrative.

In such an explanation of the development of the Gospel record, the church ('the creative community') is seen as not only having preserved some of the essence of what Jesus said and did, but also as having created much (or most) of what we read in the three synoptic Gospels. It is assumed that similar processes occurred when Matthew (employing Q and Mark and M) and Luke (employing Q and Mark and L) put their Gospels together. The theory goes by the German name of *Formegeschichte* (history of forms) or Form Criticism.

Other theorists, noting that interpreters have long discerned different theological emphases in each of the Gospels, have applied studies of ancient literary genre to their perusal of the Gospels. Such work is a refinement of the Form Criticism just mentioned and is called *Redaction Criticism.* It lays emphasis on the theological purposes of the authors of the Gospel record.

Why this discussion of the various explanations of the Gospel accounts? How do these matters relate to interpreting sermons and parables of Jesus? To answer, more must be observed concerning the theories advanced by modern critics.

These theorists all have shifted authority away from scripture to an unknown or even hypothetical Jesus of history. That shift has affected the way they have viewed the parables. Julicher, Dibelius, Dodd, Bultmann, Jeremias, Kummel, and their lesser colleagues and disciples have regarded the parables of the present Gospels as several steps removed from the dominical words of Jesus.

It is therefore not certain what such modern authors have meant when they have affirmed faith in historic Christian doctrines. WG Kummel, one of the clearest of these writers, closed his *Promise and Fulfillment* with orthodox-sounding affirmations. Yet he had just affirmed that Christ was mistaken in teaching that there would be a *parousia* of the son of Man within the lifetime of people then living. Kummel felt he could not expunge his embarrassment by critical methods.

Kummel came to such contradictory conclusions because he saw the Gospel record as being essentially distorted. In *Promise and Fulfillment* he tried to determine what the essential message (*kerygma*) of Jesus was, and what its value was, then and now. He focused on the proclamation of the kingdom of God, showing what other leading teachers and writers who shared his presuppositions said. He assumed the synoptic Gospels (including of course the parables) were the two stages removed from the actual words of Jesus. The first stage was the stage of tradition in the early church before the written Gospels. The second stage comprised the modifications made by the writers themselves in the traditions to conform to their own ideas about what should or should not be true. The result, Kummel asserted, was that the Gospel accounts were somewhat tendentious, that is, they were twisted to prove a point. In Kummel's opinion, the various critics should sort out the layers until they learn what Jesus *really* said. Only then would they be able to construct a theology on the basis of the *true* message of Jesus, relieved of the overlay that reflected the biases of the church of about AD60 and of the writers and their sources: Mark, Q, M, and L. The author said:

> 'In the *oldest* tradition of Jesus' message, to be ascertained by critical methods, we meet with the Jesus whose historical message alone confirms the corrections of the apostolic message. To set forth this

oldest message is therefore not only a historical task, but one that is theologically indispensable, and no hermeneutic mistake (WG Kummel, *Promise and Fulfillment*, p105).

In other words, we must all become committed adherents to and masters of several varieties of criticism before being qualified theologians.

Jublicher, to take the earliest of these authors, held that the parables as Jesus spoke them related wholly to incidents or issues contemporary with Jesus and His audience. Any application to later people was secondary. Other authors have held that the parables (along with about everything else Jesus presented regarding the kingdom of God or the kingdom of heaven) were related to the eschatological coming of the Son of Man to judge the world. Albert Schweitzer held that Jesus expected to usher in this coming *parousia* in His own person and failed in the mission. Some scholars have held that an eschatology fully realized among the hearers then was what Jesus meant. Still others say that the impact on the world of the powers of the world to come in the hearts of men who heard Jesus there was a kind of *inaugurated* eschatology, the coming of the kingdom. The church proclaimed this for a while, but shortly added the apocalyptic parts of the Gospels (Matt. 24, Mark 13, Luke 21) when there was no second coming. The parables of the kingdom were likewise modified to suit.

All these writers seem to have been saying in slightly different ways that, as Gentiles came into the church, the tradition (including parables) was modified to meet the new constituency, and that as the *parousia* (second advent) failed to occur, the tradition was modified to meet the new conditions. Some have spoken of how, during this period of thirty years or so, the church (that is, 'the creative community') reshaped the traditions now enshrined in the Gospels.

Almost every author of the type in this section has denied that Jesus had any specific foreknowledge of a future church and the long age of its existence. They have viewed passages directly applicable to the church as being the work of 'the creative community,' i.e., the first generation of Christians, and of the redactors. Passages such as Matthew 16:13-28, wherein Jesus plainly spoke of a future church that would come into existence after His death and resurrection, they likewise have assigned to 'the creative community' or have placed in doubt. Some have made such denials partly because their theories about his message and the manner of its incorporation in the Gospels forbade any other position and partly because they seem to have had few strong convictions about the deity of the Lord and were thus doubtful of his foreknowledge. Still others have theorized that the kenosis (self-emptying) of the Logos robbed the incarnate Christ of His divine foreknowledge.

What can be said of scholars who take such positions? Their sincerity and hard work should not be questioned. They have scoured the meager materials available for reconstructing those nearly blank three decades of history. No doubt they have come up with some valuable insights concerning the parables. Also, some have written of their devotion to Jesus. One writer, for example, has movingly reported that once the Gospels are stripped of accretions and tendentious modifications the reader finds himself listening to the veritable voice of the Son of Man Himself.

This much seems certain. Outside of the limited number of persons who read their books for professional reasons, few have found the critics' work interesting or convincing. Matthew 13 conveys much more of the ring of truth just as it reads than the Matthew 13 which emerges after the crew of critics has stripped the chapter of alleged accretions and tendentious changes. The critics themselves seem to have grasped how empty their work is. The foreword of a 1978 history of interpretation of Jesus' parables ended on this melancholy note: 'The appearance of this volume will do much to stimulate the round of advances and will contribute to its own obsolescence. Such is the reward of productive scholarship' (Robert Funk, introduction to *The Parables of Jesus: A History of Interpretation and Bibliography*, by Warren S Kissinger, p vi.)

The writer was correct in judging the lasting power of the work he was evaluating. It would not endure. But he did not pinpoint the cause of that lack of vitality. It is not the crowding of new theories that will condemn their work to early obsolescence, but their work's lack of a truly Christian sense of religious authority.

Subject Index

Scripture Index